The Making of KIND OF BLUE

ALSO BY ERIC NISENSON

'Round About Midnight: A Portrait of Miles Davis

Ascension: John Coltrane and His Quest

Blue: The Murder of Jazz

Open Sky: Sonny Rollins and His World of Improvisation

The Making of
KIND OF BLUE:

Miles Davis
and His Masterpiece

by

ERIC NISENSON

St. Martin's Press ⚜ New York

www.stmartins.com

Book design by Tim Hall

Library of Congress Cataloging-in-Publication Data

Nisenson, Eric.
    The making of Kind of blue : Miles Davis and his masterpiece / by Eric Nisenson.
        p. cm.
    Includes bibliographical references and index.
    ISBN 0-312-26617-0
        1. Davis, Miles. Kind of blue.   2. Jazz—1951–1960—History and criticism.   I. Title.

ML419.D39 N58 2000
781.65'026'6—dc21   00-044170

First Edition: November 2000

10   9   8   7   6   5   4   3   2   1

Contents

Introduction

In 1959 Miles Davis recorded his sixth album for Columbia Records, a small group session that would eventually be titled *Kind of Blue*. More than forty years after its release, it is still one of the most-sought-after recordings in the country; in fact, as late as 1998 it was the best-selling jazz album of the year. In both *Rolling Stone* and Amazon.com end-of-the-century polls, it was voted one of the ten best albums of all time—in any genre—and it is the only jazz album ever to reach double-platinum status. Yet its popularity is not the only extraordinary thing about *Kind of Blue*. In addition to being an incontestable masterpiece, it is also a watershed in the history of jazz, a signpost pointing to the tumultuous changes that would dominate this music and society itself in the decade ahead.

Beyond its historical significance, this album is for many listeners the record that lit their passion for jazz. I was one of them. *Kind of Blue* is the album that made me fall in love with jazz when I was about fifteen years old. It was not the first jazz album I had ever heard. It was not even the first Miles Davis album I had ever heard; that was *'Round About Midnight*, which I greatly enjoyed. But my reaction to *Kind of Blue* was of an entirely different order. I was immediately fascinated, even obsessed with it. The music stayed with me and seemed to follow me wherever I went, singing to me in the far reaches of my mind. As I sat in my math class, the memory of Miles's incomparable solo on "Freddie Freeloader" kept me from being bored to tears. John Coltrane's solo on "Blue in Green" would haunt me while I was strolling down the hall to biology class or while walking my dog. I could not get the music out of my mind. And after a lifetime of listening to jazz, I find that this fascination still lingers. Very few experiences remain so vividly with us from the time we are kids to the later years of our lives. But my love for *Kind of Blue* has remained a constant in my life—as it has, apparently, for many others.

It was not simply the beauty of the music that moved me; I was engulfed by the dark, melancholy mood of the album, a mood leavened by a kind of cool joy or sad irony that seemed to be an illustration of the old blues line "laughing to keep from crying." Although I have listened to *Kind of Blue* countless times over the years—so much so that I know every note by heart—when I play it now, I still have the same visceral response that I had as a boy.

Even the album's liner notes fired my imagination. Bill Evans's perceptive comments, in which he compares the spontaneity of jazz improvisation to a type of Zen painting, intrigued me and gave me the first clues to the mysterious process by which a jazz piece comes into being. Creating music spontaneously, right now, here in the moment, seemed a thoroughly magical idea, expressing an act as profound as the Zen Buddhism that I had become increasingly interested in at that time. (I would sit in study hall and, instead of doing my homework, attempt to meditate and reach satori, floating in my mind far away from the gray halls of my high school. Unfortunately, I never reached satori.)

Like Zen, the music of *Kind of Blue* seemed both simple

and profound. For me as a young person, it was like a gateway to the world of adult emotions—not just any adult emotions but those that speak to the ambiguities and tragedies of life. *Kind of Blue* reflected not only hard-lived experience but also the discipline of contemplation. This was, I thought, music created by people who knew the meaning of pain, hunger, fear, great sadness, and irrepressible joy. Moreover, it was music that seemed to express an awareness of death. I cannot point to anything specific to support this last observation. But throughout the album, I heard—and still hear—an awareness of mortality and a deep knowledge of the exigencies of living. Yet despite the undercurrent of melancholy in the music, I also felt an affirmation of life in the face of death; and these are emotions that were foreign to me as a boy. Through repeated listenings to the album, I began to glimpse something of the complexity of these emotions. Thus, for me, *Kind of Blue* was one of the stepping-stones toward emotional maturity as well as simply another beautiful piece of music.

Sadly, describing something as *beautiful* no longer carries any special weight. The overuse of words such as *beautiful, profound,* or *awesome* has impoverished our language. Commercials routinely invite us to buy products that are "beautiful": products as disparate as margarine, eyeglass frames, SUVs, instant coffee. But the unmistakable beauty of *Kind of Blue* rests on two qualities of great depth: the splendor of its sound and the starkness of its hard-won truths. *Kind of Blue* is further proof of Keats's statement that beauty and truth are inseparable.

Jazz has been called "the imperfect art," and there is much validity in that description. After all, any art form that is largely created spontaneously, in the moment, might have a number of fine qualities, but perfection is usually not one of them. And so it is with *Kind of Blue*—a flawed masterpiece, but a masterpiece nonetheless. Miles once complained that record companies should release jazz albums with all the mistakes included instead of editing them out. With *Kind of Blue* he realized his wish; the album was released, imperfections and all, without a single edit.

The diversity of musical sensibilities of the jazzmen who play on *Kind of Blue* is impressive: Miles Davis's terse lyricism, John Coltrane's intense spirals of sound, Bill Evans's introspective romanticism, and Cannonball Adderley's ebullient funk. I used to think that Adderley was the most noticeable flaw in this album, but I have completely changed my mind. The album would have been far less compelling without Cannonball's bluesy joie de vivre; the listener can almost hear him saying to the others, "Hey, lighten up, you guys!" The older I get, the more I understand that this sensibility is at least as profound as the darker moods expressed by the other musicians (though Wynton Kelly, who spells Evans on the blues "Freddie Freeloader," had a style close to Adderley's spirit).

That the sessions were something of an experiment only adds to the mystery of the album's brilliance. None of the players saw the pieces Miles planned to use until the actual sessions—with the exception of Bill Evans, who composed at least one of the tunes and probably collaborated with Miles on one or more of the others. And the tunes themselves were experimental. Instead of being based on chords, modes were used for their tonal organization. This was not the first time modes had been used in jazz or even the first time this particular band had played a modal tune. On *Milestones*, the small group session that preceded *Kind of Blue*, the title track was modal (the front line of that band was the same, but the drummer was Philly Joe Jones and Red Garland was the pianist, at least for part of the session). But that single tune was hardly preparation for the experimental pieces that Miles and Evans brought to the *Kind of Blue* sessions. This album would prove that jazz could find a tonal path apart from the European harmonic system that had been such a constant throughout music history, and it would give improvisers a new and unprecedented melodic freedom.

These matters of form are interesting, especially to musicians, and provide an additional explanation for the long history of attraction to this album. Formal elements aside, *Kind of Blue* gets under the listener's skin. Every one of the soloists creates the illusion that he is speaking to each of us as an individual, and to us only, thereby developing an extraordinary level of intimacy. Most of the solos are so eloquent that it is almost as if, on some other level—perhaps on the level of dreams—the musicians are speaking words directly into the listener's ears.

And what are they saying? That, too, is like a dream: in some sense we know exactly what they are "saying," but—by its very nature—music transcends language. Our understanding is intuitive; there is no need for a translation. This kind of immediate communication characterizes all good music, of course. But in *Kind of Blue* the phenomenon is especially vivid.

I have wanted to write extensively about *Kind of Blue* for a long time, but only when I began to research the subject and talk to the participants did I discover that the story behind the creation of the album is itself a fascinating one, and a long one. Its roots go back to the mid-forties, and it embraces the entire history of modern jazz. It is a story that offers a number of revelations about how innovation happens in jazz, about how musicians worked together during the "golden age" of jazz to keep the music fresh and to build upon and extend its great tradition. It is an error to think that the steady flow of innovation means somehow that the tradition is unimportant or that jazzmen are ignorant of its existence. One of the dominant aspects of the true jazz tradition is the desire of the musicians (though not necessarily the critics or fans) to find ways to expand the perimeters of jazz expression. And the story of *Kind of Blue* gives further credence to the importance of this desire.

In order to understand how an album like *Kind of Blue* (or any other jazz album, for that matter) was created, we must approach it from several angles: the period and overall milieu in which it was recorded, the events and musical ideas that led up to this period, the musicians who played on the dates and their individual histories and contributions to the album, and in particular the musical history and characteristics of its leader—in this case, Miles Davis.

The *Kind of Blue* story describes the roads traveled by some great jazzmen—roads that were not laid out in straight lines. For each musician there were innumerable detours, backtracking, unexpected loops and circles. And given the tight, insular world of jazz, their separate paths inevitably crossed and intertwined with one another long before the historic sessions for Columbia Records. There were disparate points for these journeys: St. Louis, Missouri; Philadelphia, Pennsylvania; Plainfield, New Jersey; Tampa, Florida; Pittsburgh, Pennsylvania; Washington, D.C.; Cincinnati, Ohio; Brooklyn, New York. From such varied beginnings each jazzman followed his own path, leading ineluctably to the shining moment when they came together in 1959 for the creation of *Kind of Blue*.

The story reminds me in a way of the great Japanese film *Rashomon*, in which four individuals, having witnessed or participated in the same event, reveal their differing visions of the truth concerning what happened. In the case of *Kind of Blue*, the "differing visions" appear not after the fact, as in the film, but come as individual contributions to the same event. The musicians on *Kind of Blue* arrived in 1959 with their own personal visions and were affected by the success of the album in different ways for years afterward. The story of *Kind of Blue* is one of ideas and dreams, of sociocultural and political change and musical evolution; it is the story of towering geniuses who for a brief moment collaborated to produce an imperishable work of art and then went their separate ways.

Not long after making this album, three of the dominant players in the band—Evans, Coltrane, and Adderley—became leaders of their own very successful groups. But each of their bands were so different that it seems nothing short of miraculous not only that they had played in the same group together but that they had been parts of the magnificent whole that was this Miles Davis sextet and, in particular, the group that created *Kind of Blue*.

Some readers may fear that telling this story with so much background detail will spoil the magic of the album. There is no way any writer or critic could do that. No matter how much we explore and attempt to understand the creative process or the actual details involved in the making of *Kind of Blue*, its beauty and truth can never be tarnished. If listening to it literally hundreds of times does not diminish its power, which has been my own experience, nothing can. I have no doubt that five hundred years from now *Kind of Blue* will speak as eloquently to those who hear it as, say, the loveliest of Mozart's string quartets speak to us today. I find this idea reassuring—that there are works of art that, even in this age of transience and packaged feeling, will last as long as life itself.

Our sense of music, our attraction to music, shows that music is in the depth of our being. Music is behind the working of the whole universe. Music is not only life's greatest object, but music is life itself.

—from *The Mysticism of Sound and Music*
by Hazrat Inayat Khan

The Making of KIND OF BLUE

1 End of an Era

Since *Kind of Blue* was not born in a vacuum, we cannot separate it from the time in which it was recorded or the dynamics of the contemporary scene. And since innovation and flux in jazz have always arisen from this community of musical philosophers and explorers, musicians with no direct connection to the album nevertheless influenced its creation—a particularly significant factor because of the album's place in jazz history. In a sense, we can divide jazz history into two segments: before *Kind of Blue* and after *Kind of Blue*. But the particular era in which *Kind of Blue* was born may be an example par excellence of being in the right place at the right time. This album could not have been produced three or four years earlier or later.

Kind of Blue was created, at least to some extent, because the most important jazzmen in the modern scene desperately wanted to change the way they played their music. This need was not purely musical; it had more than a little to do with the changes then going on in American society, especially concerning the lives of African Americans. And that is how our story begins—with a glance back to the jazz scene and social climate at the end of the 1950s.

The year in which *Kind of Blue* was recorded, 1959, can right-fully be considered the final year of the bebop era. Bop contin-ued to be played, of course, as it is to this day. But its status as the cutting edge in jazz came to an end as the decade itself ended. By then there was a restlessness among many of the most-forward-looking jazzmen and a widespread feeling that jazz had to change in order to survive.

The world of jazz during its "golden age"—roughly from the early 1920s to the early 1970s—was somewhat isolated, alienated from American society at large. It had its own val-ues, language, mores, traditions, and politics. It was not a geographical place, although its capital in the 1950s was New York City. It was a world whose entrance was jealously guarded, a world that was certainly not open to all. While all races were admitted to the jazz scene, its primary sensibility was derived from the African American experience, and its provenance can be dated back to its African roots and the subsequent experience of black people in America. It should never be forgotten that the depth and beauty of jazz have arisen from centuries of injustice, brutality, fear, and pain, none of which were passively accepted but were met with African Americans' resistance, striving, and hope for a more benevolent future.

As preparation for this project, I read a book titled *Invisible Republic*, written by the famous rock critic Greil Marcus. I read it because, like this book, its core subject is a specific recording, Bob Dylan's *Basement Tapes*. Marcus's contention is that the music of that album evokes a world within a world that is now gone, an "invisible republic" that was once alive in the traditional folk songs of America's past.

This idea of a separate nation without physical borders that is located both within and outside of America is exactly what the jazz scene once was. It was a unique society that had its origins in the years of slavery, when African Americans—coerced into an alien land—forged their own culture and developed a way of communicating with one another that would not be understood by the white slave masters. White folks took the songs and dances of the slaves to be simply mindless entertainment, not understanding that they were a form of conversation and a means of solidifying community. The words of the songs, the freedom of the dances, even the most subtle gestures, had worlds of meaning beyond the comprehension of the whites. The lyrics of the slave songs and spirituals all had at their core the ecstatic belief in the inevitability of freedom. As in Africa, music was essential to life itself, a key to survival, a way of keeping mind, heart, and community together.

There is another significant aspect of jazz originating in the African American experience. Along with the value placed on community is the value placed on individuality, which in the jazz world is of paramount importance. By "individuality" I do not mean merely the possession of an idiosyncratic style, nor do I mean "individualism," whose focus on self-aggrandizement and one's own self-interest is the very antithesis of community. The individuality to which I refer derives from respect for the *person* and, in jazz, allows each musician to create an entire *sound* that is unlike anyone else's. In a society in which black people were routinely stereotyped, being true to oneself had an intrinsic value that ran deep to the bone. Jazzmen have often been characterized as "eccentric" or even "crazy." But this is simply an expedient way for others to reject their insistence on individuality in a society in which conformity is the desired norm.

Black musicians continued to use a kind of code in their music and in the jazz lifestyle. One fine example is the long list of blues tunes with salacious lyrics that have been cleverly coded—for example, Ma Rainey's "See See Rider Blues" and Mamie Smith's "I Ain't Gonna Give Nobody None of this Jelly Roll." Heavily codified references to illegal drugs have been used in jazz and blues virtually since the inception of the music, from Louis Armstrong's "Muggles" (marijuana) up through Lee Morgan's "Speedball" (a mixture of cocaine and heroin).

In his fascinating (and often racially repellent) memoir, *Really the Blues*, the white New Orleans–style clarinetist Mezz Mezzrow provides an example of a lengthy conversation in "jive" lingo. Although it is blatantly about a drug deal, any police officer overhearing the exchange would have no idea of its meaning; the participants might as well be speaking in Hungarian. Mezzrow also recounts the story of a Louis Armstrong broadcast in which, right in the middle of an interview, Armstrong communicated to Mezzrow a request to have the best marijuana ready for him upon his return to Chicago. To anyone other than those "in the know," the musician was speaking gibberish. Needless to say, Mezzrow got the message.

Besides being one of the most important of all jazzmen, Lester Young was particularly imaginative in creating his own personal "jive" lingo. For example, "Bing and Bob" meant the police. "I got eyes" meant he wished to do something. "I feel a draft" meant he felt that somebody present was, in his opinion, a racist.

There was constant mutual influence between prevailing social currents and the lives and work of the musicians. Musical style and aesthetics were of necessity interwoven with the social fabric, a reflection of the honored place that music occupied at the heart of the social structure in African societies; thus, as society changed, so did the music. The romantic notions about art that have become accepted in Western society since the last century were alien to African culture. John Miller Chernoff writes in *African Rhythm and African Sensibility*:

> The fact that most people in Africa do not conceive of music apart from its community setting and cultural context means that the aesthetics of the music, the way it works to establish a framework for communal integrity, offers a superb approach to understanding Africans' atti-

tudes about what their relationship to each other is and should be. The judgments of competence which people make and the standards of quality of which a musician is aware are elaborations of their own conceptions about the nature of their social life, elaborations which are particularly more evident in musical activity than in many other institutionalized relationships because artistic standards involve explicit judgments on the potential of the communities within which people live.[1]

The jazz world itself was as self-contained as these African communities, and to an extent, music had the same overriding effect on the lives of those who were part of it. The insularity of this world created a kind of musical "greenhouse effect." Wherever musicians gathered and played, whether in nightclubs, on touring buses, or in after-hours joints, they nourished the growth of new ideas, challenged one another, or simply talked music.

Because it is chiefly improvisational, jazz has unique problems, as well as assets, that are not characteristic of composed music. There are still classical music snobs who point out that musical techniques that may be viewed as cutting edge in jazz are old hat in classical music. What these criticisms ignore is the profound differences between the two kinds of music. Techniques that are successful in classical music may not work in jazz, and vice versa. So jazzmen cannot simply steal ideas from other forms of music. They must work out their creative problems for themselves within the special boundaries of their music. Their passionate commitment to the progress of this music springs from the belief that jazz serves a higher purpose, that it provides musicians with far more than a career. As Sonny Rollins told me in a letter, "My whole life has been devoted to the achievement of some important breakthroughs, and I would die disappointed if I couldn't reach them. I want to live up to my promise, not just for me, but for the music."

It has been said that the jazz combo is a perfect microcosm of American democracy (at least in its ideal form): the individual is as important as the society of which he or she is a part. In jazz the individual solo is essential to the work of the group as a whole. This relationship between part and whole is especially crucial for jazz innovation, which arose out of the progress of both individual musicians and the collectivity of the jazz scene. It was an ongoing process born of the musicians' deep belief in their music and its possibilities, and a desire born of curiosity about exploring new planes of freedom. Jazzmen realized that outside of a relatively small circle of fellow believers, musicians, writers, and fans, there was little understanding of, interest in, or respect for this art form in America. And few became involved in the music because they thought they could become rich. There were other reasons to persevere; call it faith.

This closed-off community created a rare intimacy among jazzmen, but not every aspect of the scene was positive. To some extent, the heroin epidemic of the 1940s and 1950s was an offshoot of this tightly knit world. According to Sonny Rollins, using drugs was a kind of protest against the whole money system and a way of renouncing American mores. Ironically, however, even dope acted to bring jazzmen closer together in their shared misery. It was just this intimacy in the musical greenhouse of their world that gave them the ability to connect so closely that they could almost read one another's minds while on the bandstand. The smallest gestures, the subtlest facial expressions, a nod or a glance, had implications lost on most of those in the audience. While playing, jazzmen could hold conversations, admonish one another, or crack jokes, all through their music. Charles Mingus in his autobiography, *Beneath the Underdog*, describes a philosophical conversation he had with Eric Dolphy just before they were due to perform. According to Mingus, they continued the same conversation when they were onstage performing, this time using music instead of words.

This intense intimacy also spurred innovation during the "golden era" of jazz. By the end of the 1950s, many jazzmen were beginning to feel that they had reached the limit of improvisation based on the European-derived harmonic system. They were just beginning to look at the music of other cultures, particularly those of Africa and Asia. And they were responding as well to the growing civil rights movement, with its call for "freedom now!"

It is misleading to make too much of a parallel between the changes in society, in particular the lives of African Americans, and the evolution of their music. But it is even more misleading to ignore this connection. For example, the innovations of Louis Armstrong in Chicago during the mid-1920s reflected in many ways the northern exodus of millions of southern black people. The exultant sound of Armstrong's trumpet represented a new kind of freedom that they sought in the North (however illusory that goal proved to be). Armstrong's swinging rhythmic attack seemed to offer the joy of freedom itself.

During the Swing Era, a period when Armstrong's advances were being further expanded by both big bands and certain key players, New York became the center of jazz. Black musicians in the 1930s found themselves becoming somewhat more accepted into the American mainstream. When Benny Goodman fronted a trio, or later a quartet, of racially mixed personnel, it both reflected these changes and helped push them forward. The Swing Era was a period in which jazz (now labeled swing) became massively popular. But many of the most successful bands were white big bands, such as those of Glenn Miller, the Dorsey brothers, and Artie Shaw. This situation did not go unnoticed by a number of black jazz musicians. In a way, the enormous success of swing, and in particular these white bands, was confirmation of the power of black music. Of course, to some black musicians it appeared that this success was more theft than confirmation or acknowledgment, but the reality is somewhat more complicated, for white musicians had been playing jazz since almost the very earliest days of the music.

Nonetheless, by the late 1930s and early 1940s, there was a restlessness in jazz that would begin gradually and grow to enormous proportions by the time it reached its culmination in the 1950s and 1960s. And with black soldiers fighting a war against racism and fascism in Europe, the idea of returning to a home country in which they were themselves oppressed fanned new winds of change.

The revolution of the early boppers was as much social foment as it was musical. This is not to say that the growing jazz revolt came about solely through racial dynamics, especially black hostility toward whites. The idea that bebop was created to discourage whites from playing jazz—a once-popular theory—is belied by the fact that the first bebop group to play on Fifty-second Street, led by Dizzy Gillespie, included a white pianist, George Wallington. And later Dizzy hired the white drummer Stan Levey for his group.

However, the social ramifications of bebop cannot be avoided. For one thing, the boppers wanted to discard the last remnants of minstrelsy and insisted on being taken seriously as artists. Not that Duke Ellington or Lester Young or Roy Eldridge or Billie Holiday was less than a serious artist. But the boppers made a conscious effort to be treated as artists rather than as performers. Dizzy Gillespie might have clowned around onstage, but his jokes had little connection to minstrelsy. It was humor with a bite that often made his audiences uncomfortable. Most of the other boppers, however, purposely avoided any concession to their audience. If people wanted entertainment beyond brilliant and complex music, they were not going to find it in bebop.

According to the jazz composer-theorist George Russell, there was another sociocultural basis for the harmonic complexities of bop: black musicians needed to make clear the fierce intelligence that was necessary to play this music. The greater society thought of jazz as merely an offshoot of the so-called natural sense of rhythm of African Americans and believed that it lacked the sophistication of classical music. But anyone with ears could hear that bop was as challenging to the mind as any art form could be. Again, this is not to say that earlier jazz did not also require a finely tuned musical mind—of course it did: Armstrong, Ellington, Lester Young, and Art Tatum, to name a few, were inarguably musical geniuses. But bop made much more obvious the importance of the intellect in creating this music (although as we shall see, the ability to *turn off the mind* ultimately became a skill of equal importance).

Bop had been born in the mid-1940s after years of development by young, forward-looking jazzmen. During its embryonic years (from approximately 1939 to 1944) musicians would experiment at after-hours joints in Harlem such as Minton's or Monroe's. Included among the chief "Young Lions" of this era were trumpeter Dizzy Gillespie, alto saxophonist Charlie "Bird" Parker, and guitarist Charlie Christian (although Christian died in 1942 at the age of twenty-five). At these after-hours clubs the nascent boppers would challenge musicians who dared to sit in with them by playing at very fast tempos and, especially, using tunes with complex chord structures such as "How High the Moon" (once declared the "anthem of bebop"). Harmonic complexity became a hallmark of modern jazz. A musician's ability to run the harmonic gauntlet and still make a coherent musical statement was the great challenge of bop.

The use of harmonic structure had special, extramusical significance in jazz: it was the aspect of the music that was most deeply rooted in Europe. Jazz is usually considered a fusion of African and European musical sensibilities. The rhythms and, to an extent, melodies of jazz can be traced to Africa. But the use of chords comes out of the European harmonic system. And jazzmen were very aware of this—a crucial fact to remember when considering the making of *Kind of Blue*.

With this in mind, it is useful to compare the attitude of the original boppers toward European classical music and that of the later generation of jazzmen. Dizzy Gillespie once said that when the boppers listened to the great European repertoire, it was like "going to church." I find this a revealing phrase. The religious analogy implies that the great composers of classical music were patriarchal gods and that the best that jazz musicians could do was act as members of the congregation or obedient children.

In other words, they were expected to embrace the commonly held belief that classical music is the pinnacle of musical achievement for humankind and that the ultimate goal of a musician is to reach for that seemingly unobtainable level of artistry. The accomplishments of Western civilization have too often been used as a weapon against other cultures. The obvious cultural bias may rarely be stated aloud, but we know that in our society the general attitude throughout our educational system—at least until relatively recently—is that we have geniuses such as Shakespeare, Keats, Bach, Mozart, and da Vinci, to name a few. What could any society produce that would come even close to the artistic works of those towering geniuses? The beboppers assumed this cultural bias to be the gospel truth. They simply wanted to be in the same pantheon, albeit on a lower tier.

In the late 1950s and early 1960s, this attitude began to change. Jazz musicians started to look for inspiration beyond Europe and went back to their non-Western roots. (This movement was also, to some degree, a continuing reaction by mainly East Coast African American jazzmen to the cool-jazz movement.) Many began to question whether European tradition was the only yardstick they had with which to measure their own music. In 1960 Miles recorded *Sketches of Spain* with an orchestra that included several classical players. According to Miles, many of them clearly thought of themselves as superior to Miles himself and the other jazzmen. But

Miles bluntly told them that he could do everything they could and that they could not do something he could—which was to improvise, at least to improvise at any significant length. Many jazzmen began to wonder whether trying to achieve the harmonic complexity of classical music was a desired goal after all, especially for a music such as theirs, based primarily on improvisation.

These were the early years of the Black Power movement in which African Americans, no longer kowtowing to the standards of white people, asserted their belief in their own culture. This steadfast commitment reflects one of the distinguishing characteristics that separated Malcolm X philosophically from Martin Luther King Jr. Malcolm had no faith in Western culture and believed that African Americans should distance themselves as far away from it as they could; King continued to hope for solutions within the Euro-American system. Once again, this parallel with the growing movement in jazz away from European harmonic complexity is far more than coincidence. It is evidence of a major shift in the attitudes of masses of American blacks. As usual, jazzmen were far ahead of the curve; but they were not ready to dispense completely with European harmony. One musician, John Coltrane, took it to its maximum complexity before turning his back on it and choosing another route altogether. *Kind of Blue* was the deciding factor in his turnabout.

There were those who felt that the harmonic and rhythmic sophistication of bop ruined jazz as "people's music," and they resisted the ride. Many of the jazz listeners as well as the artists themselves claimed that the new jazz divested the music of its charm. And, in fact, jazz *did* lose a portion of its popular audience with the inception of bop. It was no longer music to dance to, although early on many tried. The boppers often played dances in the 1940s, and there were those who attempted to create ballet using the new music. But eventually modern jazz became primarily a small-club phenomenon, where audiences listened intently to this subtle and complex music. Dancers had to look elsewhere for suitable music, eventually finding it in rhythm and blues and in rock.

Any study of the late Swing Era makes it clear that the bebop movement was inevitable. Musicians ranging from Benny Goodman and Artie Shaw to Coleman Hawkins, Lester Young, Don Byas, and Art Tatum were pushing the harmonic or rhythmic envelope and were already pointing the way toward the modern jazz era. Jazz was simply growing up and moving in new directions.

With the advent of bebop, small groups came to dominate the jazz scene. There were still big bands, and for that matter there were big bands that played modern jazz. For the most part, though, modern jazz was small group jazz. Most often a performance of modern jazz consisted of a statement of theme followed by a series of solos. Sometimes even the melody itself was dropped, and the musicians simply improvised on the chord changes.

There were exceptions to this routine, however. John Lewis, the musical director of the Modern Jazz Quartet, for example, developed complex arrangements that proved small groups could do more than simply play a series of solos. And composers-arrangers such as Charles Mingus and George Russell worked to put jazz improvisation in a more formal context, giving their performances direction and coherence. On the other hand, Sonny Rollins developed an improvisational style in which solos were not just a series of melodic ideas but rather possessed form and overriding logic. Instead of playing on the chord changes only and discarding melody when he started to improvise, many of his solos used the melody itself as a way of imposing form.

After the initial bop revolution, modern jazz went through two important permutations in the 1950s. The first was the cool, or West Coast, jazz movement. This lyrical, languid, pastel jazz is bop without the heat. It is associated mainly with white jazz musicians, though the most important influences were Miles Davis, Lester Young, and in his less incendiary solos, Charlie Parker himself in the work he did with strings.

One reason cool jazz is associated with white jazzmen is that the music often seems as much influenced by European classical music as by the jazz tradition. To many people it was jazz in which the African American elements had been bleached away, although there were a number of black musicians who played in West Coast groups, such as Sonny Clark or Chico Hamilton. Actually, Hamilton's popular group was the apotheosis of the movement. His group included a classically trained cellist and often performed suites and complex arrangements that at times gives off the musty odor of the conservatory.

Cool jazz is associated with white jazzmen for yet another reason. As anyone who has read my earlier books knows, I have little use for the revisionist segregation of jazz history, but there is no doubt that much cool jazz lacks the harsher truths heard in bebop. It is jazz minus the tortured history one can hear in even the most joyous playing of the great black jazzmen, as well as in the music of white jazzmen who empathized with that sensibility.

A particularly key influence in the advent of cool jazz was a nonet that Miles Davis led in the late 1940s and early 1950s. The collection of this group's recordings would be titled *Birth of the Cool*, and from then on Miles would routinely be identified as a cool jazzman no matter how far he advanced from the style of those earlier recordings. Even when he was playing the often cacophonous music of his fusion groups in the 1970s, he was still dubbed a cool jazzman. For that matter, *Kind of Blue* has occasionally been called a great cool-jazz album. To a degree this is understandable since the album has a surface serenity not unlike that of much cool jazz. But beneath that surface are deeper and darker emotions; these complex layers of feeling and thought give *Kind of Blue* its continual fascination and help explain why it remains so powerful, even after multiple listenings.

In the 1950s there was a movement on the East Coast that in some ways was a reaction to the cool-jazz movement. Dubbed hard bop, it is far more bluesy and strong-edged than West Coast jazz. It is inevitably portrayed as an attempt to bring jazz back to its African American roots, which is true to an extent (although in a mirror reversal of West Coast jazz, there were a number of important white players of hard bop). Out of hard bop developed a subgenre usually called soul jazz. This is music even more centered in the blues than most hard bop, and it became very popular. Usually featuring an organist who had been influenced by Jimmy Smith's funky style, the tunes generally have titles referring to down-home black life, such as "Back to the Chicken Shack" or "Members Don't Get Weary." But this music soon became mired in clichés, and the plethora of soul jazz albums, with few exceptions, became unrecognizable from one another. Ironically, there are also those who classify *Kind of Blue* as one of the ultimate products of the hard-bop movement—a view that is merely a knee-jerk reflex among commentators who need to pigeonhole. The truth is that *Kind of Blue* is beyond easy categories.

By 1959 bop—in one form or another—had been dominating the jazz scene for almost fifteen years. But there was a new kind of restlessness, a feeling of anticipation that yet another fresh wave of change was about to engulf jazz. The prophets of this change were musicians such as Rollins, Mingus, Jimmy Giuffre, and George Russell. By this time cracks were becoming obvious in the bop aesthetic. When improvisational geniuses like Parker, Gillespie, or pianist Bud Powell had performed, bop seemed limitless. But by the end of the 1950s, many less-than-stellar musicians had mastered the rhythmic and harmonic disciplines of bop and were playing solos that just "ran the changes"—playing through the harmonic structures without creating coherent musical statements.

By the late 1950s a number of important musicians were becoming dissatisfied with the status quo and were actively seeking ways of giving jazz renewed life. One of the most important of these musicians is the bassist-composer Charles Mingus, who in the notes for his wonderful 1959 album, *Mingus Dynasty,* wrote about Ornette Coleman, even though at the time he had not actually heard Coleman play. Mingus had, however, already heard about Coleman's innovations. Coleman, in order to play with a new melodic freedom, was playing music that mostly discarded conventional harmonic structure. He had previously recorded two albums in Los Angeles before coming to the East Coast, but they were largely overlooked at the time. Mingus knew that Coleman, or somebody like Coleman, was inevitable. Mingus was well aware that he and many other musicians who were not satisfied with conventional harmony were looking for a way to expand their ability to create melody unhampered by the prison of chord changes. Mingus himself had already explored atonality and other harmonic forms in his search for new areas of freedom.

Mingus was not the only musician looking beyond the frontiers of bop. Sonny Rollins had practiced with Coleman while on his first trip to Los Angeles in 1957. Rollins was not shaken by Coleman's direction, because he himself had been thinking along similar lines. In some ways Rollins's famous "Blue Seven," recorded in 1956, is an indication of the shift in Sonny's direction. After he left Max Roach's group in 1957, he usually performed with only bass and drums in order to provide himself with the greatest possible melodic freedom. A new revolution was on its way, and the best musicians in jazz knew it.

At the same time, African Americans in general were becoming increasingly impatient, confronting head-on the racism and segregation that, despite the gains following World War II, still held them in place as second-class citizens, in both the South and the North. Again, it is certainly not a coincidence that the idea of freedom, especially for African Americans, was itself in the wind, especially in the late 1950s.

It is ironic that the 1950s in general were a period that has often been described as tepid, bland, and conformist; nothing could be further from the reality of that decade's tumult and hard-won achievements in the African American experience. During that "tepid" decade, among other groundbreaking events, Rosa Parks made her courageous stand, and following it the amazing (and successful) grassroots bus boycott in Montgomery, Alabama, took place. The U.S. Supreme Court ordered the end of school segregation, with fierce opposition in many states, and federal troops had to be sent in to Little Rock, Arkansas, to ensure the safety of black children as they entered the desegregated high school. To America's crushing shame, the crime of lynching was still a menace, the most widely publicized case being that of Emmett Till in 1955. Under the leadership of Dr. Martin Luther King Jr., the civil rights movement picked up momentum; eventually, espe-cially for the people on the front lines, that movement—"the Movement"—would become a juggernaut, a relentless force.

These parallels between the lives of African Americans bat-tling for their freedom as citizens and that of jazz musicians for their freedom from European harmony are too close to be mere happenstance. The disenchantment of black Americans with the status quo following World War II was mirrored in the gathering anger that revealed itself in the changes in jazz. *Kind of Blue* is a product of this striving for both social and musical freedom—which is one reason this album is so deeply textured.

Miles Davis clearly had his finger in the wind by the late 1950s. At the time, Miles had become one of the most influen-tial of all jazzmen, and his home had become a favorite gath-ering place for musicians. It was often the center of lively discussions about any number of subjects, but the usual focus was on expanding the vocabulary of jazz and dealing with innovation and change. Many musicians looked to Miles almost as if he were a prophet, which in some ways he was. He was always on the crest of the latest wave of change, although very often, as we shall see, his actions were in reaction to innovation rather than in accordance with it. Miles always had his own agenda, like the greatest musicians, and was constantly on the lookout for ideas and jazzmen who could help him achieve his goals.

It is worth noting that Miles had been a forward-looking musician even as a teenager in East St. Louis. He had also been acutely sensitive to the frustration and untenable situation of black people in America. Miles's intuition about the course of jazz evolution and its connection to the changes in American society were among the reasons *Kind of Blue* had so much impact on the jazz scene and the future of what Duke Ellington called "the great American music."

2 Miles's Mode, Part One

One night early in the 1980s, Miles was talking about his past work. This kind of reminiscing was rare for him because he preferred to live defiantly in the present, and he at least pretended to no longer care about his past accomplishments. He was irritated with anyone who harped continuously about his former achievements. He insisted that his only interest was in the work he was doing at the present time. The past, he told those who kept referring to it—especially journalists—was dead and buried. Sure, it was great back then. But that was *then*; he was living, and creating, in the here and now.

For whatever reason, Miles was willing to talk about the past on this particular evening. Perhaps the reason for this shift in behavior was that he was with only a couple of friends, one of whom had known him since the 1940s; or maybe it was simply that the hour was late, and it was one of those times when the past comes to haunt the mind. Miles admitted that some of the music he had created long ago was close to his heart. When the old friend asked him what the best music he had ever created was, he answered without a moment of thought: *Porgy and Bess* and *Sketches of Spain*. This was no surprise; he had collaborated on those albums with his closest friend, Gil Evans, and—after the great works of Ellington—those albums are without a doubt the finest orchestral pieces in all of jazz. His friend asked him which album meant the most to him from the dozens of classics he had recorded with small groups. Miles answered, just as quickly, *"Kind of Blue."*

Probably no jazz musician has been more written about (and photographed, for that matter) than Miles Davis. By the time he was thirty-two, when he recorded *Kind of Blue*, he was already something of a legend; yet a considerable number of his greatest achievements still lay in the future. His is such an enormous presence throughout the past fifty years of American music that it is almost impossible to write about any aspect of modern jazz without taking him into consideration. I have written about him in all four of my previous books; there is simply no way one can ignore him.

Despite all the books, including his autobiography (as well as my own book *'Round About Midnight: A Portrait of Miles Davis*), he remains an enigma, a figure who both personally and artistically is so elusive that trying to define him is a bit like attempting to capture mercury. I believe that this is how Miles wanted it. Being the accomplished boxer that he was, he knew the importance of always being on your toes, ready to dance away from being cornered or held tight. One thing is certain: Miles was always calculating his odds, always working on his strategy as both an artist and a public figure. Perhaps Sonny Rollins is right when he says that improvising is largely intuitive—which does not mean, however, that strategy does not come into play. Except for Duke Ellington, no other jazz musician understood so well the importance of strategy in the creation of his music.

As many of my readers know, I had been friends with Miles for a while during the 1970s and early 1980s. My first book was based mainly on our conversations over the few years that I knew him. People often ask me what my favorite "Miles story" is, and I always choose this one: I was visiting Miles, and we had an argument about what day of the week it happened to be. This may sound strange, but at the time Miles was using massive amounts of cocaine and staying up for days at a time; then he would crash by taking barbiturates. All his friends, including me, tried unsuccessfully to make him refrain from such self-destructive behavior, but he was headstrong. Sadly, he felt that this was all he had left to live for. He was having painful health problems, and drugs were probably a kind of self-medication. Consistent with his image as the "Prince of Darkness," he always kept his home dark; it was hard to tell whether it was three in the morning or three in the afternoon.

Anyway, Miles asked me what day it was. I told him it was Wednesday. He replied, using one of his favorite expressions, "You're a lying motherfucker." (He always put the emphasis on *fuck* in *motherfucker,* giving the line a personal lilt.) From there on, we debated which day of the week it was. Finally I remembered I had that day's *New York Times* in my briefcase. I took it out and showed it to Miles; needless to say, it confirmed that the day actually was Wednesday. Miles shook his head and sat down. Then he said, "Do you see all those awards on my wall, Eric? The reason I won them is because I can't remember anything worth a damn."

Miles, like many jazzmen, had a fascinating and subtle way of talking in shorthand; often his words had layers of meaning that were not immediately apparent. It took me a few moments to figure out, metaphorically, exactly what he meant: not remembering his past work forced him to be constantly inventive in the moment of creation. The past was dead, buried, forgotten; as Bob Dylan put it, true artists "don't look back." (Miles was a great admirer of Dylan, incidentally.) When jazz fans wondered why he didn't attempt, say, a *Kind of Blue II*, the reason is obvious: it was simply not possible. Miles's own reply to those who asked him about playing music from his past was always, "Why do you want me to do that again? Didn't I do it good the first time?"

Of course, there was more to his genius than simply "forgetting" the past. I have a friend who cannot understand why Miles is so admired, why he is considered to be on the highest tier of jazz achievement when he was obviously not a great virtuoso like Clifford Brown or Dizzy Gillespie. The answer is simple—Miles's music deeply affects people; he is able to reach a part of us that other musicians, no matter how accomplished their technique, cannot touch. This quality is part of the mix that accounts for the album's seemingly ageless popularity. Isn't that a prime goal of art—to communicate one's deepest feelings to the audience? *Kind of Blue* does just that, communicating not only Miles's feelings but also the mood usually associated with him.

What is that mood? It is dark, melancholy, bluesy, introspective, yet with a rare kind of joy at its center. I am tempted to say also that the mood is "innocent," by which I mean that the expression of emotion has a yearning quality and a simple straightforwardness that, despite its sophistication, seems almost childlike. The closest any other musician has come to achieving this mood is Louis Armstrong in "West End Blues" and Charlie Parker in "Parker's Mood." I believe that it is a deeply spiritual expression, although Miles never claimed to have any interest in spirituality. He had lost all interest in religion when he discovered, as a boy, that the churches in East St. Louis were racially segregated. Nevertheless, Miles's expressiveness, at least to me, embodies the sound of hope: no matter how dark our journey, there is always a light to lead our way. Perhaps that hopefulness in itself is childlike, but how can anyone who has experienced life's pain fail to find solace in the levels of emotion expressed on *Kind of Blue*?

Where and how did this mood originate? I believe that looking even briefly at Miles's life, we can clearly trace the emotional geography that he translated into music. We can also see how Miles became a kind of existentialist hero, insisting always on making his own choices, always finding his own route, and committed to being the exact person and artist that he strove to be without making allowances for the expectations of others. If he was an innovator, it was always in the service of his effort to understand who he was and who he was becoming, and to create the music that reflected his own evolution. We cannot understand *Kind of Blue* without attempting to grasp the sometimes elusive identity of Miles Davis, both as a man and as an artist.

Miles Davis (he was actually Miles Davis III) was born in Alton, Illinois, on May 24, 1926. Both his father and grandfather had been prominent in the black community. When the family moved to East St. Louis, his father became a very successful dentist and dental surgeon. Unlike so many black jazzmen, Miles did not grow up in poverty. His family was well-to-do, wealthy enough for his father to buy a ranch on which he raised hogs.

Miles was spoiled by his parents; he wore only the best clothes and early on had his own car. He first started playing the trumpet at the age of thirteen, when his father bought him a horn. One of Miles's father's patients was a trumpeter and music teacher named Elwood Buchanan, who became the young musician's mentor. Buchanan instructed his students to play with as little vibrato as possible: "You'll wind up getting old and start shaking anyway." Miles quickly became proficient on the instrument, but when he participated in music contests at his school, he inevitably lost to white players who, at least according to Miles, were clearly not as accomplished as he was. This experience helped forge his distinctive personality and his strength of will. As Miles told an interviewer: "It made me so mad that I made up my mind to outdo anybody white on my horn. If I hadn't met that prejudice, I probably wouldn't have had as much drive in my work. I've thought about that a lot. Prejudice and curiosity have been responsible for what I've done in music."[1] If some people

wonder where Miles got his supposed "arrogance," this statement should make the answer obvious.

Miles became close to a number of other trumpeters in St.
Louis (which at that time was known in the jazz world as a
trumpet man's city), including Clark Terry, whose quick,
vibrato-free style was a key influence on Miles. According to
Miles, even in his early years as a musician, he was fascinated
with the evolution of jazz. Despite his youth, he displayed an
unusual farsightedness about the future of the music, and he
was always curious about the latest innovations. When he discovered that Billy Eckstine was bringing his big band to St.
Louis, he was overjoyed to be able to see and listen to two
jazzmen he had heard so much about through the musicians'
grapevine: the alto saxophonist Charlie "Yardbird" Parker
and trumpeter Dizzy Gillespie. Miles knew that these two
men were the leaders of the burgeoning bebop revolution,
although Miles himself had at this point never heard bop. On
the opening night of the Eckstine band, one of the trumpeters
became sick, and Miles, mainly because he had a union card,
was hired on the spot to replace the ailing sideman while Eckstine was in the area. Billy Eckstine would later say in an
interview: "When I first heard Miles, I let him sit in so as not
to hurt his feelings, but he sounded terrible; he couldn't play
at all."[2] This contradicts Miles's insistence that at the time,
he was an accomplished musician. Nevertheless, Bird was
impressed enough by the youngster to invite him to New
York, offering to take him under his wing.

Actually, Parker's invitation does not necessarily contra-
dict Eckstine's statement. I think there is little doubt that
Bird had his own reasons for wanting Miles to come to New
York besides whatever musical ability Bird detected. Having
a young man who idolized him and who had a constant supply
of cash was of great importance to Bird, because even this
early, Parker had a heavy drug habit that could be maintained only with a reliable source of money. I am sure that
the saxophonist was able to hear Miles's incipient musical tal-

ent, but he certainly had other motives, which Miles would soon discover.

After he graduated from high school in 1944, Miles moved to New York, supposedly to attend the Juilliard School of Music; at least that is what he told his father. He wound up spending very little time at the school, however. His real "school" was hanging out with Charlie Parker and spending most of his time on Fifty-second Street—"Swing Street" to the musicians who performed there. In a single block there were small jazz clubs, one after another, in which some of the greatest of all jazz artists regularly played: Coleman Hawkins, Art Tatum, Billie Holiday, Roy Eldridge, Don Byas, even Count Basie's band somehow managed to fit onto the tiny stage of one of the clubs.

Whatever ulterior motives Bird might have had for his relationship with Miles, he was genuinely dedicated to the education of the young trumpeter. For example, he brought him to the home of Thelonious Monk. Monk had been termed "the high priest of behop." (And this was true in more than one way—Monk's love for a variety of illicit substances was notorious.) From Monk, Miles was given early training in what *not* to play, a lesson that would eventually be crucial to his own mature musical conception.

I believe, however, that Miles learned an even more valuable lesson from Monk. Monk's piano style has at times been derided for its purported lack of technique. Upon hearing Monk, my father once said, "A four-year-old could play better than that." Certainly, Monk's style would have shocked most piano teachers. He did not use the balls of his fingers; he played with his fingers flat on the keyboard. He often used his elbows and never displayed the technique of, say, Art Tatum or Oscar Peterson. However, Monk's sound is as immediately identifiable as that of Ben Webster, Lester Young, or Miles himself. There are those who have heard Monk play, when he wants to, in what may be called a "legitimate" style, performing with surprisingly conventional technique. But Monk understood that the most important thing in jazz is to establish your own distinctive sound, one that is uniquely yours. Technique exists for one reason only—to create a sound that reflects the musician's inner self. The rest is extraneous. In order to be a great jazz artist, you must find out who you really are; only then can you create music that expresses your truest self.

This perspective is markedly different from that of European music, in which for each instrument there is a standard set of techniques that a musician must try to master. Nobody with a style as idiosyncratic as Monk's would ever have made it in that world. Monk really reinvented the piano, twisting the entire technique and approach to the instrument until it fit his personal conception. Of course, this was nothing new. Louis Armstrong reinvented the trumpet, using a broad vibrato previously unheard on the horn. Coleman Hawkins was dubbed the "inventor of the tenor saxophone." Of course, he did not really "invent" his instrument, but he did create a way of playing the tenor sax—previously used mainly for slap-tongued vaudeville effects—that turned it into a perfect instrument for personal jazz expression. These were vital lessons for the young Miles Davis, ones that he took to heart. They are the lessons that saved him as a musician and eventually helped to make him as a man.

Besides creating a personal sound, Monk was also subverting a Western instrument for his own purposes. The piano is simply not made to be played the way Monk played it. Most of the greatest jazzmen, in the service of creating a personal sound, have similarly subverted the traditional techniques associated with their instruments. Certainly this is true for every musician who plays on *Kind of Blue*.

In 1945 Miles played on Charlie Parker's first recording date under his own leadership for Savoy Records. It is one of the classic recording sessions in the annals of jazz. Parker, bursting with ideas, creates one astonishing solo after another, climaxing in the fast-tempoed "Ko Ko," perhaps his single greatest achievement—although Bird played so many brilliant solos that it is difficult to choose one such highlight. At this time, Miles's ability certainly bears out Billy Eckstine's earlier opinion (rather than Miles's own memory of his skill at handling the trumpet). His playing is barely adequate and often sounds shaky and uncertain, hardly swinging at all. When Dizzy Gillespie sits in for the introductory passages of "Ko Ko," the contrast between the two trumpeters is almost embarrassing.

It is here that we come upon a mystery: How did this basically incompetent trumpeter eventually become such a brilliant artist? Within four years or so, he could keep pace with virtually any player in jazz. With such poor soloing on the 1945 Bird session, it is a miracle that he did not turn tail and head right back to East St. Louis. I think it says something quite remarkable about Miles that he did not. In 1946 Parker went to California as part of a group that included Dizzy and the vibist Milt Jackson, a group supposedly arriving as bearers of the bebop gospel. Parker wound up staying in Los Angeles and eventually had a nervous breakdown due to his inability to score heroin and his attempt to use alcohol as a way of preventing a violent withdrawal from the drug. In 1946 Miles joined Benny Carter's band in New York for the express purpose of getting to the West Coast and hooking up with Bird again. Miles recorded some sides with Parker for the small Dial label. Although he sounds better than he had on the 1945 "Ko Ko" date, it is nevertheless hardly the work of a convincing soloist.

After drying out at California's Camarillo State Hospital, Parker returned to New York and quickly put together a quintet that included Miles. According to Miles, he himself was the one who rehearsed the band and kept it together because Parker was so involved in his chaotic lifestyle. For Miles the challenge of playing next to Bird, one of the most magnificent virtuosos in jazz history, was so great that, in his own words, "I used to quit every night." We can only imagine how harrowing an experience this must have been for the young trumpeter. There are stories of Parker literally pushing Miles onstage; he was paralyzed with fright at the thought of attempting, once again, to keep pace with the saxophonist. Miles was forced to either find a way to survive this trial by fire or give up the whole idea of being a jazzman. To Miles, no doubt, the thought of going back to East St. Louis and working on his father's hog farm or becoming a music teacher (a quite horrifying thought from a kid's point of view) must have been soul-withering.

During this experience he was compelled to face the hardest truths about himself, and he had to either forge his own way through sheer willpower or simply surrender. Undoubtedly this is when Miles, both as a man and as an artist, intuitively gravitated toward an existentialist perspective of life. It is possible that he was drawn in this direction during his first trip to Paris, where he became friends with both Jean-Paul Sartre and Simone de Beauvoir. Though he had not read their philosophical works, he understood the crucial idea that one does not come into the world with a ready-made identity or essence; one must create oneself. Thus, Miles Davis was forced to reinvent himself, to decide who and what he wanted to be and then actually bring that self into being.

It was in this period that Miles developed his tough exterior, his "arrogance." The part of him that was shy and vulnerable had to be protected by a thick skin. He had been quite the opposite when he first arrived in New York—something of an innocent who did not use any drugs, did not drink, and didn't even chase women. (In fact, Miles was actually married at the time, although he had left his wife behind in East St. Louis.) So, out of the welter of complications in his life, he made a conscious choice to develop some of what would later became known as the more notorious aspects of his personality: the use of invectives and hard language, the cynical (and often hilarious) sense of humor, the quickness to anger. In the world he had chosen for himself—the fractious and often down-and-dirty New York jazz scene—this external hardness was the only way to survive for someone as deeply sensitive as Miles. He allowed only those who understood his artifice to get close to him. Those who saw only his surface and believed, for example, that he was an antiwhite racist or a vicious bastard, he did not want to deal with anyway.

Miles once told me, "If they took away my legs, my arms, even my cock, as long as they left me my mind, I would find a way to get everything back." It was his brilliant mind and his stubborn determination that enabled him to weather the ordeal he went through in his early days with Parker. Through this searing apprenticeship, Miles developed into a persuasive and stylistically original soloist. The sides that this group recorded in 1947–48 for both Savoy and Dial (including the first date led by Miles, in which Bird played tenor instead of his customary alto sax) reveal that Miles had greatly improved and was developing the style for which he would become famous. Although he clearly had a long way to go, the melodic inventiveness and flowing logic, the use of the middle register, and the introverted lyricism are all in evidence.

Miles eventually left Parker's group, frustrated by both the battles he and Max Roach went through to get Parker to pay them and dealing with Parker's out-of-control lifestyle. After Bird died, Miles said to Roach, "The motherfucker died before we could get even, Max."

Miles gigged around as much as he could. He had become a well-known musician on the Fifty-second Street scene and began leading his own groups. During this period he increasingly wanted to learn how to compose and arrange. He chose another perfect mentor for learning these crafts: Gil Evans. Evans had been writing arrangements for years, and Miles especially appreciated Evans's ingenious arrangement of "Donna Lee" for the Claude Thornhill band, a tune that the trumpeter had written for the Parker group.

Evans had a basement one-room apartment near Fifty-second Street, and it eventually became the place for a kind of jazz Bloomsbury. Musicians would squeeze into this small apartment and discuss the latest directions of the modern jazz scene. Among those who hung out there, in addition to Miles and Evans, were the baritone saxophonist and composer Gerry Mulligan, alto saxophonist Lee Konitz, pianist-composer (and eventually musical director of the Modern Jazz Quartet) John Lewis, the great bop drummer Max Roach, the composer John Benson Brooks, and a composer-arranger and onetime drummer named George Russell. At times, Bird himself would take a breather from his tangled life and join the group.

Years later this is how Gerry Mulligan remembered the scene: "With all the great bands that were around [New York], big and little, it was an exciting time musically. And everybody seemed to gravitate to Gil's place. Everybody influenced everybody else, and Bird was the number-one influence on us all. Gil lived in a basement on Fifty-seventh Street near Fifth Avenue. Actually, it was behind a Chinese laundry, and had all the pipes for the building as well as a sink, a bed, a piano, a hot-plate and no heat."[3]

It was in this funky environment that ideas were hatched, ideas that would have a profound influence on the course of jazz for years to come. Many years later *Kind of Blue* would indirectly become one of the important fruits of the relationships germinated in this group.

By this time, the late 1940s, many musicians had climbed on the bop bandwagon, and jazz was inundated by imitators of Bird and Dizzy, and bop clichés could be heard in most of the clubs on Fifty-second Street. The more forward-looking musicians, including Miles, were working in the direction of new ideas to be built on the beachhead that bop had established.

In one of my books, *Blue: The Murder of Jazz*, I wrote that there is a "Miles myth" that goes something like this: Miles

Davis personally invented cool jazz, then created hard bop, modal jazz, freebop, and fusion. But Miles really "invented" none of these movements. All innovation in jazz can be traced to far more than one "inventor." Certainly, Miles found ways to incorporate the ideas of the more progressive musicians into a convincing and personal music. I believe there were key reasons that Miles was such a continually restless artist. Some have already been touched upon—his refusal to "look back," the "art of forgetfulness" in which he forced himself to find fresh musical territory, and his indefatigable curiosity. But perhaps the most important and overriding factor was his disdain for musical platitudes and easy licks. If nothing else, changing the ground rules of the music forced the soloists to come up with new conceptions, which is what Miles lived for. Whenever a style became stale, musicians often trotted out shopworn phrases or even whole solos rather than create fresh ideas. But if the ground was constantly shifting beneath their feet, they were forced to approach their improvisations from novel directions, to go deeper and play more inventively. This kind of strategy is a constant throughout Miles's career, one that, as we shall see, was very much a force behind the creation of *Kind of Blue*.

Miles's restlessness, both for him and his colleagues in the jazz Bloomsbury, led to the first development that emerged directly from the caucuses in Evans's apartment: a band led by Miles that would explore new musical areas and eventually become one of the chief influences for an entire jazz movement destined to dominate the early 1950s.

Its founders wanted this band to be large enough to accommodate intricate arrangements, with as much room for tonal color as possible without forfeiting the intimacy, and freedom for improvisation, of a combo. Miles liked the lush arrangements that Evans had done for the Claude Thornhill band; he especially enjoyed Evans's use of dense tonal colors. It was decided that a nine-piece group would be ideal. However,

Evans became sick and was able to do only a couple of the arrangements. Most of the others were done by John Lewis and Gerry Mulligan (although one of the most famous tunes composed for the group, "Israel," was written by the trumpeter John Carisi).

The sound that this group produced was unlike anything else in jazz history, although its ambience bore a slight resemblance to that of the Claude Thornhill band. Unlike orthodox bebop, the rhythmic thrust was mainly behind the beat, and the tonal colors were more pastel than those of red-hot bebop. The solos, although as harmonically sophisticated as bop, had a detached and more reflective quality than the burning intensity of the music created by the boppers.

Years later Gerry Mulligan wrote the liner notes for a reissue of *Birth of the Cool*. This is how he characterized Miles: "Miles [was] the bandleader. He took the initiative and put the theories to work. He called the rehearsals, hired the halls, called the players, and generally cracked the whip."

Miles, befitting a leader, is the most prominent soloist on these sides. One can clearly hear the mature style that we all associate with him. In particular, his work on "Israel" is a perfectly constructed solo, and in years to come Miles's solo would often be used as part of the arrangement when big bands played the tune. This is the Miles we are all familiar with, the Miles whose virtuosity is replaced by lyricism and depth of emotion. In addition, his tone has a burry quality, not nearly as brassy as that of most jazz trumpeters. Some critics have denigrated Miles for virtually turning the trumpet's sonic quality into something closer to a woodwind.

Unfortunately, this band was truly ahead of its time. It was not able to find an audience and had only a single stand at a jazz club, the Royal Roost. However, they did record several sides for Capitol Records that, when they were eventually collected into a single LP, were titled *Birth of the Cool*. This was not just record-company hype—the band was to an extent instrumental in the advent of the cool, or West Coast, jazz movement. Despite being one of the founders of the cool jazz movement, Miles would soon go on to new, and fiercer, areas of music-making.

3 Miles's Mode, Part Two

Birth of the Cool is vital to our story because it is an early example of a pattern that Miles would set for the rest of his career. In many ways the music was a deliberate attempt to cool the flames of bop. By emphasizing lyricism, using softer-edged tones and tight arrangements rather than simply a series of solos, the nonet played modern jazz that lacks the ferocity and roiling quality of orthodox bebop.

Those involved in the group were not the only ones taking this "cool" approach. Other musicians also aimed for a lyrical quality. About the same time, for example, the pianist George Shearing formed a quintet that played what was called "bop for the people." This music, too, employed many of the harmonic advances of bop but was nevertheless cooler in texture and possessed a singable melodicism.

Ironically, Miles and the nonet were not rewarded for playing more accessible bop. However, the cool jazz, played mainly by white musicians, was greatly influenced by Miles's band and would find a large, primarily white audience in the early 1950s. But Miles himself would have little interest in cool jazz after the nonet disbanded. A further irony is that the music of the group was arguably superior to anything done later during the years of the cool-jazz movement.

Now we come upon another mystery. In almost any history of jazz, Miles's development is usually portrayed like this: he was originally influenced by Dizzy, but when he discovered that he lacked the ability to play on that kind of virtuosic level, he developed a style in which his lack of technical mastery was not important. Thelonious Monk's development is often portrayed in a similar manner—in both cases these artists' evolution is based on their ability to make tasty musical lemonade out of the lemons of their limited technique.

At one time I myself believed this version of history, but I have since come to a very different conclusion. Miles had always maintained that one of the most rewarding musical experiences of his life was his practice sessions with the young trumpeter Fats Navarro. Navarro, who would die from drug-related causes when he was only twenty-six, was a brilliant trumpeter, a great bop virtuoso second only to Dizzy Gillespie. He was also the chief influence on Clifford Brown, another magnificent trumpeter who was fated to die young.

Miles claimed that he himself could play on the same virtuosic level as Navarro and that Navarro, in turn, was able to play ballads as soulfully as Miles. I was always very skeptical about this. How was it possible that the guy who, in Billy Eckstine's words, "could hardly blow [his] nose, let alone [his] trumpet" in the mid-1940s became a virtuoso on the same level as the prodigious Navarro? Yet Sonny Rollins has told me that he heard Miles and Fats practice together, and it was one of the most exciting musical experiences of that genius's life. And now we even have aural proof that Miles's unlikely-sounding story was true.

The Birth of the Cool sides that the band recorded for Capitol were done in three sessions, two in 1949 and the third in March of 1950. In August 1949, five months after the second *Cool* session, Miles went to Paris to perform at the Paris Festival de International Jazz. He was coleading a group with one of the most important composers and arrangers to arise out of bebop, Tadd Dameron, who played piano in the group. The intent of the festival was to provide an overview of jazz history; the Davis-Dameron group was the representative of bebop.

Dameron had been leading some of the most interesting modern jazz groups of the era, often using Fats Navarro. Perhaps as a result of the Navarro influence, Miles played with a virtuosity that is astonishing. At times he is easily comparable in technique with Navarro, who, as previously noted, was one of the most technically adept of all bop trumpeters. Miles plays on the full range of his horn—high, fast, and with brassy brilliance. The contrast between this performance and his style on the Parker recordings of the time and, especially, his solos on the recordings of his nonet is startling. The nightly trial by fire of his years with Parker had forced him to evolve at an amazing pace, especially when one remembers his incompetent soloing in the very first session with Bird, Miles's solo debut on records.

So what was going on here? In some ways the answer is simple—Miles *chose* the style he pursued. He had not been exaggerating when he said that he was able to keep up with Navarro (which also means, of course, that Sonny Rollins's memory about those sessions is accurate). He was not forced to play the way he did because he lacked technique, at least not at this point. Rather, he developed a style that reflected his inner being. Every aspect of his style was in place because that was Miles's deliberate choice.

Much later in his career, Miles said in an interview that he always tried to keep in mind the context in which he was playing and would always try to adapt his own style to what was going on in the current musical environment. He said that if he had played with Count Basie, his performance would have been far different from, say, that of his own small groups. Undoubtedly, he developed a style playing with Bird that offered a contrast with Parker, giving the music of the group both variety and depth. This contrast—between virtuosic saxophone and lyrical trumpet—would be a pattern for most of his small group work for years to come. After a blistering solo by John Coltrane or Sonny Rollins, Miles's solos, with their use of space, melancholy lyricism, and pliant tone, could be devastating. Of course, this was no accident—perhaps more than anything else, Miles's sensitivity and intuition in the use of contrasting aural textures was almost equal to the grand master of sonic architecture, Duke Ellington.

So here, in this contrast between Miles's playing in Paris and that of the nonet sides, we have the first solid evidence of his skill as musical strategist. Perhaps when he walked the tightrope next to Charlie Parker night after night, he realized that he must make hard choices and then put himself and everything he had behind those choices. He would never again let himself become cornered—because now he had a secret: his knowledge of his own freedom, despite the difficulties of a racist society or the many complexities of the kind of music he had chosen to explore. He knew there would always be choices, and perhaps this knowledge caused him to be what some people called arrogant. Even if he *was* arrogant, though, it was an attitude based on ultimate self-knowledge and the freedom that comes from such knowledge.

It was just about this time, the late 1940s, that Miles became addicted to heroin. It is strange that it happened after Miles left Charlie Parker's group. Drug addiction had become a plague throughout the jazz world during this period, so it was not surprising that Miles finally succumbed. Being an addict was, in the words of Dexter Gordon, "part of the [jazz] social scene at the time."[1] In the bebop subculture, drug addiction was almost mandatory for admission. There were a few, like Dizzy Gillespie, who remained untouched by the dope epidemic, but most young jazzmen felt that heroin was necessary to play at the level that bop demanded. According to

Sonny Rollins, using dope also reflected the profound alienation of young jazzmen from mainstream American society. As Sonny put it: "Using drugs was, in a strange way, a negation of the money ethic. Because guys were saying, 'I don't care about this, I don't care how I dress or how I look, all I care about is *music*.' Using drugs was kind of a way for the boppers to express what they thought about American capitalist values."[2]

Perhaps Miles did not become addicted while he was with Bird as a natural consequence of his awareness that Parker's life had become a mess. By the late 1940s Miles's career was no longer in high gear, probably in part because of the disappointing reception that the nonet had received from the jazz public.

Whatever the reason, after he became addicted Miles was increasingly undependable, and club owners were reluctant to hire him. Throughout the early 1950s Miles got very few gigs. However, he did record under his own leadership for the Prestige label. During the first years of his relationship with the label, he did a series of inconsistent sides in which a number of up-and-coming young players were heard, including saxophonists Sonny Rollins and Jackie McLean, pianist Walter Bishop, and drummer Philly Joe Jones. On one date he had both Sonny Rollins and Charlie Parker playing tenor sax.

Nevertheless, the early 1950s were the lowest years of Miles's life, both personally and professionally. It was in these years, however, that he discovered his mature voice and developed a depth of feeling that can be attained only through struggle and hard experience, what jazzmen call "playing your dues." I wonder whether the darker shades of feeling in *Kind of Blue* would have existed if it had not been for these years of nightmare.

Finally, in 1954 Miles made up his mind that he had had enough of addiction. As he put it, "I made up my mind I was getting off dope. I was sick and tired of it. You know, you can get tired of anything. You can even get tired of being scared."

Miles decided to get straight by himself. He simply stopped using dope and sweated it out over a few horrible days of sickness and devastating pain. But he made it through. I do not think it is going too far to say that this experience gave him the inner strength to take control of his life and music. It is the kind of experience that ultimately touches a person's mettle and strengthens his resolve to take his future into his own hands. Now nothing could prevent Miles from going down any path he chose.

Not long after the ordeal of kicking dope, Miles led a remarkable recording session for Prestige. Part of this session was released under the title *Miles Davis and the Jazz Giants*, and the name was not just public relations ballyhoo. In addition to the superb Prestige in-house rhythm section of bassist Percy Heath and Kenny Clarke (the founder of bop drumming), the other musicians on the date were Milt Jackson and Thelonious Monk. Every track is sterling, but on Milt Jackson's medium blues "Bags' Groove," Miles plays a perfectly constructed solo in which he creates an atmosphere unlike that of any other musician. He had redefined the blues on his own very personal terms. It is a shattering solo whose cool exterior barely conceals the heat of its emotions. This is music created by someone who had seen and inhabited the darkest side of life yet was able to create from the experience something of rare beauty. At this point we are obviously listening to a master improviser. The solo is a clear precursor to Miles's playing on *Kind of Blue* five years later, in which he was able to produce solo statements that had a similar melodic logic and emotional ambience.

The following year Miles played at the second Newport Jazz Festival in an ad hoc group that included baritone saxophonist Gerry Mulligan, Thelonious Monk, and tenorman Zoot Sims. The climax of this group's performance came when Miles played a gorgeous version of Monk's famous " 'Round Midnight." It was the talk of the festival, and after the show

George Avakian, an A&R man for Columbia Records, asked Miles whether he would be interested in recording for the company. This was the break that Miles needed.

Shortly after the Newport show, Miles put together a regular working group. He chose Philly Joe Jones, one of the rising stars in jazz, as his drummer. The pianist was Red Garland, who was known for his lightness of touch and an ability to create singable melody. One reason Miles chose Garland was that the pianist could, when he wanted to, play in a style similar to that of a Chicago pianist named Ahmad Jamal. Jamal had a unique style that, according to some critics, was not much more than cocktail music. What Miles admired about Jamal was his feather-light touch and ability to use large blocks of space in his playing, implying rather than stating musical ideas. However, there were people who were not entranced with Jamal's music. The critic Whitney Balliet describes a typical Jamal performance: "Everything was blotted out but the attempt to guess when he would next lift his hands to hit the piano. It was trying work."[3] (I have often wondered whether Jamal was an enthusiast of John Cage.) But under Jamal's influence Miles expanded what he had learned from Thelonious Monk about space, and this would be one of the earmarks of Miles's genius: his understanding of when, and how, to make silence work.

Miles chose a talented teenager, Paul Chambers, as his bassist. His problem was finding an appropriate tenorman. First choice was Sonny Rollins, but Sonny was off the scene, cleaning up his own heroin habit. So Jones and Chambers convinced Miles that the right man for the job was a journeyman tenor player named John Coltrane. Miles had actually played with Coltrane early in the decade in a band that also included Rollins. But it was only for a single gig, and Miles had not been all that impressed. Reluctantly he decided to hire the Philadelphian for the group. This quintet would eventually be considered one of the greatest in jazz history.

Miles made several recordings with the group, including

four albums that came out of two marathon sessions that he had done in order to satisfy his contract with Prestige. The way Miles recorded these albums demonstrates another career pattern. He merely had the group play its usual repertoire in single takes, just as if they were in a live performance. Miles's philosophy of recording was never to do more than one take of each tune, if possible—two at the most. There are some jazz musicians (including Coltrane, when he recorded under his own leadership) who insist on doing take after take, hoping to come as close to perfection as possible. But for Miles, doing innumerable takes meant losing the spontaneity and freshness of thought that to him was what gave jazz its edge. This was also the philosophy that he brought to bear in recording *Kind of Blue*, most of which was recorded in the first take—an awesome feat.

Miles's work with this group eventually made him one of the most popular figures in jazz. His ballad performances—which he played with a Harmon mute—created a poignant and intimate sonic effect and were especially important in winning him a large audience. As Joe Goldberg wrote about Miles's performance of ballads, "When Miles played ballads, mute tight against the microphone (he seems to play microphone as much as trumpet) he reveals an area of tenderness and sensitivity which is rarely visible in his public aspect. These performances, in the emotion they evoke, are comparable to nothing in jazz."[4]

Well, Goldberg's point is not entirely correct, at least if you consider Frank Sinatra a jazz singer, which I do. Miles was a great admirer of the crooner, and I believe that Sinatra had been a major influence on the trumpeter's ability to create such intimacy with his audience. Like Sinatra, Miles projected a strongly masculine persona, which made the tenderness and poignancy of his ballads especially moving. Miles seems to be speaking through his music to say something that is deeply personal. For a man embarrassed to expose the most sensitive aspects of his being, this kind of performance is extraordinary indeed.

But Miles was also famous for his fluffs, and in his ballads these little slip-ups make him seem even more vulnerable. I have often wondered whether Miles deliberately made fluffs in certain spots as a calculated effect. Knowing what a master strategist he was, I would not find such a ploy improbable.

By this time Miles had mastered the most remarkable aspect of his style, the use of silence: he was able to condense complex musical ideas into a kind of shorthand, implying more than he stated, knowing when holding back was more meaningful than simply filling the space with notes. As Miles himself put it, "You don't have to play all the notes; you just have to play the pretty ones." This technique made the contrast with his saxophonist, John Coltrane, even greater than it had been in Bird's group. Trane often seemed to be creating byzantine towers of notes that overwhelmed the ear and mind. Add to this Red Garland's light and straightforward approach to melody, along with Jones's dominating drums, and the brilliance of Miles's calculations for his group become obvious.

Virtually every musician who has ever played with Miles can testify that he rarely gave them much direction. Miles hired only musicians who, from his perspective, had something to add to his music. If they were playing with him, it meant that they were already good enough and did not need his input. It was not just that Miles did not want to provide direction; more to the point, he fervently believed that spontaneity can be achieved only if a musician finds his own way. When a musician is playing genuinely personal, idiosyncratic music, he can improvise with a true sense of discovery.

Despite its success, the group had its problems. Coltrane was struggling with his horn, and at times he seemed to falter. The birth pains of his burgeoning mature style were partly responsible. Undoubtedly his addiction to both heroin and alcohol played a large part as well. The entire band, in fact—with the exception of Miles himself—had similar problems, so much so that the group became known to jazz fans as the "booze and dope band." The musicians were a constant source of irritation to Miles; they would show up late or nod off on the stand and were constantly demanding advances from Miles so they could score their dope. Finally, Miles disbanded the group in March of 1957.

Now that Miles was with a large record company, he was able to do some projects that were simply not possible with the record labels he had recorded with earlier in his career. In particular, he wanted to do a large-scale orchestral piece with his old friend Gil Evans. The resulting album, *Miles Ahead*, is magnificent, one of the great big-band jazz albums in the history of the music. Evans was not really a composer. Rather, as George Russell has put it, he "recompose[d] existing material." He had a command of orchestral colors second only to that of Duke Ellington, and there are even times when he surpasses Duke. Miles switched from trumpet to flugelhorn for this date; the bigger horn gave his tone an even softer texture. His soloing on this album clearly shows the influence of Jamal: Miles uses notes extremely economically, playing simple, perfectly phrased, melodic ideas and using space to constantly imply more than what he is actually playing.

At this point Miles's career took two divergent paths. One was that of his small group work, for which he demanded genuine spontaneity, both in live performances and in the recording studio. The other was the series of orchestral pieces on which he collaborated with Gil Evans—the most famous being *Porgy and Bess, Sketches of Spain*, and *Miles Ahead*. As we now know, the recording of those albums was painstaking. Evans was a perfectionist who was never able to feel satisfied with a less than superlative rendering of his charts. Miles and Evans rarely performed outside the studio, although there were exceptions (such as Miles's famous Carnegie Hall concert of the early 1960s, when he performed both with his small group and with a large band led by Evans).

Miles had a fascinating approach to playing with the Evans ensemble. He would talk about his playing on these albums as if he were a Method actor—that is, he felt he had to assume a specific role when playing this music. For example, he said that when he played "Bess, You Is My Woman Now" for the *Porgy and Bess* album, he had to think of exactly what Porgy was trying to say: "I had to think the lyrics, repeating the refrain over and over again in my head. I mean, how many times can you say, 'Bess, you is my woman'? You can say, 'Bess, you is my woman,' 'Bess, you is my bitch,' 'Bess, you is my whore. . . .' It fucked me up." And he had an even more complicated problem recording *Sketches of Spain*—"Here I was, a black man from East St. Louis trying to think like a Spaniard, like a matador in Spain. I had to think like he would for every note I played."

Miles never talked about this kind of role playing for his small group work, and I am sure it had no part in his creation of that music. While on the bandstand with his small groups, he not only felt free to be completely himself but also knew that the creation of music reflecting one's unique sensibility was an almost sacred aspect of the African American musical tradition. With Evans's work, he had to take on another personality in order to fit his playing into Evans's dramatic arrangements, as if he were a singer in an opera. Actually, Miles had to go beyond what an actor does because the actor's main concern is to convince his audience that he is the character he is portraying. For Miles, this preparation was all internal. He had to convince *himself* that he was another person so he could play with the same integrity that existed in his small group work.

As Miles's star continued to rise, so did the criticism from both jazz writers and some fans. Miles never talked to his audience, never introduced the tunes or the other players.

Unlike Dizzy Gillespie, he did not crack jokes onstage, and at times he actually turned his back to the audience (although Miles claimed that he did this just to better hear the drummer). Yet his supposed arrogance did nothing but increase the public's fascination with him.

Criticism of his taciturn stage manner greatly irritated Miles. After all, he pointed out, classical performers were never expected to introduce tunes or the other musicians. Miles thought of banter in particular as a sort of minstrelsy. For him, all he owed his audience was the best music he could make. Why would they want anything more? Many people wondered whether Miles was actually more of a showman than he would admit. After all, this sort of insolent behavior had become part of his legend, but Miles was at heart a shy man who was not comfortable with his admiring public. He became a master at keeping his fans at bay, but by so doing he earned the reputation of being a misanthrope.

Much of Miles's growing fame related to extramusical facets of his life, such as his wardrobe. He was always on top of the current wave of men's fashions, and his choice of clothing complemented his stunning good looks and undeniable charisma. Even people with little interest in jazz often had one or two of his albums. Particularly among college students, owning a Miles Davis album was proof that they were hip. With his beautiful girlfriends, expensive clothes, and cars, Miles was to a degree hijacked by the Hugh Hefner mentality of the time. However, when he spoke for the very first *Playboy* interview (which at the time was a coup for the magazine, since Miles rarely indulged the press), he revealed that he was not exactly on the same wavelength as the typical *Playboy* reader. Miles was brusque and often cutting in his denunciation of American racism, making it clear that he had no interest in having anything to do with "the kind of man who reads *Playboy*." His angry feelings about the racism of most white men was at the time considered shocking. It certainly was not what anybody would have called a great career move. Unlike so many prominent individuals who learn how to parse their public statements, Miles usually spoke with blunt honesty.

Miles was now in a unique position for a modern jazzman, and with unique opportunities. He had become enormously popular. He could have merely continued pursuing the music that had made him famous, featuring ballads like "My Funny Valentine" or "When I Fall in Love," or the kind of medium-tempo tunes that his group played so well, such as "Bye Bye Blackbird" or "Diane." He could have played it safe and remained a major star and celebrity. Like Louis Armstrong or Dave Brubeck, he could even have eventually played Las Vegas. But that sort of fame and success was unthinkable to Miles. *Time* magazine discovered just how unthinkable when it attempted to do a cover story on Miles. After Miles threw their photographers out of the Village Vanguard, they decided that maybe they should do a story on a more amenable modern jazzman. (Strangely enough, they chose Thelonious Monk, who talked in riddles; but at least he allowed them to photograph him.)

Miles was far too mercurial to allow himself to be trapped into a static identity, especially one constructed by someone else, including the public. More than most people, he was able to come to terms with himself, to be comfortable with being exactly the kind of man he wanted to be without concessions to anyone. He had disdain for a society that made him rich but kept him stereotyped simply because of the color of his skin. More than that, his insatiable curiosity continued to drive him forward. He fully understood that in his art form, standing still was a kind of death. Moving forward was all he knew how to do.

Yet in some ways Miles was musically conservative. He did not want jazz to develop so far into left field that many listeners would feel that they had been left behind. Despite his supposed contempt for the audience (something he vigorously denied), he always wanted his music to be accessible on at least some level.

After he disbanded the quintet, Miles did a number of projects without a working group, including the first album with Gil Evans and the sound track for a French film directed by Louis Malle titled *Elevator to the Gallows*. It is a lovely sound track that gives some indication of the direction in which Miles was moving. The simplified chord progressions and indigo mood of a number of the tracks are prescient of the emotional ambience and harmonic conception of *Kind of Blue*.

Back in America, Miles decided to put together another quintet. He rehired Garland, Jones, and Chambers, but Coltrane was not available. He was playing with Thelonious Monk. Miles wanted Sonny Rollins; however, he was no longer a sideman but the leader of his own group. Miles finally hired a young alto saxophonist from Florida named Julian "Cannonball" Adderley. Cannonball was a large, jovial man with, in Miles's words, a "very special spirit." Miles generally had contempt for overweight people, but he made an exception with Cannonball. The saxophonist was, like most modern alto players, heavily influenced by Charlie Parker, but his tone was fuller and his playing had a funky quality that made his sound immediately identifiable. He often sounded as if he were influenced by rhythm-and-blues saxmen such as Earl Bostic or Eddie "Cleanhead" Vinson.

For a short while Miles's group was a quintet. But in late 1957 Coltrane left Monk and early in 1958 joined Miles's band. By this time Coltrane had gone through an astonishing metamorphosis, both as a man and a musician. His voice was now so strong, his conception so intense, that he seemed to overshadow all of the other musicians in the group. Some leaders might have been uncomfortable with a sideman who played such long solos and who had become such a commanding force in the band. But not Miles; he once said that he was "too vain" to lead a group that was not at the top of the game.

He realized that having as powerful a player as Coltrane simply enhanced his music. Miles was also wise enough to understand that Coltrane's ferocity offset his own subtlety and use of space.

In two sessions—in February and March of 1958—Miles recorded what would be the only album of the sextet with Coltrane, Adderley, Garland, Chambers, and Jones. It is a great album, but the sessions were chaotic. The members of the rhythm section were on their way out, and Jones and Garland did not show up to record all the music. Miles was bringing a new drummer, Jimmy Cobb, into the band and was looking around for a pianist to take Garland's place. One of the pieces was a tune based on a simple scale rather than chord changes. It was the first taste of things to come. (Originally this tune was titled "Milestones" but was changed to simply "Miles" when somebody remembered that Miles had recorded a different tune also called "Milestones" with Charlie Parker in the 1940s.) Both Miles and Adderley—although Cannonball treats the tune as if it had the usual kind of harmonic progression—have little problem navigating within this early modal piece, but Coltrane seems hesitant and unsure of himself. But as discussed later, Coltrane was going through a confusing time from a musical point of view.

There were further indications of Miles's direction in his next project. In July and August of 1958, Miles recorded his second large orchestral piece with Gil Evans. The movie of Gershwin's *Porgy and Bess* was due to be released, and Columbia Records wanted some of its artists to record music from the folk opera. This was during an era when jazz recordings of show tunes were in vogue. André Previn's jazz interpretations of the music from *My Fair Lady* had been especially popular, and a number of jazzmen followed suit. Miles never used such gimmicks. He was not interested in playing show tunes simply because it was a popular trend. The music from *Porgy and Bess,* however, is of an entirely different order, containing some of the most beautiful American music ever composed; and it fits well with jazz interpretation. Evans and Miles virtually recomposed the score, making it seem to listeners that they were hearing the familiar songs almost for the first time.

Miles and Evans both wanted to experiment with using simpler chord changes. One piece, their version of "Summertime," made use of only one chord. It is also one of Miles's most stunning performances. By this point, Evans was creating dense tonal colors that were unlike anything else in music. On "Summertime," Miles plays simple melodic phrases that are answered by the thick textures of Evans's arrangements. Although far different from the way "Summertime" is usually played, it nevertheless has the dusky, humid atmosphere that the tune is meant to convey. The *Porgy and Bess* album is one of Miles's greatest triumphs, one of the most gorgeous albums ever recorded. The simplified harmonic structure of this and some of the other tunes on the album give further clues to Miles's future course.

According to Coltrane, during the years he was in the quintet, Miles was obsessed with complex harmonic progressions. But when he returned to the Miles group, the trumpeter was following a very different path. In a revealing 1958 interview, Miles told Nat Hentoff: "I think a movement in jazz is beginning away from the conventional string of chords, and a return to an emphasis on melodic rather than harmonic variations. There will be fewer chords but infinite possibilities as to what to do with them. Classical composers—some of them—have been writing this way for years, but jazz musicians seldom have. . . . The music has gotten thick. Guys give me tunes and they're full of chords. I can't play them."[5]

One of the classical composers Miles was referring to was the Armenian Khatchaturian, who uses scales that, as Miles said, "were different from the usual Western scales." Khatchaturian was heavily influenced by Armenian folk music, which like much native music throughout the world is basically modal.

Miles could smell revolution in the air, but he was not ready to throw out the entire idea of tonal organization. In a way, Miles's restraint was reminiscent of that of a prominent man from an entirely different sphere of influence: Franklin Delano Roosevelt. Roosevelt is portrayed by those on the right as virtually a socialist. But FDR's New Deal reforms actually had the effect of *preventing* socialism from sweeping the nation. By making capitalism a little fairer, Roosevelt managed to prevent class revolution.

Like Roosevelt, Miles was an innovator but not a radical. Despite his supposed arrogance toward the audience, his aim was always to make jazz a more communicative art form. Miles did not want a revolution against all methods of tonal organization, although he realized that jazzmen were increasingly desperate for the freedom to improvise with fewer restrictions. So Miles needed to find a way to give musicians that freedom without resorting to the kind of musical anarchy that would, with the "new thing" movement, become a reality in the 1960s.

Miles was always lucky. Just when he most needed it, he found a wonderful solution to his problem, one that had been right under his nose for many years. The solution was the theory of a jazz composer Miles had known since 1944, George Russell. Not only was Russell an old friend, his theory had arisen out of a question that Miles himself had asked many years ago.

4 The Lydian Odyssey of George Russell

Earlier I mentioned that the four key musicians responsible for the creation of *Kind of Blue* were Miles Davis, John Coltrane, Bill Evans, and George Russell. Many of you are probably baffled by my inclusion of this last name. After all, George Russell does not play on the album, he is not the composer or co-composer of any of the tunes, and he is not even mentioned in the original liner notes. Yet Russell is in many ways as important to the making of *Kind of Blue* as the other musicians. Without him the album would never have been created.

Russell's contribution to jazz is unprecedented. Although he has composed and arranged some of the most fascinating and powerful music of the modern era, his real lifework is not as an instrumentalist or composer-arranger; it is as a theorist, and it is in this light that Russell views the concept he has been developing for more than half a century (as I write in the year 2000). He is the author of the only major theory to arise out of jazz—though he does not consider himself the *inventor* of his theory so much as its *discoverer*. A "jazz theorist" may suggest the image of someone who has spent all his time in an ivory tower, but Russell's theory has had an enormous, concrete effect on the evolution of jazz. Earlier we discussed the "subversion" of Western musical instruments by African American jazz musicians such as Miles Davis, Coleman Hawkins, and especially Thelonious Monk. George Russell has gone even further—his theory subverts the basic structure of Western music. Russell approaches the fundamentals of Western musical philosophy from the perspective of jazz. As the authors of *The Penguin Guide to Jazz on CD* put it: "Like all great theoreticians, Russell worked analytically rather than synthetically, basing his ideas on how jazz actually *was* and not on how it could conform with traditional principles of Western harmony. Russell's fundamental concern was the relationship between formal scoring and improvisation, giving the first the freedom of the second, freeing the second from being esoteric, 'outside' some supposed norm." Moreover, his theory has not only influenced jazz but has also strongly affected composers in other idioms as well.

If the name of Russell's theory—*The Lydian Chromatic Concept for Tonal Organization*—sounds dry and academic, just think of the music that it made possible: for example, in addition to *Kind of Blue*, there is Bill Evans's beautiful "Re: Someone I Knew," Coltrane's *A Love Supreme* as well as his famous version of "My Favorite Things," and Russell's own classic works, such as "All About Rosie." It is simply impossible to imagine the jazz of the past forty years or so, let alone the creation of *Kind of Blue*, without the contributions of George Russell.

Russell's role in jazz history is unlike that of any other great innovator. Significant bursts of development in jazz have emerged from years of evolution rather than from preexisting theories. For example, only after bebop had become a fully mature style did anyone attempt to define it or develop a theory for playing it. Similarly, it was not until long after Ornette Coleman had been playing his unique style that he came forth with a theory to explain it—his so-called harmolodics. George Russell's theory, on the other hand, exemplified a very different process: George was something of a prophet in that he foresaw a time when inevitable changes would take place in jazz if it continued along the same evolutionary path. He knew that jazz was concerned with two issues of the soul and heart: individual expression and freedom. And he knew that eventually jazz musicians would need to be liberated from the bonds of Western harmonic structure. Yet for many years Russell was a lone prophet in the wilderness. He simply had to wait until jazz had grown sufficiently and found itself compelled to turn to his theory for the sake of the music's continued evolution.

As you might imagine, the life of a jazz theorist and composer is even more difficult than that of a jazz instrumentalist, and George has had a bumpy road since he first became a professional musician in the 1940s. Like so many jazz musicians, Russell certainly paid his dues, and like the music of the best jazzmen, his theory has grown over the years, becoming more expansive and continually gaining depth and universality. The theory is now as much an expression of George Russell the man as the music of Miles Davis and John Coltrane is an expression of them. Yet despite his importance, Russell is an obscure figure in his own country, while he is something of a celebrity in Europe and Japan. It is scandalous that he has received so little attention here, especially given the enormous popularity of albums such as *Kind of Blue* and Coltrane's *A Love Supreme*.

George's unceasing dedication to his theory is inspiring in this day and age. He has not tried to become rich from his theory, insisting on publishing it himself rather than selling it to a commercial publisher. His tenacity is reminiscent of such other American mavericks as Charles Ives or Harry Partch. Given Russell's singular place in jazz history, his odyssey is especially fascinating.

George Russell was born in Cincinnati, Ohio, on June 23, 1923. His biological father was a white professor of music at Oberlin College; his mother was an African American student at the college. She was very light-skinned and came from a wealthy black family in Kentucky. They actually owned an entire town. George comments: "I was adopted a few days after I was born. My mother's family was very conscious of its social status, and in those times it [having a baby out of wedlock] was a disgrace. They insisted that their daughter put her baby up for adoption."

Russell was adopted by a middle-class black family. His adoptive father was a cook on the B&O Railroad. His adoptive mother was one of the first black nurses to graduate from Meharry Medical College. Both of his parents loved music; his father, when he was home, delighted in playing the piano and singing. George's mother worked for a doctor who had a practice in their largely black middle-class neighborhood. (It is interesting to note that the doctor was an outspoken advocate of birth control despite the laws of that period.)

Because both his parents worked, George spent most of his childhood at the homes of neighbors or at a nearby boardinghouse, which proved propitious for the direction his life would eventually take. George recalls, "The boardinghouse that I stayed in housed mainly musicians. They'd have their instruments on the floor of their rooms, and they would practice all the time."

George's interest in music accelerated when his mother took him on boat rides in vessels that came up from New Orleans. The boats, on which jazz bands regularly played, would travel the Mississippi River to St. Louis, then they would take the Ohio River and go up to Cincinnati and Pittsburgh. "So my mother took me on the boats, where we heard all these bands. Eventually we heard the great Noble Sisle, probably the greatest name in the history of American music! I was tickled pink when the drummer for the great Noble Sisle fell for my cousin, who was staying with us for a while. I really got interested in the drums from listening to Sisle play. Then when I became a Boy Scout, I was a member of the drum and bugle corps and that, in turn, led me to playing the drums for a neighborhood band we called the Rhythm Club."

At this time, Cincinnati was a hub of musical activity. As Russell remembers, "Cincinnati was a hell of a music center. A lot of it had to do with the boats, which were transporting various bands. Cincinnati was called the 'graveyard of bands' because the audience had a reputation for being so demanding. They demanded that the band be damned good."

One of Russell's musical associates was the nephew of the great pianist Art Tatum; and George often had the opportunity to hear Tatum play. That in itself must have been a musical education for George, especially given Tatum's harmonic precocity. The famous Mills Brothers had ties to the neighborhood and often rehearsed there, too. George also got to know Jimmy Mundy, who was a tenor saxophonist but became more famous as a composer and arranger. (He wrote several charts for Benny Goodman, Earl Hines, and others.) Mundy perceived Russell's fascination with music and told him, "George, you know you belong in music."

George found high school to be a discouraging experience. Why? Because the high school he attended was integrated— an incredible irony! "That was the first time I realized I was colored, and there was one insult after another. I remember one incident while I was singing in the school choir. We were invited to sing at the YMCA and then swim in the pool. But they took the two of us who were black aside and told us that we could not go swimming after we sang. Most of my teachers discouraged me. My music teacher even told me that I would never make it as a professional musician."

But George went on to play drums in a band made up of fellow students that was led by a pianist-composer named Harold Gaston. By the time he was fourteen, he was playing drums in a local beer joint behind a female singer. Increasingly he lost interest in school, and when he was about fifteen he was expelled for dressing "outlandishly." His life as an iconoclast was just beginning.

George never had any formal musical training. For a while he studied with the church organist, Professor Rider: "He was very strict; he was more German than black! He would crack you on the knuckles when you made a mistake."

But most of Russell's education came from simply absorbing the music he heard all around him: "I found myself being really captivated and fascinated with the jazz that I heard back then. I listened a lot to Jimmy Mundy, Jimmy Crawford, Count Basie, and Papa Jo [Jo Jones, Basie's great drummer at the time]. They were on the jukebox, and the kids sang the tunes, all the solos; we wanted to hear anything that was new. I told Professor Rider that if I had anything to say, it had to be said my way, something personal to me. I lived in a very sophisticated neighborhood. Jack White, one of those early bandleaders who did not have any profound influence on jazz, listened to me and taught me. Lena Horne lived in my neighborhood, and I learned from her, too."

It is pertinent that George Russell never went to a conservatory or took formal lessons. If he had, he would have approached music from the point of view of the European tradition rather than that of jazz. Certainly it would have been more difficult for him to rethink the basic concepts of Western music if early on he had been trained in a conservatory. He did not even take lessons to play the drums, yet as a youth he was able to get jobs as a drummer.

If there had been any doubts in Russell's mind about devoting his life to music, they were erased while he was still a teenager: "I was working at a department store and got a letter from Wilberforce University saying that they would give me a scholarship to play the drums for the Wilberforce Collegians, the college orchestra, if I was interested. Back then the black universities scouted for jazz musicians just as they scout for athletes now. About 1938 or '39 I was at Wilberforce playing in their band. We traveled everywhere because we went along with the football team. For example, when our team played football against the black university of Ken-

tucky, we also had a battle of the bands between the Wilberforce Collegians and the Kentucky State Collegians. There
were players who would become big names, like Ernie
Wilkins or Willy Cook [who played with Count Basie], and
Lucky Thompson. Luck, the first time I met him, was with
the Alabama State Collegians."

Russell points out that Wilberforce is historically important to jazz because, among other reasons, so many great
musicians have played in the Collegians at one time or
another. Coleman Hawkins, Benny Carter, Fletcher Henderson, Horace Henderson—the list goes on and on. Russell
recalls: "Ben Webster was in that band at one time. I met Ben
Webster years later in Denmark. He was pretty rough when
he was drunk, and he had been drinking when I met him. He
looked at me and said, 'Who's this nigger?' I said, 'Ben, I went
to Wilberforce.' He said, 'You were at Wilberforce?' And then
everything was all right.

"I was with the band for one semester when they fired me.
So I went back to Cincinnati and got my time together.
Wilberforce had hired another drummer, but he was so bad
that they begged me to come back. I wound up playing with
them for two years. But in 1941 or so I was called up for the
draft. I went down for my physical with this pianist who
played in the band. We talked with a Marine colonel there
and volunteered for the Marine Corps if they would let us
play in the Marine band. The recruiter was very sweet, very
nice. But when I suddenly heard my name being called, they
told me I had been rejected."

The reason Russell was rejected would change his life in a
variety of ways: he had tuberculosis. "I guess it was kind of
inevitable. After all, I had been going to school at Wilberforce
as well as working from twelve to eight in the evening. And
before that, I had been working two jobs while I was in
Cincinnati. I would play drums at night, get home by three,
and then get up at six-thirty for my other job. And while I was

living at Wilberforce, I was staying in a place with no heat. I
began to spit up blood."

George was hospitalized, which became a turning point in
his life for reasons other than his health: "Harold Gaston, the
bass player, was also a patient. In that hospital he taught me
the rudiments of chords, after which I wrote my first arrangement without a piano and sold it.

"At the hospital the lunchroom where we ate was segregated. Harold and I and a couple of other patients began to
rebel about this situation. They put one TB patient in jail for
doing this. And then there was something else. One of the
nurses liked to cavort with the male patients. She was discovered in a compromising situation in our room, so the head of
the hospital told us, 'It's time for you to go.' I had to go, but I
was not cured. I was still sick."

Both Russell and his friend Gaston got jobs playing at a
downtown club. In this environment they disregarded their
doctors' warnings and smoke and drank alcohol. Harold Gaston got sicker and eventually died.

Then Russell got a big break—he was hired by Benny
Carter. At that time Carter was considered one of the greatest alto saxophonists in jazz. He also played clarinet and was
even a fine trumpet player. Carter had a number of excellent
musicians in his band, and for Russell this was just the opportunity he needed: "I traveled all over with that band. That is
where I met a lot of young players. For example, [trombonist]
J. J. Johnson was in that band. Finally we wound up in New
York City. I was a steady drummer; I had a good beat. But I
wasn't a show drummer, and at times Benny really wanted
that. So Benny told me he would keep me until he found a
drummer who could fill the whole bill.

"As soon as I hit New York, I went into one of the little
clubs on Fifty-second Street and listened to some music. It
blew me away." The band Russell heard was Charlie
Parker's. It was the first time Russell had heard bebop; he

was thrilled by the new music and realized that New York was where he belonged.

Shortly after this experience, Russell went to Washington, D.C., with the Carter band. "It was at the Howard Theater where Benny called me and said, 'I hate to tell you, but I have to let you go.' And I asked, 'Why?' He told me, 'I have a new drummer. His name is Max Roach.' So I went back to Cincinnati and did a little work around there. While I was there, I went to hear the Ellington band play in Dayton. On the train back to Cincinnati, all I could think about was the figure of Ellington standing in the train. The car was filled with soldiers and members of his band, and there was Duke standing the whole way. When the band got to Cincinnati, a number of them found hotels, but four of them didn't. And those four were Ray Nance, Skippy Williams, Betty Roche, and Al Hibbler. I took them home, and they stayed with me and my mother for four days. Ellington treated me and my mother wonderfully."

Shortly afterward, Russell decided he had to leave home: "I finally left because I couldn't stand the whole ugly racial thing there. I told myself that I had to get out of there. I went to Chicago."

While he was in Chicago, he almost became a member of Duke Ellington's band: "Duke asked me to join his band. His regular drummer, Sonny Greer, was sick then. I sat in with the band at the Downtown Theater in Chicago. But Ellington did not count off the tempo; he just gave a downbeat, and I started playing in the time I thought it would be in. The band and I were in different tempos! It was strange. I was really being a dummy, because if I had just skipped the first beat and waited to see where they were, there would have been no problem. Still, Ellington asked me if I wanted to join the band, so I must have righted up the tempo somewhere. I really am not a native drummer; I am only a passable drummer. After hearing Max play, I no longer wanted to play drums. By that time, though, I was committed to something else—being a composer."

Despite turning down Ellington's offer, Russell was forced to play with a band in Chicago in order to survive. The bassist Eugene Wright, who eventually became famous playing with Dave Brubeck's quartet, had a band called the Dukes of Swing. During the three months that Russell spent with Wright's group, he wrote his first composition, a tune called "New World."

George continues: "Benny Carter and his band were at the Sound House Theater in Chicago, so I went down and saw Benny and showed him my tune. Benny pulled the whole band off the stand, took everybody into the basement, and we rehearsed 'New World.' It sounded wonderful. It was really unbelievable. Benny gave me some big money, and that started the whole thing. I was determined to be a composer and arranger."

Russell went back to New York intent on this new career path. He sold "New World" to several bands, but the revenue from those sales was the only money he had. He became friends with the drummer who had taken his place in the Carter band, Max Roach, one of the few drummers who can safely be called a genius. "Maybe Max felt bad because he had taken my place, but I was not jealous or anything like that. He befriended me and took me on Fifty-second Street to meet everybody. Very quickly the guys accepted me. We all became quite chummy. I had written this one arrangement, and it really knocked Max out. Dizzy really loved it, too. That's when I first got to know Bird. Nobody was like Charlie Parker. All I can say is that he lived every minute of every day. He wouldn't go to sleep; he participated completely in life during the day and whatever that day brought—then he would finally collapse. That's the way he lived."

Russell got a room on Forty-eighth Street and Sixth Avenue, not far from "Swing Street"—the block of Fifty-second Street where so many clubs regularly presented the greatest jazz musicians of the day. According to George, "The owners of the Three Deuces were really beautiful men. They found out from the other musicians that I was okay, and I was admitted free. We'd be in the front row and sit up on Bird every night. Then during intermission, some of the musicians would come to my place for their 'refreshments,' needles and all. One time Bird offered me some, but being aware of the fragile state of my health, I had to refuse. He even asked me to play drums with his band. If I had done that, I would have died for sure, because those guys were living on the edge. So I had to say no to Bird, but it hurt. You just didn't say no to Bird. He was a gentleman—he didn't force it or anything. He acted like 'This is a wonderful dessert I made and I'd like you, if you would like, to have a taste.' "

Among the musicians Russell became friendly with was a very youthful Miles Davis. "I first met Miles in Chicago when he was with Billy Eckstine. Then when I moved to New York we spent a lot of time together. This was early in 1945. He invited me up to his place. We used to have sessions together. He was interested in chords, and I was interested in chords. We would sit at the piano and play chords for each other. He'd play a chord and I'd say, 'Ooh, that's a killer.' And then I would play a chord. At one of these sessions I asked Miles what he was looking to accomplish. He told me, 'I want to learn all the chord changes. How can I go about doing this?' And I thought about that. I didn't challenge it. At times Miles could be very definite, but at other times he could be really obscure. I just said to myself, 'He already knows the changes. What could he need?' Even then Miles was noted for outlining each change, identifying it with the melody. In other words, he wouldn't have even needed the piano player, because Miles's melody was dictating what the chords were. He wanted a new way to relate to chords. But this question of his—about how he could learn all the chords—eventually saved my life." Miles's question would also lead almost fifteen years later to the making of *Kind of Blue*.

About this time Russell moved into a small place with some friends, but the place had no windows. For George—with his breathing problems—this was anathema. So he wound up sleeping in parks, particularly Gracie Park, where the mayor's mansion is located. Needless to say, sleeping in parks was disastrous for Russell's health, and after a while his condition began to deteriorate. When he went to an uptown hospital, the doctor told him that he was okay. Yet a short time later he collapsed from a hemorrhage. He was soon ensconced in Bellevue Hospital for three weeks. He was so sick that a priest came to give him last rites. "I told the priest, 'Let me level with you—I don't want your blessing. If I'm going, I might as well level with God because I do not believe in him.'" But Russell's period as an atheist was brief.

Russell survived this ordeal and was sent to a sanitarium. "I ended up at St. Joseph's Hospital, 143rd Street and Brooke Avenue in the Bronx. I was in a room with fifteen other guys who had TB. I stayed there for fifteen months, the first six of them in complete bed rest. So I thought, 'I've got to start doing something constructive.' I lay there thinking about what Miles had meant—because I already had the feeling that chords have a scale of unity, and they have a scale closer to them, to the sound of the chord, than any other scale. And that started me on the path that is here before me right now."

When Russell was finally released from the hospital, Max Roach took him under his wing and had George move in with him and his mother: "I lived off New York City welfare. The city had a program for young people who were TB survivors. That gave me enough money to live on until I was strong enough to get a job, and it gave me the opportunity to study for a new occupation. Max's mother kind of adopted me, and I stayed there for nine months." This was a perfect situation for Russell to continue to work out the details of his theory:

"Mrs. Roach used to say, 'Max, that boy never sleeps!' Max told her, 'He's working on his theory.' I'd be working on it every night until around four in the morning."

After moving out of the Roach home, George was approached by Dizzy Gillespie. Gillespie was putting together his first big band and was planning to do a concert at Carnegie Hall; it would be the first time a modern jazz band played that hallowed venue. According to Russell, "Dizzy told me: 'I have a song, and I want to make it into something bigger.' He asked me to take his tune and turn it into a suite."

The name of the tune was "Cubano Be, Cubano Bop," and it was the first time modern jazz was fused with Afro-Cuban rhythms. Yet for George Russell this piece had even greater significance: "I wrote the first section based on a C seven flat nine chord. By that time I knew what the parent scale was. So all the melodies and all the harmonies came out of the B flat auxiliary diminished scale. That was the first modal piece that I ever consciously wrote, back in 1947."

At this point Russell was living in a sleazy hotel in the Bowery: "It was the bottom of the rung. I used to walk home, and I would trip over people lying on the sidewalk." Dizzy wanted George to conduct the band for the Carnegie Hall concert in which "Cubano Be, Cubano Bop" was to be performed. In order to do so, Russell was forced to walk all the way from the Bowery to Fifty-seventh Street. After the concert John Lewis, who was the pianist with the Gillespie band and had found out where George was living, insisted that Russell move in to his home in the Jamaica section of New York City.

It was at the Carnegie Hall concert that Russell first met Gil Evans: "Gil was impressed with what I had done with 'Cubano Be, Cubano Bop,' and he introduced himself to me after the concert. He said, 'Drop by my place whenever you get the time.' His place was a one-room apartment in the basement of the St. Regis Hotel. All the pipes of the St. Regis went through Gil's apartment. Pretty soon I started hanging out there all the time. There were a lot of great musicians who were drawn to Gil's place. It was kind of a haven for a lot of people. Miles and Max, of course, and the composer John Benson Brooks, Gerry Mulligan, John Lewis, Lee Konitz, and [singer] Blossom Dearie. We all knew something of the Claude Thornhill Orchestra [for which Evans had done several arrangements] because that was a very special band.

"When you walked into Gil's place, you never knew who would be there. Bird might be there, lying in bed because that was about the only piece of furniture Gil had. And a lot of records. We talked music, music, music, and I often discussed my theory with Gil. He was very interested. Back then, I would show the theory to anyone who was interested. Most of them didn't pay much attention, because I didn't have a name or anything at that time. A lot of musicians knew about me, but I was kind of floating around. Gil would never have invited me to his place if he hadn't been impressed with my writing. The thing he did most beautifully was his work as an orchestral composer. He himself didn't really compose all that much, but he had an incredible talent for coloring things." Many years later Evans recorded some of Russell's compositions.

As already noted, Miles's *Birth of the Cool* band came together out of the get-togethers in Evans's apartment. But as Russell points out, music was not the only thing discussed in that cramped room: "People were always coming in or out of that place because it was a refuge for a lot of them. Gil became a kind of guru. All of us would come to Gil with our problems, and he always seemed like a wise man who could go to the depths of your problem and straighten you out real quick. It must have taken a lot out of him. Sometimes he would get really boggled with everyone's problems. One day he left the apartment and just walked all around New York: down to the tip of the island, going over to Staten Island, and then coming all the way back to Harlem. And then back again. He just walked. One time he wound up knocking on the door of a friend of his. Her name was Lil, the woman he married soon afterward."

Evans's marriage spelled the end of the little haven under the St. Regis. Russell was present on the final day: "I was there with Dave Lambert [who would eventually become famous as a founder of the jazz singing trio Lambert, Hendricks and Ross]. He was with his wife and baby because that's where they had been sleeping. A cop came and told us, 'You're all gonna have to vacate. You don't live here anymore.' So I said, 'But this man has a baby.' The cop just said, 'You shut up, or I'll take you downtown.' And I shook my head and thought, 'This is really ruthless.' "

It was all over—perhaps the closest thing to a jazz Bloomsbury that ever existed. It was finished, or at least it seemed to be. But musicians continued to find places to congregate and discuss music. For example, the mid-Manhattan bar Jim and Andy's became a favorite haunt of jazzmen. Some of the musicians gave out the bar's phone number as if it were their own. From the mid-1950s on, Miles's home became another gathering place for jazzmen. But there would never again be quite such an intimate haven as Gil Evans's tiny apartment.

Russell continued to eke out a living with occasional arranging jobs and compositions, but most of his energy continued to be devoted to working out his theory. One of Russell's earliest and most famous compositions was "Ezz-thetic," which he named after the boxer Ezzard Charles. "I took an arrangement of it to Bird while he was playing with strings at Birdland. He really liked it, but his manager, Teddy Reig, thought it was too uncommercial for Bird to record it. But Bird used to play it with strings all the time."

A few years later Lee Konitz [with Miles Davis playing trumpet] recorded "Ezz-thetic." And Russell himself recorded the tune a couple of times, the first in his landmark *The Jazz Workshop* album, and later as the title track of an album he made for the Riverside label. It has become a jazz classic, frequently recorded by a variety of jazzmen.

Russell also had the opportunity to do an arrangement for another jazz legend, Ella Fitzgerald: "In about 1948, after I wrote 'Cubana Be, Cubana Bop,' I was approached by Ella Fitzgerald. She wanted me to write an arrangement, so I showed up at the Decca studio with her; but I had sort of overwritten. I had written what she should sing on some of my choruses. She got mad as hell, and she said, 'I give you brothers a chance, and you mess me up every time.' She did this in front of the musicians. I was really embarrassed. And she said, 'Let's just use the first chorus of this.' And that's what they did. They used the first chorus, then she had worked out her scat improvisation. I found out that's how she works. She had worked out her supposed improvisation at home, and she didn't need what I had written for her. But she did use the first chorus. And she paid me something like seventy-five dollars, grudgingly. It eventually sold about ten million records. It was one of her most famous recordings, 'How High the Moon.' Later I ran into her and the bassist Ray Brown, her husband at that time. They said, 'George! Come have dinner with us.' They were going to a new club across the street from Birdland. So this was very funny—I had written her best-selling record!"

Shortly after the end of the Evans haven, Russell got a job working at a drugstore. But he continued to write and do some arranging and, of course, continued to work on his theoretical work, the Concept. For a while his living situation improved greatly: "I met a woman who really liked me, but she was living with her husband. She had me move in with her and her husband in their place on Park Avenue! So I was very comfortable right then."

Needless to say, it must have been quite a contrast to the Bowery flophouse he had been living in earlier. It was while living in the luxurious Park Avenue setting that he composed a piece that became a kind of legend itself: "A Bird in Igor's Yard." The Igor referred to in this title is Igor Stravinsky. This composition was Russell's successful attempt to fuse

Stravinsky's polytonality with Charlie Parker's bebop—a piece clearly ahead of its time.

Russell left his job at the drugstore so he could concentrate on his music. He wanted to see whether he could make a living by writing music and work on the Concept on the side. At least he wanted to attempt it. But the reality turned out to be something else: "There was a guy who had a band that more or less imitated the Glenn Miller sound. The guy wanted all the writing for the band to have clarinet leads. This was during a time when real commercial music was making a noise. So I took an arrangement and made kind of a symphony out of it. But this guy didn't like it because it wasn't commercial enough. He said, 'Take it home and do this and that to it, and we'll see if we can play it.' That didn't feel right to me, so at this point I said to myself, 'Okay, you can either do this or get a job outside of music and concentrate on the Concept.' By that time I knew that the Concept was for real, and I knew that I wouldn't lose anything by getting out of music, because any music that could give me a living would be compromised. I just could not do it. So I got a job at Macy's and I stayed there for two years." Russell was, luckily, assigned to the wallpaper section of the store. Since not many people bought their wallpaper at Macy's, he had plenty of time to focus on the Concept.

By the early 1950s Russell's luck with living quarters had turned again, and he was back in a hotel only a step above the place he had lived in when he was on the Bowery. He was hired by the alto saxophonist Hal McKusick to write some arrangements for an album for RCA Victor. When Jack Lewis, the A&R man for the session, heard it, he told Russell, 'That's wonderful.' He was enthralled with Russell's work. Later Lewis visited Russell at his hotel, which was half a block from the Victor studios: "Lewis was so shocked by my living conditions that he told me, 'George, you've got to get out of here!' Then he said, 'I wouldn't do this ordinarily, but I'm going to give you an album, and I am going to pay you much more than I would ordinarily pay in order to get you out of here.' So that's what happened, and after that I never had to accept anything outside my own work."

With the advance for the album, Russell was able to get a decent apartment and live in relative comfort. While he was planning for the album, he had a fateful meeting that would eventually help change jazz history and make *Kind of Blue* possible: "I had met a singer from Chicago named Lucy Reed. She had asked me to do a few arrangements for an album she planned to make. I think Gil [Evans] did a few for her, too. She was in town and called me up on a Sunday and told me that she wanted to discuss something with me. She asked if she could bring a friend, which I said would be fine. She came up with this male friend of hers. I thought he was a business-man of some sort. He was very quiet, and he wore glasses. It was one of those quiet New York Sundays. I couldn't think of anything to do, so we took the Staten Island ferry, and we had a sandwich or something. All I got out of this guy was that he played piano, and he had been in the army. He also had been in the South, although he didn't have a particularly southern accent. Eventually the conversation sort of lapsed and finally I said, 'I have a piano at home. I'd love to hear you play.' We went back to this one-room apartment, and he sat down at the piano. And from then on, I closed my mouth. I mean, I was absolutely amazed. Out of this sort of nonperson came all this incredible technique and feeling and sense of orchestra-tion. So I said, 'Whoa—we have to work together.' "

The pianist, of course, was Bill Evans. At the time, Evans was struggling, playing whatever gigs he could find. And Rus-sell did work with him. Evans was the pianist on *The Jazz Workshop*, the album Russell did for Jack Lewis at RCA. The interesting thing about Evans is that, even very early on, he seemed to play naturally in a style that had modal implica-tions. His son, Evan, says that in his earliest practice tapes, recorded while he was very young, there is a strong sense of modality. Bill Evans would become famous for playing "rootless" chords, which implied an advanced harmonic conception and which adapted well to modes.

The *Jazz Workshop* album is one of the greatest albums of the 1950s, just a rung or two beneath *Kind of Blue*. The musicians on the album, besides Evans's trumpeter Art Farmer, saxophonist Hal McKusick, guitarist Barry Galbraith, drummers Paul Motian and Osie Johnson, and the bassist Milt Hinton, were among the cream of the New York jazzmen. They were all sophisticated enough to work with Russell's challenging compositions and arrangements while also being superb improvisers.

In its way, Russell's *The Jazz Workshop* was a precursor of *Kind of Blue* in that it subjected some fine jazzmen to tunes based on modes that Russell was using as substitutes for chord progressions. Yet the album, like *Kind of Blue*, is not just a dry experiment. The music, both in the writing and improvising, is passionate and at times almost frightening in its reckless force. For the listener the experience is like being a passenger in a speeding car. At the same time, despite the reckless feeling, there is an overall sense of control. It is clear that on *The Jazz Workshop* a finely tuned musical mind is shaping the performances. Bill Evans's playing on the album is spectacular and quite different from the impressionistic lyricism for which he eventually became famous. Here he plays with a driving energy that at times is almost hair-raising. The other soloists approach the same level of brilliance. Like Evans, Art Farmer's solos on this album have an intensity missing from some of his later work. The alto saxophonist Hal McKusick plays way above his head, although it is clear that he is deeply influenced by the cool altoist Lee Konitz; he also plays with a vigor and drive absent from much of his work on other albums. In any case, there is little doubt that the freedom Russell's modes gave to improvisers ignited their imaginations; this would also be the case for *Kind of Blue*.

Compelling as we might find the soloists, it is Russell's writing that is the greatest revelation. Russell himself, like a superb soloist, has created a "sound" unlike that of any other jazz composer or arranger. His arrangements are some of the most intricate and inventive ever written for a small group, yet he is able to frame perfectly all of the improvisations so that they are indivisible components of the arrangement, not just a string of solos. Although this album was considered avant-garde in its time, the music is always accessible and, more often than not, viscerally powerful.

All the tunes on the album were composed by Russell while he was working at Macy's, and the way he composed them was, to say the least, remarkable: "I'd come home after the day job and I would immediately start writing. And all of this work was a way of testing the evolution of my theory. I know this sounds kind of mystical, but answers would come when I'd ask the theory a question. If the theory got stuck, I would say: 'I want an answer by tomorrow morning.' When I got out of bed in the morning, I would have the answer. My ideas were continually growing. They weren't static. And each time an idea got bigger, I would write it and then test it with a piece of music.

"The theory and I grew together. And we are still growing. My atheism was disappearing, to be replaced by a firm belief in higher forces because the ideas were truly alive. Whenever I heard a musician do something that I could not explain, I went back to the theory in order to figure it out."

Not long after recording *The Jazz Workshop* album, Russell was given a commission from Brandeis University to compose a longer piece of music. This piece would be performed in concert at Brandeis along with the work of several other jazz composers, including Charles Mingus, J. J. Johnson, John Lewis, and Jimmy Giuffre. There were also pieces written by so-called classical composers, among them Gunther Schuller, Milton Babbitt, and Harold Shapiro. All the compositions were supposed to be written as a fusion of jazz and classical music. This was part of a movement that Schuller (who had played French horn briefly in Miles Davis's *Birth of the Cool*

nonet) called the "third stream." It was a controversial movement at the time; many of those in the jazz scene thought it
pretentious, if not downright useless. Miles, for example, said
that the third-stream movement made him think of "looking
at a naked woman that you *don't like*."

Yet many of the pieces written under these grants were
quite fine. Regardless of how Miles Davis felt about the genre,
J. J. Johnson's "Poem for Brass" is a lovely piece, with a simple lyricism similar to Miles's own work on the *Miles Ahead*
album—his collaboration with Gil Evans. And Mingus's
"Revelations" is a typically brilliant and ferocious composition by the great bassist-composer. But it was Russell's piece,
"All About Rosie," that was the undeniable hit of the concert.
Russell got the initial idea for the piece from John Benson
Brooks: "John loved folk music and the idea of mixing it with
jazz. One day he played a tape of Alabama children's songs
that Alan Lomax had made. One of the songs was 'Rosie, Little Rosie, Rosie's in a Hurry.' "

Russell used the thread of this simple tune to embroider a
complex three-part piece, one of the most memorable of
"long" jazz compositions. Each section is enthralling, and the
entire piece swings like mad. It is obvious, at least on the original version, that Rosie worked up the imaginations of the
soloists, which included Art Farmer, the saxophonist John
LaPorta, and Bill Evans. The original version is now available
on the Columbia/Legacy album *The Birth of the Third
Stream*. One of the solos on this version is legendary—Bill
Evans's taut, tightly constructed blues solo. This solo helped
establish Evans's growing reputation—at least among musicians. And the piece itself established George Russell's reputation as one of the most important jazz composers of the
modern era.

Russell's next important work was the album *New York,
New York* for Decca. This album is unique in that it was one
of the earliest "concept" albums. All the tunes—some of them
standards, some composed by Russell—are about New York

City. For this session—Russell's first big band venture—he worked with top musicians of the New York jazz scene, including alto saxophonist Phil Woods, tenor saxophonist Benny Golson, bassist Milt Hinton, drummer Osie Johnson, John Coltrane, and Bill Evans. In addition, the jazz singer Jon Hendricks wrote some patter tunes (what would be called rap today) that link together all the sections into a suite. Russell's arrangements with their fresh tonal colors are some of the most original big band charts of the day, making *New York, New York* a rival for the orchestral albums of Miles Davis and Gil Evans.

Bill Evans once again plays brilliantly throughout *New York, New York,* as he always seemed to when working with Russell. "His time was impeccable," recalls Russell. "I mean his time was like Philly Joe's; he was always right on it. It is a curious thing about Bill and the Concept. I know he was interested in modes, but it seemed as if he didn't want to acknowledge the Concept. I have a piece that he wrote called 'Twelve-Tone Piece,' which is harmonized traditionally, but the melody's a twelve-tone row. I have his outlining of the piece, and he's got all these different modes on the piece. So he did think modally. He always said that the Concept influenced him. But he never directly told me that."

New York, New York was a relatively successful album from a commercial point of view, and it has become Russell's most popular work. If one assumes that a piece of music based on theory is necessarily dull and lifeless, such preconceptions wither when listening to *New York, New York*. Like virtually all of Russell's pieces, it is challenging and original but immediately accessible. I find most of Russell's works among the most exhilarating in all of jazz, whether or not one is aware of the underlying theory. I have to wonder if the rather chilly thought of theory-based music turns off potential listeners before they have even given Russell's works a chance.

By now, Russell had developed a "sound" as idiosyncratic

as any of the great jazzmen, but that was never his aim: "I rebelled against style. I didn't want to get stuck with one particular style for a lot of reasons. One of these reasons is that I could see that styles are not permanent. They tend to quickly become 'out of style.' Suppose in the 1960s I had wanted to join up with the 'freedom riders,' the free-jazz guys of that period, and go all the way outside. I couldn't do it. I didn't believe that was all there was to music. I wanted to be more like a panmodalist, a panthinker, *pan* meaning *all*. I wanted to be free to be this or be that, to have a mixture of different things. That would be my 'style,' and that is the way I want it."

Russell continued to get together with Miles, and they challenged each other with chords. "One night Miles and I had dinner together, and we had a very serious discussion about modes. At the time, Miles was seriously looking for musicians to replace some of the guys in the band with substance-abuse problems. So we sat down at the piano and played chords. I played a chord for him, and he asked me where I got it. I tried to show him where the chord came from. And he got very interested because, by that time, I could translate any chord in terms of the Concept, and I could show Miles what its parent scale was; the scale formed a unity with the chord. Then Miles understood it. He saw that in the Concept there was an objective explanation for the chord. He saw that traditional music overlooked verticality and unity. Unity was not a factor. When musicians are talking about harmony, they mean progressional harmony. They were ignorant—and still are—about a vertical concept. The Lydian Concept is based on the unity of chord and scale. That night, when Miles saw how he could use the Concept, he said that if Bird were alive, this would kill him. And it was just what Miles needed for the direction his music was taking."

The fact that the leading jazzman of the time had been won over to George's Concept may have seemed like a kind of ultimate triumph for Russell. The irony, of course, is that Miles had been the musician who first set Russell off on his long intellectual and musical odyssey. But Russell still felt that he had a long way to go. He felt that his theory was in an embryonic stage, fifteen years after he first conceived the basic premise while hospitalized in a TB ward. He would continue to live a bifurcated life: on the one hand he continued to write and arrange, but his primary work continued to be his theory, which would always be the center of his life.

Whether or not you understand the details of Russell's theory (as presented in the Appendix), there is one thing of paramount importance about it. In sharp contrast to Western theory, Russell was attempting to bring a unity to musical theory. I do not believe that this attempt, or the profundity of the Concept, is an illusion, nor is the fact that Russell's theory was born of the aesthetics of jazz (although Russell has applied it to classical music, and it has influenced some modern composers in that tradition). Since the Eastern belief in the unity of all things is at the heart of much non-Western religion and philosophy, it should not be surprising that this first, and only, musical theory derived from the jazz tradition is based on the concept of ultimate unity. Improvisation based on modes instead of chord changes gave jazz musicians a new freedom; now their choices could be open-ended rather than shackled by the chains of chord progressions. The theory brought jazz closer to its non-Western roots and gave jazzmen the opportunity to fly into what Sonny Rollins called music's "open sky."

Russell says: "I am not an intellectual. I refuse to be one, and I hate to be classified as one. All of these ideas already existed. I was just stuck with the Concept until it revealed itself completely."

Russell's struggle was long and laborious. But in 1959 he would, finally, begin to receive the recognition for the value of this theory to which he had devoted his life. That recognition came from the making of *Kind of Blue.*

5 Trane's Passionate Journey

For John Coltrane, recording *Kind of Blue* was one of the most significant events of his life as a jazzman. In retrospect, Coltrane must have felt that recording the album was like the inevitable end of one journey and the beginning of a new one. It would set the course for the rest of his career and propel him toward the innovations that would change jazz and define his career as a leader. The path by which Coltrane arrived at *Kind of Blue* is as important to understanding his music as an awareness of the path that he would take thereafter.

A few years ago I wrote a book about John Coltrane titled *Ascension—John Coltrane and His Quest*. I still believe most of what I wrote about Trane then. Despite any changes that have occurred in my thinking about Coltrane since writing *Ascension*, he is a pivotal figure and is far too important to ignore in telling the story of *Kind of Blue*. There are many who believe that Coltrane's voice dominates the album. I am not certain of that, but it is true that on *Kind of Blue* we hear for the first time the direction he would pursue after leaving Miles's group.

My thinking about Coltrane has evolved since completing *Ascension*. One of the important lessons I have learned from listening to jazz all these years is the inevitability of change, including my own feelings about the music and the players who have mattered most to me. It is impossible to fight against change, so the best way to deal with it is to embrace it. Thus, when I write a book, all I can claim is that it represents my ideas and feelings about its subject at the time. Those ideas and feelings are not immutable but are, rather, in a constantly fluid state. This is especially true for my ideas regarding someone like Coltrane, since nobody embodies the idea of evolution and perpetual change more than he; as Coltrane changed, so did my thinking about him, and those ideas continue to evolve. I believe this has been true for most of his devoted listeners.

In addition to my responses to the music itself, I have found that the ideas of others have helped sharpen my own point of view, their opinions sometimes acting as a challenge, at other times solidifying and reinforcing my perspective. Probably one of the main reasons for the current turn in the evolution of my feelings about Coltrane and his music is the series of conversations I have had with my friend Nick Catalano. To name a few of his activities, Nick is a professional saxophonist, a jazz writer (he has a column in a New York weekly newspaper), and a professor at Pace University in New York. He also recently published the definitive biography of Clifford Brown. Though he is extremely knowledgeable about jazz and has an appreciation of its development that is both broad and deep, he does not care much for Coltrane; nor is he much of a Miles Davis fan, either. Discussing Coltrane with Nick has in some ways strengthened my love of Trane's music, but it has also caused me to reconsider it. In particular, I wonder whether in my enthusiasm I have overlooked Coltrane's tendency to be self-indulgent in some of his music, focusing on his own inward journey instead of communicating with an audience.

Ascension is concerned mainly with Coltrane's spiritual quest and how it affected his life and music. The decisive experience in this quest occurred in 1957. Until then he had been a journeyman saxophonist, respected but not considered especially original or innovative; in addition, he was a hopeless drug addict and alcoholic. But after his spiritual epiphany of 1957, he became within just a few years the most important artist in jazz. This amazing transformation is one of the most fascinating stories in jazz history.

Coltrane's epiphany was the starting point for a spiritual quest that created in him a new and different reason to play music, a reason that went beyond simply communicating with and moving his listeners. For him, playing improvisational jazz became a journey within, an attempt to use the intensity that he brought to his music as a form of trance. To be more precise, he played in order to sustain that inward journey, seeking nothing less than the mind of God. That is why he played solos of such great length (half an hour, sometimes even much longer) and with such apocalyptic fury. It was impossible for those in the audience to be merely passive observers; all one could do was hold on for dear life. The experience of listening to Coltrane's music was more like a trip in a rocket ship to some strange corner of the universe than anything resembling "entertainment." Later in his career, Coltrane would go even more deeply within himself, this time to a place where he seemed almost to lose track of the difference between music and pure sound.

Thus, the puzzling question about Coltrane is this: Was he an artist or a kind of shaman, or was he simply self-indulgent? The answer is by no means apparent. One thing is certainly true, however: after Charlie Parker, Coltrane is one of the two most significant and influential saxophonists in the jazz scene. (The other is Sonny Rollins.) During the 1960s in particular, Coltrane cast a long shadow, and not merely over the world of jazz. He became a cultural hero to both African Americans and the young people of the counterculture. Much of his music during his ascendancy is undeniably beautiful, sometimes even breathtaking, but his performances could at times be brutal experiences for many listeners. However one feels about it, there is little doubt that the course Coltrane pursued during the most important years of his career began with *Kind of Blue*.

John Coltrane was born in Hamlet, North Carolina, on September 23, 1926, the same year as his future boss, Miles Davis. He began playing the alto saxophone in high school but was no prodigy. After his mother moved to Philadelphia, John followed suit and wound up studying at a local conservatory. When he was nineteen he entered the navy, where he played in the navy band. Some rare Coltrane recordings in the 1940s reveal that at this time he was, like most modern jazz musicians, deeply influenced by Charlie Parker. There was no clue that this young man would eventually become one of the most original and innovative musicians in jazz history.

After leaving the navy, Coltrane switched to tenor sax and became a journeyman musician, getting occasional jazz gigs, briefly playing in a band led by Miles (which also included Sonny Rollins). Like many tenormen of the time, he was also under the influence of Dexter Gordon and Sonny Stitt (that is, Stitt's tenor style). For the most part, though, Coltrane was forced to play rhythm-and-blues gigs in order to make a living. Being an essentially shy and introspective man, Coltrane hated the more "show biz" aspects of rhythm and blues, such as "walking the bar," a nightclub act in which the saxophonist literally walked on top of the bar while supposedly wrapped up in the fervor of his music. One time when Coltrane was forced to walk the bar, a friend, tenor saxophonist Benny Golson, walked into the club. Coltrane was so mortified that he immediately jumped off the bar and left the club, never to return.

Coltrane played for a while in a band led by the rhythm-and-blues saxophonist Earl Bostic and then later with Johnny Hodges, who for a time led his own band while on leave from the Ellington orchestra. Coltrane said that he learned quite a bit from both Bostic and Hodges, and I think their influence is evident. Rhythm-and-blues saxmen like Bostic brought a sweat-drenched intensity to their playing that was echoed in Coltrane's music in the 1960s. As for Hodges, the altoman's rich, golden sound carried a message about the possibilities latent in music that surely affected Coltrane's own conception.

About this time Coltrane, like so many of his jazz contemporaries, became addicted to heroin. His addiction began partly as a means of dealing with physical pain. He suffered from serious dental problems, the pain of which was greatly exacerbated when he played. (Sonny Rollins has suffered similar dental problems throughout his career.) In order to get through a gig, he used both dope and alcohol, and he soon found himself with a dual addiction.

Despite these problems, Coltrane got his first big break about this time (the early 1950s): he joined Dizzy Gillespie's quintet. On some sides that Gillespie recorded during this period, we can hear Coltrane's tenor for the first time. (He had recorded as part of the Hodges band but took no solos.) Only with the benefit of hindsight do we hear that familiar Coltrane voice. At this point, however, he could have been one of dozens of tenormen from this era. Undoubtedly he would have evolved much more quickly had drugs and alcohol not cut so deeply into his time and ability to concentrate.

Despite Coltrane's tenures with Gillespie and Hodges, two of history's stellar jazzmen, it was Miles who in 1955 would make Coltrane a well-known figure in the jazz scene. After his triumph at Newport, Miles put together a working band. His first choice was Sonny Rollins for the saxophone chair, but Sonny was busy remaking his life in Chicago after kicking his own heroin addiction. Miles's drummer, Philly Joe Jones, encouraged him to hire Coltrane. Apparently Miles was not particularly enthusiastic about the idea, probably remembering Coltrane's performance in the early 1950s band, which had also included Rollins. He finally relented, however, and hired Coltrane.

At first Miles's audiences were unhappy that the man they had assumed would be the saxophonist in the group, Sonny Rollins, had been replaced with this little-known tenorman. Nevertheless, they gradually grew to accept Coltrane, and the group became one of the most popular in jazz—despite being dubbed the "booze and dope band" since every member of the group, except for Miles, was addicted, or dual-addicted like Coltrane. Coltrane became a spectacle in the band—not, unfortunately, because of his stellar playing. He would nod off on the bandstand, his nose running. He would often show up late and constantly pressured Miles for cash to feed his habit. His playing evolved, but only to a small degree. He sounds authoritative on the blues during this period, but on some of the tunes he seems to be have trouble working within the harmonic framework. On a tune like "Diane," performed in the marathon recording session for Prestige, he seems to falter, inventing lyrical ideas but having trouble putting them into a coherent musical statement.

After Miles broke up the band (mainly because of the erratic behavior of Coltrane and the other members of the group), Coltrane seemed lost. To those who saw him during this period, it appeared that the question was not whether but how soon he would die; there was little doubt that he was doomed. He dressed like a hobo and spent most of his energy maintaining his dual addictions. One of the most humiliating incidents occurred during a Thelonious Monk recording session. Coltrane had nodded off and was so out of it that Monk had to call his name loudly, "Coltrane! Coltrane!" at the point where Trane was supposed to solo. Many musicians respected Coltrane's obvious talent, but at this juncture he seemed utterly hopeless, another jazz tragedy.

Then something remarkable happened. Coltrane went home to Philadelphia and—like Miles himself at an earlier point—made the decision to clean himself up, and to do it on his own. At his mother's house he lay down in a bedroom and instructed his wife, Naima, to bring him only water while he went through the agony of kicking both heroin and alcohol. It was during this horrendous withdrawal that he experienced the spiritual epiphany that changed his life. In the middle of this ordeal, he felt touched by God. He made a bargain with God: if God would get him through the pain of withdrawal, he would devote his life and work to a spiritual quest. And that is exactly what he did. There is one thing about Coltrane's ordeal that I find particularly interesting: although Coltrane had successfully kicked both alcohol and heroin, he also wanted to stop smoking tobacco. It was almost as if he wanted to be wholly purified; but smoking proved to be the one habit he was never able to kick.

Shortly after returning to the jazz scene, Coltrane was hired to play in Thelonious Monk's quartet. Monk was slated to play a lengthy gig at the now defunct Five Spot Cafe in New York's East Village. Unlike most clubs, the Five Spot permitted musicians to play for several weeks or even months at a time. It was during this gig that Coltrane began to make rapid strides in his evolution as a player. Monk encouraged him to take long solos, and Coltrane enthusiastically embraced Monk's suggestion. Night after night Coltrane played long, serpentine solos, developing one of the most original voices in all of jazz. He said that performing with Monk was very tricky, feeling at times as if he were "stepping into an empty elevator shaft." But the listeners who heard the group live were enthralled. The premier bop trombonist J. J. Johnson said that listening to the group was the "most electrifying sound [he had] heard since Bird and Diz."

During this stand with Monk at the Five Spot, Coltrane developed a style that Ira Gitler has very aptly described as "sheets of sound." This is a technique in which Coltrane plays long series of arpeggiated chords, almost as if he were determined to find every possible chord permutation within a single solo. It creates a spectacular effect, like fireworks for the ear. Melody is sometimes virtually ignored; the pure sound of those roiling arpeggios is the substance of these solos.

There is a photograph of Coltrane from the late 1940s or early 1950s in which he is seen at a club watching Charlie Parker play. Looking at his face, one can see that he is thoroughly fascinated with Bird's playing, so entranced that the cigarette he is holding has burned almost to the filter. It is either burning his finger or close to it, but he is in a kind of trance. Experiencing the transformative power of Parker's playing, Coltrane might have experienced an early premonition that this music could elevate and save his soul.

After the spiritual awakening that occurred while going through withdrawal, Coltrane felt even stronger about the healing and saving grace of music. At first his path seems rooted in harmony and the world of chords. At the core of bebop is the challenge of creating fresh melodic ideas through complex and difficult chord progressions. As noted previously, the European classical tradition was seen by the boppers as a kind of "church," and Western harmony was a kind of catechism, one that laid down the ultimate laws of music, which were ironclad. The challenge for a jazz musician is to create idiosyncratic music and fresh melodic ideas within the boundaries of Western theory.

Bop offered the musicians more harmonic latitude but, to some extent, also deprived them, because the harmonic structures required for bebop were far more complex. Charlie Parker once said that he could play "anything" with chords. Perhaps he already knew that some musicians were beginning to balk at the constraints of Western harmony, even back in the bop era. We shall see that there was at least one musician who was looking for such alternatives even in the 1940s. (It should also be pointed out that Lennie Tristano experimented with "free jazz"—improvisation not based on any kind of structure or even a specific meter—in the late 1940s, but it was a one-time experiment.)

One must wonder whether Coltrane was basically "practicing on the bandstand," something he would also be accused of later, at the height of his "sheets of sound" period. In its own way, Coltrane's music at this point is totally abstract since there is very little melodic flow; it is harmony for its own sake. Yet he played with ferocious intensity, and perhaps it is this intensity that keeps his performances from sounding like nothing more than a saxophonist practicing his music. A more accurate description—albeit one tinged with an element of mysticism— might be that of a saxophonist fervidly seeking his salvation in chords, as if, should he be able to play every possible harmonic permutation, he might find the mind of God.

This was the first, but certainly not the last, time that Coltrane would be accused of self-indulgence. Clearly, he seems to have had an agenda other than simply communicating with his audience. He seems to be thoroughly obsessed with chords during this period, like a scientist whose entire focus is on atoms and who perceives all matter only in terms of its molecular building blocks. There are stories about Coltrane sitting at the piano between sets and playing chords night after night, and then going home and practicing until he fell asleep with the horn in his mouth. It is almost as if Coltrane had taken the burden upon himself for bringing the harmonic advances of bebop to their logical conclusion.

The question of whether Coltrane is self-indulgent—in the music of this period or, even more so, in his later work—gets to the heart of the nature of jazz improvisation. Coltrane used to describe his musical quest as "cleaning the mirror," looking deeper and deeper inside himself in order to discover, finally, both his true self and that of God. But is that what jazz, or any art form, is for? Is it a means for an artist to exorcise his demons, a kind of therapy or method of self-investigation? Or is it intended to be a form of communication between artist and audience?

Later in Coltrane's career, especially in the final two or three years, these questions became even more relevant. By that time Coltrane seems to have lost interest in any structure at all for his music, and his playing seems based completely on striving for apocalyptic catharsis. There is no easy explanation for listeners' responsiveness to this wild show, for Coltrane was immensely popular. Could a music so arcane, so seemingly self-referential, be truly popular—with other jazzmen as well as with fans? Obviously many listeners in both groups found great value and beauty in his music. I certainly was one of his avid admirers. Perhaps a key to the puzzle has something to do with the vision of a man nakedly baring his soul, and the inherent risk of that act. Maybe his music was a catharsis for us, too. But is that necessarily good art?

To make things even more complicated, Coltrane in the recording studio was different from the man in public. The saxophonist was notorious for playing take after take while recording, attempting to achieve perfection. This is exactly the opposite of Miles Davis's approach.

Coltrane had the ability to take the ideas he had been exploring in live performances and truncate them for his solos in the recording studio. Perhaps one reason he maintained his popularity is that his best recorded solos have far more formal logic than his long-winded live solos (although his studio work, needless to say, lacks the overwhelmingly visceral effect of the live performances). Unlike a musician such as Sonny Rollins, who does not enjoy recording in the studio and does not usually play nearly as brilliantly there as he does in his personal appearances, Coltrane thrived in the studio. He used recording sessions to tighten musical concepts he had been exploring and to put them into a logical formal context.

In late 1957 Monk disbanded his quartet, and by 1958 Coltrane was back with Miles. Like many jazz musicians, Miles had been spending time at the Five Spot and was greatly impressed with Coltrane, especially since the saxophonist was clean. By the time he rejoined Miles, Coltrane had absorbed the influences of the jazzmen who had most affected him. Now he had gone far beyond them, creating a sound and style unlike that of anyone else in jazz.

After Coltrane joined Miles's sextet (with Cannonball Adderley playing alto sax), he was surprised to discover that Miles's own musical thinking had evolved in a rather unexpected way: "On returning to Miles's group, I found Miles at another stage in his musical development. There was one time in his past when he was devoted to multichorded structures. He was interested in chords for their own sake. It now seemed as if he was moving in the opposite direction, using fewer and fewer chord changes in a song. He used tunes with free-flowing lines and chordal direction. This approach allowed the soloist the choice of playing chordally or melodically."[1]

This new direction must have been somewhat bewildering to Coltrane. After all, it was Miles who first set Coltrane off in his obsession with harmony, and Coltrane felt deeply committed to continuing in that same direction.

Coltrane's evolution continued at an amazing rate. He seemed to be attempting to make up for all the time he had lost during the dark days of his addictions. He became even more of a workaholic, spending time doing little else but practicing and working out chords on the piano and playing gigs. In contrast to his naturally reserved personality, his playing became increasingly explosive and electrifying. His solos grew longer and longer. At one point Miles asked another musician to find out why Coltrane played such long solos. Coltrane replied, "I don't know how to stop." Miles told the musician, "Tell him to take the horn out of his mouth."

The first recordings of the original Davis sextet include Coltrane and Adderley as well as the original quintet rhythm section of Red Garland, Paul Chambers, and Philly Joe Jones (Garland does not play on every track; Miles is the piano accompanist on some tunes). By this time all the elements of Coltrane's style were in place: that diamond-hard tone, as recognizable a sound in jazz as that of Coleman Hawkins, Lester Young, or Louis Armstrong; the surging rhythmic thrust and harmonic complexities; the non-Western lyricism and the tidal waves of emotion. This sextet recorded "Milestones" (or "Miles," as it was eventually retitled), the title track on the only album performed by the group and Miles's first recorded modal tune. Only the three horns solo on this piece. Miles and Cannonball seem to thrive on the melodic freedom they have been given, but Coltrane sounds uncomfortable, as if he were blindly feeling his way. To most listeners, his hesitancy would seem to bode ill for his ability to play modal pieces in the future; of course, that turned out to be anything but the truth.

Several months after the *Milestones* session, Coltrane made his only recording with George Russell, the big band album *New York, New York*. Trane had continued to record in a wide variety of contexts, although by this time he was regularly recording under his own leadership. He plays on only one track, Russell's reimagining of the Rodgers and Hart standard "Manhattan." The big band was a stellar one, including Phil Woods, Milt Hinton, and Coltrane's bandmate in the Miles sextet, Bill Evans. As Russell recalls, after Coltrane came to the session, he took Russell's score for the tune and sat in a corner studying it. This caused Russell and the other musicians some consternation, since the musicians were being paid for their time, and they were all among the most illustrious, and expensive, musicians on the New York scene. Nobody was especially happy that Coltrane had chosen to delay the session. Some of the musicians at first thought he had trouble actually reading the score. But that was not the case. Rather, he was working on Russell's chord progression, reharmonizing them in accordance with the harmonic advances he had been working on.

Shortly after the session, Coltrane visited Russell at his apartment in Greenwich Village. The two discussed Coltrane's solo on "Manhattan," and Russell told the saxophonist, "You know, John, you really do not have to go through all that in order to play the chords you want to use, because the Lydian scale includes them all. You don't have to think about reharmonizing the tune. You have the freedom to play whatever you want." Of course, we can never know exactly what effect this conversation had on Coltrane or his development as an improviser, but when he performs on *Kind of Blue* a few months later we hear, for the first time, the great modal player who would dominate the 1960s jazz scene. He was not, however, simply throwing away the harmonic effects he had been exploring since 1957. He had discovered that he could stack chords on the scales or simply play straightforward melody. No longer having to think his way through the harmonic jungle of post-bop, he was able to access his deepest emotions and develop into one of the most passionate and profoundly spiritual musicians ever to walk this planet.

For Coltrane, *Kind of Blue* was not the only important record date in 1959. Later that year he recorded *Giant Steps* for Atlantic. As the Italian musician-writer Enrich Merlin has pointed out, Coltrane was clearly at war within himself when he recorded *Giant Steps*. The title tune seems to be the final outcome of his intense obsession with chords. Even now the tune is used to put jazz musicians on their mettle; the chord structure is like the definitive harmonic test. Yet on some of the other tunes, like his classic ballad "Naima," Coltrane seems to be under the influence of Miles in using streamlined harmonies (although, interestingly enough, the tenorman does not really improvise on this version of the tune).

A few months after the *Kind of Blue* sessions, Coltrane recorded *Giant Steps*. Following the performance of *Giant Steps*, though, Coltrane became devoted, for the most part, to modal playing and composing. We ask the same question about Coltrane as we did for Miles: what was going on here? I think it is simple—at the time of *Kind of Blue*, Coltrane felt that he had not yet brought his obsession with conventional harmony to its ultimate point. With the tune "Giant Steps" he did so, and now the bebop era had finally come to its close.

We can only imagine the battle that must have been taking place within Coltrane's mind. Had his obsession with chords met a dead end, or did he decide that it was, finally, fruitless?

One can only speculate; perhaps Coltrane felt he had taken the mantle from Charlie Parker and had completed the great saxophonist's work. Certainly he had taken the harmonic challenges of bop as far as they would go. Now it was time to move on to a whole new world of freedom.

It is important to note that after Coltrane went out on his own as a leader, his name was associated with the Black Power movement—though we have no evidence that he actually participated in it or had any political concerns at all. Certainly a number of the young free-jazz musicians he played with in the 1960s identified themselves with the more militant wing of the civil rights movement. The tenor saxophonist Archie Shepp is one example, and many of those young musicians consciously wanted to liberate jazz as completely as possible from its ties to the European musical tradition. Of course, the key aspect of that tradition in jazz expression (other than the instruments themselves) is its harmonic theory.

For Coltrane, the issue was whether to give up on all the harmonic devices he had been working with and simply become a completely melodic, horizontal player. Perhaps that is why he sounds so hesitant on Miles's first modal piece, "Milestones." Coltrane would discover, however, that he did not have to discard all he had achieved. This critical discovery set him on the course he would begin to explore the following year, when he left Miles and went out as a leader of his own group—and that critical discovery would come with the recording of Kind of Blue.

6 The Lonely Road of Bill Evans

When Bill Evans died in 1980, he was not a particularly controversial figure. Most musicians and critics regarded him as not only one of the most lyrical of all jazzmen but also the most influential jazz pianist since Bud Powell. Evans influenced a range of jazz performers, not just other pianists. Virtually every musician who heard him absorbed aspects of his harmonic conception and the innovations of his best groups. Yet in the past few years, Evans has become the center of a disquieting controversy. There are some people who argue that he was not really a jazz pianist at all, that his conception was outside the "true jazz tradition." They say that he did not "swing" and that the blues was foreign to his style. Such criticisms are really euphemisms; what the naysayers mean, of course, is that Evans was white and that his music reflects his white sensibility; and since jazz is an African American art form, only African Americans can play it with any kind of idiomatic validity.

The strangest aspect of this contention is that Evans influenced, or was admired by, as many black musicians as white ones. Herbie Hancock's style, for example, plainly reflects the Evans influence. Pianists such as Larry Willis and Ronnie

Matthews have been very clear about their debt to Evans. Moreover, jazzmen such as Miles Davis, Charles Mingus, George Russell, Cannonball Adderley, Ahmad Jamal, John Lewis, and Oliver Nelson, to name just a few, hired, played with, or simply expressed great admiration for Evans. That is a fairly imposing list of musicians, all of them African American. Miles Davis, a man who was inordinately grudging with his praise, said: "I sure learned a lot from Bill Evans." Miles made comparably strong statements about very few other musicians. Still, one critic has disparagingly compared Evans with Wynton Kelly, the pianist who took Evans's place in Miles Davis's group; but Kelly himself was influenced by Evans, especially in the way he played ballads.

If anything, Evans's success demonstrates the universal legitimacy of the jazz aesthetic. Bill Evans understood that aesthetic better than most, and he worked consistently to fulfill and honor it. He understood that on the most profound level jazz was born of the African American experience. He realized the overriding importance of individual expression, of achieving a *sound* that is one's own, and of discovering freedom through improvisation.

Clearly there are problems for white jazzmen, which would be dishonest to deny. One of these problems is racism. Since racism is endemic to our society in both subtle and blatant ways, it is virtually impossible for anyone to be unaffected by it. In order to develop an authentic grasp of the nature of jazz, an aspiring musician must possess deep empathy for the African American experience. I do not use the phrase *authentic grasp* on the superficial level of those who criticize Evans because the blues is purportedly absent from his work (although Evans, in fact, was greatly influenced by a jazz pianist steeped in the blues—Horace Silver). Without that critical grasp of the nature of jazz, white musicians come face-to-face with their own bigotry. They must accept black jazzmen as leaders and major innovators. For most white men and women in this country, it is difficult to accept black people as their equals, let alone as their leaders. Nonetheless, if one rejects the idea that the ability to play jazz derives from an inherent racial superiority (a notion that has, strangely, begun to find currency again), I think it is obvious why there are more great African American than white jazzmen. Closer to the truth than the idea of an inborn capacity to play jazz are the realities of history, a history of closed doors. Until fairly recently, a brilliant black musician had very few options. A career as a classical performer was virtually out of the question, nor were blacks permitted to work in the studios. Jazz was the one place where their virtuosity was welcomed and rewarded and where they could establish serious careers as musicians. Certainly Art Tatum, to name just one great musician, could have had a distinguished career as a concert pianist. Indeed, he created awe among many classical pianists; unfortunately for the world of classical music, such a career was closed to him.

For Bill Evans, classical training turned out to be something of a straitjacket. Performing classical music involved principles that were instilled in him at an early age and continued to influence him through his years of study at a university conservatory. Evans realized that the technique required to play classical music was, if anything, a hindrance to playing jazz. In an interview not long after he left Miles's band, and using a literary rather than musical analogy, he stated: "[William Blake] . . . was like a folk poet, but he reaches heights because of his simplicity. The simple things, the essences, are the great things, but our way of expressing them can be incredibly complex. It's the same thing with technique in music. You try to express a simple emotion— love, excitement, sadness—and often your technique gets in the way. It becomes an end in itself when it should really be only the funnel through which your feelings and ideas are communicated. The great artist gets right to the heart of the matter. His technique is so natural it's invisible or unhearable. I've always had a good [technical] facility, and that worries me. I hope it does not get in the way."[1]

Evans understood a central truth about jazz: a jazzman has to develop a way of communicating that is highly personal and idiosyncratic. In order to improvise freely, Evans had to learn how to trust the richness of his intuition rather than rely solely on his store of technical knowledge. He had to discard much of the method and many of the ideas about musical expression gained from his academic exposure to Western classical music. In fact, he had to reinvent himself as a musician. His ability to achieve this transformation was not simply a personal triumph for Evans himself; it was also a triumph for jazz.

Bill Evans might have pursued any career he desired. His teachers believed he could have become a leading classical pianist, but Evans chose jazz and proceeded to adapt himself—both physically and mentally—to becoming a jazzman deeply immersed in that tradition. He was knowledgeable enough about the jazz life to understand that a career as a jazzman would be far more difficult than pursuing classical music. He nevertheless made his choice and then committed every fiber of his being to realizing it. Other musicians have emerged from the classical tradition and attempted to play jazz, but most of them lacked even a superficial understanding of the jazz idiom and played a jazz-classical pastiche that was not satisfactory for either tradition. Evans, with his deep understanding of the nature of jazz expression, was able to take only what was helpful from his study of classical music and apply it to his chosen work. He brought fresh vistas to jazz that would change the music in a number of significant ways; and just as important, he created some of the most stunningly beautiful, and moving, music of the past fifty years.

According to Evans, his discovery of the concept of improvisation was serendipitous. He was playing with his high-school band when, by accident, he added a couple of notes to one of the arrangements. Immediately, the idea of creating spontaneous musical ideas became a new and exciting possibility.

When he was seventeen, Evans attended college at Southern Louisiana University in Hammond, a small town near New Orleans. Years later he would tell an interviewer that his time in New Orleans was the happiest of his life. "[It was] the first time I was on my own. Louisiana impressed me big. Maybe it's the way the people live . . . there was a kind of freedom, different from anything in the North. The intercourse between Negro and white [musicians] was friendly, even intimate. There was no hypocrisy, and that's important to me. I told this to Miles . . . and asked him if he understood what I meant. He said he did."[2]

While studying classical music at SLU, Evans was part of a small dance band that traveled around the area performing for anyone who would hire them. While learning the European canon, then, he was also developing as a jazz musician. Several pianists influenced the young Evans, including Earl Hines, Lennie Tristano, and Nat "King" Cole, a particular favorite. As a jazz pianist, however, Bud Powell was by far the most critical influence. Powell's impact can be heard throughout Evans's career. Powell adapted the complex musical language of bebop, in particular that of Charlie Parker, for the piano. With his right hand Powell played his melodic ideas while with the left he played chords. With a few exceptions, virtually every jazz pianist since Powell has been directly influenced by his style—the early boppers Al Haig and George Wallington, the pianists who emerged in the 1950s such as Tommy Flanagan, Cedar Walton, Barry Harris, even Oscar Peterson. Leading pianists of the past thirty years, such as Herbie Hancock, Chick Corea, and Marcus Roberts, clearly exhibit the influence of Powell (although for Hancock and Corea the relationship to Powell is probably more indirect, since Evans himself informs their styles to a large degree). Even Cecil Taylor has been influenced by Bud Powell, albeit mainly through the emotional intensity that he brings to the keyboard.

It was not simply Powell's harmonic and rhythmic sophistication that impressed Evans; the bop player's work was suffused with a melancholy lyricism that was all his own. One sometimes has to wonder whether a jazz improviser such as Powell (or Evans, for that matter) ever realizes how naked his inner world appears to sensitive listeners. Whatever emotional release Powell found in playing was not enough, for he had severe psychological problems throughout his life, spending lengthy periods of time in psychiatric hospitals. Perhaps it should come as no surprise that such emotionally vulnerable men, who make a living by publicly laying out their deepest feelings, wind up seeking a wide array of ministrations, many of them far from beneficial in the long run. Evans's own attempts to deal with the emotional pressure of playing this music would eventually turn out to be tragic.

After graduating from SLU, Evans joined the army. The armed forces have often proved an uncomfortable place for jazz musicians. Lester Young's ordeal provides the most famous example. Some people insist that the postwar changes in his playing were the result of his terrible experiences in the army, where he was sent to the guardhouse for possession of marijuana and beaten because his wife was white. Evans also had a difficult time as a soldier. Although his duty was mainly to play in the military band, Evans, who apparently had issues of low self-esteem throughout his life, left the service confused and disillusioned. Many of his problems in the army, however, were an outgrowth of the criticism directed at his playing, which seemed unorthodox and needlessly idiosyncratic for the narrow demands of military music. Evans left the army feeling far less sure of himself as a musician than he had during his years in college.

Instead of beginning a career after leaving the army, Evans moved into his parents' home, bought a grand piano, and spent every day working on his playing. He was determined to become a jazzman despite the hardships he faced. "It did not come easy," explained Evans years later. "I did not have the natural fluidity, and I was not the type of person who just looks at the scene and, through some intuitive process, immediately produces a finished product. I had to build my music very consciously."[3]

Evans was, in fact, encountering one of the chief paradoxes of jazz improvisation: during the act of improvising, the musician has to have absorbed and digested the necessary technical knowledge so that he can improvise without depending consciously on all that he has learned. In other words, one must first work at achieving a personal conception and then be able to act on it without deliberate thought. Sonny Rollins put it this way: "[In an interview] Coltrane was saying that he studies and practices up to a point. But, he said, after that point it is you . . . it is something else. I mean, you first do your preliminary stuff when you are actually performing, but then you forget it. That is how I would describe it. When I am on stage, I don't have to concentrate. I don't have to think about which chord goes here and how this chord is run and all this kind of stuff. Then the music gets to the point where it plays itself."[4]

This form of creativity is perhaps even more difficult for someone who has been involved mainly in the classical music tradition. When a classical pianist approaches a piece of music, he must work hard to think through how to play it, exploring it repeatedly and making a variety of decisions. But the jazz musician in live performances is unable to do this detailed advance planning because he is creating the music at the same time he is playing it. Everything—the harmony, the use of pedals, the rhythmic thrust, all of it—is invented in the moment; and once it's played, it is too late to change it. When Evans was originally told that he could have a fine career as a concert pianist, he was apparently tempted. Eventually, though, he chose the music he had fallen in love with: jazz. In his biography of Evans, *Bill Evans: How My Heart Sings*, Peter Pettinger says that for Evans, jazz was the easier course. From a superficial perspective, that may have been true, but in the long run jazz was a far more difficult road for a musician of Evans's temperament. He was not comfortable with show business and, more than that, was compelled to turn his musical thinking in a totally different direction from what he had been trained to follow in the conservatory.

Evans is not the only conservatory-trained musician who had to make this transition from classical music to jazz. Cecil Taylor and John Lewis, to name just two (black) jazz pianists, also studied classical music in programs similar to Evans's course at SLU. John Coltrane studied at a conservatory in Philadelphia; and Miles Davis, though he spent most of his time hanging out on Fifty-second Street, took some classes at Juilliard.

Interestingly, the same critics who attack Evans also dismiss Taylor because they believe that his playing is too heavily influenced by modern classical music. One can undoubtedly hear elements of composers such as Varèse and Bartók in Taylor's work, but, as Miles famously said, "So what?"

The notion that jazz is a pristine art form destroyed by introducing "outside" elements is absurd. Jazz was born of a merging of African American folk music and the Western musical tradition. It was never "pure." And unlike the blues, it is not a folk art, at least not anymore. It is a fine art; therefore, each artist brings to it his own sensibility and experience as well as concepts from the entire constellation of world music—just about anything goes. If freedom is one of the salient characteristics of jazz, and I believe it is, then an artist must be at liberty to tell his own story, sing his own song.

The fact that Evans's playing is not informed by the blues (except when he plays blues) should be irrelevant. Why should all jazzmen sound the same? What is wrong with an art form that allows for the sensibilities of diverse people, not confined to a single strand of humanity? By way of analogy, who would suggest that all novels must exhibit the same sensibility as the first British novels—which would mean that the novels of all other peoples are not the "real thing" and probably worthless? The triumph of Bill Evans is his ability to create music that reverberates as deeply within us as that of any other jazzman, which is all that matters.

Classical music requires the performer to fuse his own emotions and sensibility with that of the composer. Yes, one's own responsiveness and insight come into play when interpreting the compositions of others, but with jazz there is *only* the individual performer's sensibility. In his autobiography the composer and onetime jazz pianist Hoagy Carmichael wrote: "To me, jazz in its purest form is simply the mind in contact with itself—to steal Aristotle's definition of intuition."[5] Evans worked hard to achieve this kind of expression, but he actually went beyond that to demonstrate an entirely different set of artistic assumptions—assumptions that were alien to Western culture itself.

Evans was something of an intellectual. He had studied philosophy and was knowledgeable about literature. It is clear from some of his published letters that he had the makings of a fine and insightful writer. Yet he understood that jazz improvisation is based as much on the depths of the heart as the perceptions of the intellect. The jazz musician has to be able to subordinate his conscious mind and let intuition take control of his music-making. (It should be noted that Evans was not the only well-read jazzman: Sonny Rollins is an avid reader, as was John Coltrane. Charlie Parker was extremely knowledgeable in a number of areas other than music, as are many other jazzmen. But Bill Evans had more difficulty than they did in allowing his intuition to take over when he played. Undoubtedly this was partly the result of his background and training in the Western musical tradition.)

The jazz sensibility—the entire basis of the music—has arisen from two main sources: the assertion of one's individuality and the search for freedom. Needless to say, these concerns are central to the African-American experience. No matter how oppressive his life in American society, the jazz musician on the bandstand can express his true person, and he has the freedom to take his music in any direction he feels like. It is out of the exigencies of living that a jazzman develops the intuition necessary to improvise. The urgency of these concerns is not central to the experience of most white people in America.

Somewhere along the way, Evans discovered Zen Buddhism. Zen would become something of a fad in the late 1950s, thanks to the Beat generation. Kerouac and Ginsberg were fascinated by Zen, and their admirers embraced Zen—though most of them probably had no genuine understanding of what it meant. Evans discovered Zen long before the emergence of the fad, and his attraction to it was, I think, obvious. The idea of disengaging the mind and allowing the deepest aspects of our being to guide us toward an ultimate reality is a central tenet of Zen.

In his famous liner notes for *Kind of Blue*, Evans compared the making of the album to a Japanese Zen method of painting:

There is a Japanese visual art in which the artist is forced to be spontaneous. He must paint on a thin stretched parchment with a special brush and black water paint in such a way that an unnatural or interrupted stroke will destroy the line or break through the parchment. Erasures or changes are impossible. These artists must practice a particular discipline, that of allowing the idea to express itself in communication with their hands in such a direct way that deliberation cannot interfere.

The resulting pictures lack the complex composition and textures of ordinary painting, but it is said that those who see will find something captured that escapes explanation.

This conviction that direct deed is the most meaningful reflection, I believe, has prompted the evolution of the extremely severe and unique disciplines of the jazz or improvising musician.

For Evans, Zen must have seemed like a miraculous insight into the nature of his dilemma—that is, the intrusion of intellect into the province of intuition. A "thoughtful," deliberative solo may be musically elegant, but it will lack the emotional and spiritual depth, as well as the spontaneity, that give the best jazz its beauty and power. Zen offered Evans a method of disciplining the mind to grow quiet and to let the spirit reign in the improvisational moment.

Evans eventually moved to New York City and began to pursue in earnest a career in jazz. Since he was not an outgoing man, this move must not have been easy. He played whatever gigs he could find, and eventually he was given a semiregular job playing with the clarinetist Tony Scott. Modern jazz clarinetists are something of a rarity; besides Scott, Buddy DeFranco, and Jimmy Guiffre, most post-bop jazzmen ignored the "licorice stick," probably because it was so difficult to play boppish runs on the horn. Scott had a rather eccentric career, but in the mid-1950s he acquired enough gigs for Evans to be able to play on a more or less steady basis. (Interestingly, several years later Scott would enjoy great success with an album titled *Music for Zen Meditation*; it was one of the first New Age albums.)

Besides his work with Scott, Evans played as often as he could in a wide variety of contexts. He became an important player on the New York scene because he was able to read music and play from charts superbly; and, of course, he was also a brilliant improviser. Orrin Keepnews, who had created his own record company, Riverside, heard Evans and was impressed enough to give the pianist his first record date as a leader, which would be titled *New Jazz Conceptions*. The album was a bomb, hardly selling at all. At the time, Evans was a completely obscure figure except to a handful of musicians who had played with him. On this album he sounds like a fine but not especially original discipline of Bud Powell. In retrospect, we can perceive the aspects of the style that would eventually make him one of the great stylists in all of jazz. At this point, however, his playing was in an embryonic state; he had not fully allowed his intuition to take over when he played.

When Evans first met George Russell, it was one of the most fateful moments of his life because its ultimate outcome would be his tenure with Miles Davis and the launch of his own career as a leader. By 1965, when Evans first recorded with George Russell on the classic *Jazz Workshop* album, he had become one of the select performers in the jazz scene who had the ability to play some of the most challenging music of the time.

I find it of interest that Evans's playing during this early part of his career was far more muscular than when he became a leader a few years later. One of the most astounding displays of this muscularity is on the *Jazz Workshop* album. One of the pieces, titled "Concerto for Billy the Kid," was written expressly for Evans. Playing at a furious tempo, Evans takes a soaring solo that should once and for all destroy the commonly held belief that he was nothing but an introspective, romantic artist. On the CD edition of the album, there is an alternate version of the piece. This Evans solo is totally different, but both versions are equally astonishing. Here is an appropriate place to examine Evans's rhythmic conception. Some critics have accused him of "not swinging," but such criticism ignores his unique rhythmic conception. In many ways, his approach to rhythm reminds me of Coltrane; neither man "swings" in the traditional sense. But as Russell has pointed out, Evans's rhythm is implacable; he never rushes or strays behind the beat. Even when he is performing solo, he stays glued to a steady tempo.

Perhaps some of Evans's muscularity reflects the influence of Horace Silver. Silver's style, like that of Evans, derived from Bud Powell. But Silver's style was more percussive, perhaps because of the influence of Thelonious Monk, whose playing has a strong percussive quality. Silver's playing was also drenched in the blues, another stylistic earmark. Silver was one of the godfathers of the "soul jazz" movement, although his best music is more complex than the simple funk of soul jazz. Silver was a particularly strong influence on Jimmy Smith, who, in turn, spawned an entire generation of funky organists.

It is of some significance that Evans had, according to his own statements, listened to and learned from Silver. As previously noted, Evans has been assailed for the "lack of blues" in his work; yet the influence of Silver, whose music is well known for its grounding in the blues, is unmistakable—at least in Evans's early playing.

Although it is true that Evans's performances rarely exhibited zany, overt reference to the blues, at the rare times when he did play blues, he was able to find a personal way of working within that form. In the early 1960s Evans played on a classical session led by the saxophonist-composer-arranger Oliver Nelson that would be titled *The Blues and the Abstract Truth*, an album that has often been compared with *Kind of Blue*. In the primarily blues program on the Nelson album, Evans is wonderful, playing his own idiosyncratic blues. At times, however, he seems to be trying a little too hard to make his performance appropriately "funky," almost as if he were trying to prove his blues credentials to the other (black) musicians in the band.

In certain contexts, Evans could play blues superbly. His famous solo on the original version of "All About Rosie" greatly helped establish him as an important up-and-coming player. Rather than attempting to "get funky," he played the blues in his own distinctive voice, which is why it is so effective. Evans was gradually learning to trust his own instincts and not to try consciously to emulate anyone else. Perhaps because of the influence of Zen, or just from paying his dues, he was learning, in his own words, "the severe and unique disciplines of the jazz or improvising musician."

Evans was on the shortlist of musicians who could play music that was considered avant-garde at the time. For one brief period, he even played with the always volatile Charles Mingus and recorded a classic album with the bassist titled *East Coasting*. Mingus had often complained about his need for musicians who could play his music as he wanted it to be played and yet still be creative improvisers. This combination of traits was, of course, one of Evans's strengths. Like Miles, Mingus was often accused of being "Crow Jim," i.e., anti-white. But Mingus hired white jazzmen throughout his career and often expressed admiration for the best of them. He was a hard taskmaster; anyone who ever heard him during his heyday in the late 1950s or 1960s knew that he was capable of firing a sideman while still on the bandstand—sometimes in the middle of a set! Evans did not play with Mingus for a lengthy period of time, which given Evans's quiet, introspective personality, is not surprising. But he did have the ability to work with an amazing diversity of groups, yet always seemed to make apt and inventive musical statements no matter what the context.

George Russell vividly remembers the circumstances under which he recommended Evans to Miles Davis. Miles needed a new pianist because he had decided to fire Red Garland, whose abuse problems had increasingly annoyed the trumpeter. Russell told Miles that he knew of a fine pianist. Miles asked, "Is he white?" Russell said that he was. "Does he wear glasses?" Miles asked. Russell told him that, too, was true. "I know that motherfucker," Miles said. "I saw him playing at Birdland, and you're right. He can play his ass off!"

Miles asked Russell to bring Evans to the club in Brooklyn where the trumpeter was performing. As Russell remembers it: "He had Bill sit in for one set, and after it was over, Miles went up to him and told him he was going to Philadelphia the next week. And that is how Bill learned that he was in the band."

Being in Miles Davis's group was the ultimate gig for a young jazz musician at the time. And this group was spectacular, arguably the greatest jazz group of modern times. Besides the legendary Miles, the band consisted of John Coltrane, then reaching his first peak; Cannonball Adderley, the latest hot alto saxophonist on the scene; Paul Chambers on bass; and Philly Joe Jones on drums. Evans rightly felt that he was surrounded by giants. He was also, of course, the only white musician in the band. On the one hand, this may have been flattering to Evans, but it presented difficulties, too. There was a degree of resentment toward white jazzmen among certain musicians and part of the black community. When Sonny Rollins hired the great white guitarist Jim Hall, he received more than his share of flak from these quarters—though, to Sonny's credit, he ignored it.

For Evans, the worst part of being the only white in this band was exacerbated by Miles himself. Yet Miles was anything but a bigot; after all, his closest friend and favorite musical collaborator was Gil Evans. When I once discussed this with Miles, he told me, "How can they say I hate white people when my first band was almost all white motherfuckers?" He was referring of course, to the *Birth of the Cool* nonet, which did consist primarily of white musicians. But as has already been noted, Miles loved to prod and test those around him. For example, he constantly hurled ludicrous anti-Semitic comments toward me, once telling me that he was having a party and the honored guest was Yasir Arafat. His nickname for me (well, one of them) was "Jewish bastard." I knew that Miles was not an anti-Semite; he once told me that the one country he hated to tour was Germany "because of what they did—all of them." If I had become angry or upset over Miles's jabs, it would have shown him that I did not have the perceptiveness to understand where he was coming from, and he would have wanted nothing to do with me. It was Miles's personal radar; it was how he kept at arms' length those he did not want to associate with. There was another reason, of course, why Miles used these barbs: he simply got a kind of sadistic enjoyment out of making others uncomfortable. There was an undeniably cruel streak in his nature, particularly toward women, that sat cheek by jowl with the sensitive, vulnerable aspect of his personality. There are some who believe that cruelty is often the mark of the greatest artists. If that is so, Miles was definitely not lacking in that quality. (I think, incidentally, that there is a decidedly cruel streak in his music.)

Miles constantly aimed derisive comments at Evans. According to Jimmy Cobb, when the band was traveling somewhere and Evans tried to give them advice about the right direction for their destination, Miles would say, "We don't need your white opinions." As thin-skinned as Evans was, these sneers must have reached their mark, especially when he already felt the pressure of playing with this brilliant group. For Miles, the insults were probably a way of testing Evans's mettle, of making him strong enough to handle the pressure. Miles was a genius at knowing the right buttons to push. In addition to Miles himself, Evans had to deal with hostile audiences, especially when the crowd was mainly black. At those gigs, many refused to applaud Evans's solos, although the other members of the band received a hearty response.

The subject of white jazzmen is complex and beyond the scope of this book. However, I think at least this should be said: a white jazzman, like a black jazzman, has only the truth of his own life to use as grist for his music. If he is a genuine artist, he will be able to use his own experience in the act of artistic creation regardless of the nature of that experience. As already noted, great jazz improvisers must ultimately be able to use fully their intuition, a subtle mental process that goes beyond, and is fundamentally different from, mere cognition. Although jazz itself is the fruit of blended musical traditions, the centrality of the African American experience to this music is undeniable. In order to develop the special intuitive depth required in the act of jazz improvisation, the performer must understand the two key issues that arise from that experience: the desire for authentic personal identity and expression, and the search for freedom. The reason these issues are so vital to blacks in this country is obvious. As a member of a stereotyped minority, an African American must answer the need to express one's selfhood; the need for freedom is equally obvious.

For a white jazzman, as for most white Americans, these issues are not nearly as critical—at least on the surface. A white jazzman must eventually deepen his ideas, thoughts, and feelings about the notion of selfhood and freedom. If he does, he comes to realize that his presumed individuality in this conformist society is an illusion. By the time most Americans are adults, the socialization process has robbed us of self-knowledge, of understanding who we really are. Just as illusory, in a spiritual sense, is our supposed freedom. Many people in our society believe, at bottom, that they really do not have choices at all, that their lives are predetermined. They are the round pegs forced to fit into the square holes that have already been prepared for them. So the white jazzman, like a handful of other white Americans, must come to realize that the African American struggle is, spiritually, his own struggle, too. Out of that realization comes the sensibility on which jazz improvisation rests. Bill Evans undoubtedly made certain choices in his life out of a desire to achieve that sensibility, including his unwitting path to self-destruction. He was certainly not the first artist (and in particular, not the first jazzman) to believe there was some connection between that path and creativity.

For Bill Evans, the path to self-destruction, like that of many other jazz musicians, was drugs. During his tenure with Miles, Evans became a heroin addict. No one is quite certain who in the band introduced him to the drug, but it was almost certainly Philly Joe Jones. This must have seemed ironic to Miles: he had fired Red Garland and, eventually, Jones because of their habits. Jones was to heroin, in a manner of speaking, what Timothy Leary was to LSD; he had no compunction about sharing his habit with others. (Evans and Jones did become close friends and played together at various points throughout Evans's career. His classic second album for Riverside, *Everybody Digs Bill Evans*, was a trio with Philly Joe and the bassist Sam Jones.)

Evans's addiction, however, is not easily attributable to any single person or set of events. The pressures involved in the racial climate were certainly a factor, since he was more sensitive about his race than most other white jazzmen. Perhaps he even believed that in some way his addiction would legitimize his status within the jazz community, that he would be treated as "one of the guys" rather than as an aloof, introspective intellectual. Moreover, Evans's addiction was likely a form of rebellion against his middle-class upbringing, a deliberate act, perhaps, that would pull him deeper into the jazz culture. In one interview Evans said he liked using heroin because every day when he first took the drug, it was like being born again. Needless to say, this was unfortunate, and eventually it would lead to his premature death—albeit from a different drug: cocaine. Yet as tragic as this choice was, it is further evidence of Evans's desperation to connect with the jazz culture.

After Philly Joe was replaced by Jimmy Cobb, the great sextet that would record *Kind of Blue* was in place. For Evans, this must have been similar to Miles's experience with Charlie Parker—a nightly trial by fire. The difference between the two situations, however, was that Evans was far better technically equipped than Miles had been. Still, Evans was challenged in every way. Miles liked to play some tunes at a supersonically fast tempo. In some of the live recordings of this group, we can hear Evans's performance resembling those on the Russell recordings: muscular bop. Although in his later career Evans rarely played at fast tempos, he had no problem performing such tunes with Miles. One of the chief differences between Evans and Garland, at least in terms of the ensemble, is that Evans's comping seems to retard the tempos somewhat. This was best for Miles, whose playing was more lyrical and reflective. But Cannonball and Coltrane rolled over the beat, seemingly ignoring Evans's comping.

The greatest challenge for Evans must have been trying to find his own voice. He was surrounded in this group with three horn players who had all established their own sound, which must have been a spur to Evans's own development. In previous books I discuss the primacy of "sound" for jazz players. It is not just one's tone; it is the entire conception, the totality of how one plays the instrument and works with the music. All of these factors produce that personal sound. Miles, Coltrane, and Sonny Rollins, to name three great jazzmen, have all testified to the idea that creating a truly individual sound is essential to jazz expression. Miles Davis put it this way: "Getting a sound is what is the most important thing about playing. [Melodic] ideas are a dime a dozen." The sound that one achieves is almost a living thing; it is the ultimate reflection of the jazzman's soul.

Playing in Miles's band has often led good players to become great, partly because Miles worked so steadily. But their development also reflected Miles's understanding of how to bring the best out of his musicians. He put them in musical situations in which they had to play above themselves. In his autobiography he describes this process of forcing each member of the group upward. In addition, Miles rarely gave his musicians specific directions. Playing week after week, several sets a night, a jazzman was given the freedom to develop his own voice.

The first time we hear the "classic" Bill Evans style is also the first time the sextet recorded in the studio. About a month after Evans joined the group, Miles brought them to the Columbia studios. He needed tracks for half an album. The first side of the eventual LP was the beautiful score Miles had composed and improvised for the French film *Elevator to the Gallows*. Miles chose three standards—"On Green Dolphin Street," "Stella by Starlight," "Love for Sale"—and the old children's tune "Put Your Little Foot Out," which he retitled "Fran Dance." The group's version of "Love for Sale" was not released until the late 1970s. As Miles said about Evans, he did not play chords; rather, he played sounds. For Miles, that was about the highest praise he could offer any musician. In this session, after years of unceasing effort, Evans finally established his own sound and conception. His introduction to "On Green Dolphin Street" launched a sound never really heard before: lush, shimmering chords that in themselves speak profoundly to our emotions. Biographer Peter Pettinger describes this moment in Evans's career: "These . . . tracks marked the first great milestone in the pianist's lyrical development and in turn set the tone for the more famous album, *Kind of Blue*, to be made by the same musicians ten months later."[6]

These tracks proved that Evans did, indeed, complement Miles's own vision for his group. Evans gives the music a more sophisticated harmonic conception—a quality that was missing when Red Garland was at the piano. This is not to deny Garland's contributions to Miles's first great quintet, for his presence was considerable and his work at the piano always had an undeniably straightforward charm. Both Miles and Coltrane, however, were exploring new harmonic frontiers, and it was necessary that the group have a pianist who appreciated their direction and could keep pace with them.

It is notable that all the tunes recorded at that Columbia session had medium or slow tempos. "Love for Sale" has a faster tempo than the other tunes, but even here the tempo is only medium fast. Evans felt most comfortable at these medium tempos and when he became a leader rarely recorded tunes with an up tempo. But Miles loved to play fast tunes and so did the other members of the band. Listening to Evans on the live recordings of the band is almost like hearing a different musician from the one who emerged on the "Green Dolphin" date. He can play, and play very well, at these fast tempos; his solo on the tune George Russell wrote for him, "Concerto for Billy the Kid," is breathtaking. But Evans at this time was concerned with developing his own voice, and his conception did not fit well into tunes with fast tempos. Luminous lyricism was at the heart of Evans's style, and for him that was best served by ballads and medium swingers. Thus, it was not because Evans could not play at swift tempos—he could play brilliantly at any tempo—but as he more closely approached his own soul as an artist, he increasingly wanted to play music that helped him express his deepest emotions and ideas.

Miles Davis had similar choices in the 1940s. Although he could play, when he wanted to, like the virtuosic Fats Navarro, he made a series of choices and created a conception that most truly reflected his own being. All great jazz musicians go through the same grueling process. Evans's style was "busy being born," and at this point in his career, tending the birth was his chief concern. As he developed, Evans grew away from others' conceptions. The same thing was happening to Coltrane and Cannonball; they also were developing strong individual ideas and would soon become among the foremost leaders of jazz groups in the 1960s.

Evans's need to address the nature of his own voice is one reason for his leaving the band after only eight months. Playing with Miles would always be one of the greatest experiences of his life, but he felt that he had to leave. In addition to his growing individuality as an artist, he was also tired of the incessant touring. Undoubtedly, putting up with Miles's constant "testing" and jazz fans who resented him also took their toll. Finally, his addiction to heroin probably had something to do with his leaving the band. Evans was now, ironically, the only member of the band who still had a habit.

After he left Miles's band, Evans went to Florida to stay with his parents and renew his energy and commitment to music. In December of 1958 Evans recorded his second album, *Everybody Digs Bill Evans*. On the cover of the album are enthusiastic endorsements of Evans by some of the leading musicians of the day, including Ahmad Jamal, Cannonball Adderley, George Shearing, and Miles, who states, "[Bill Evans] plays the piano the way it should be played." On this album Evans's work is equal to the extravagant praise; it is his first great work as a leader. One of the tunes has garnered special attention, "Peace Piece." Based on a two-chord vamp, Evans improvises with a crystalline melodicism that turns unexpected corners. In some ways it is a precursor of the works of New Age pianists such as George Winston, but it has an emotional depth lacking in their music.

The rest of the *Everybody Digs* album is almost as good. At times Evans displays the muscular bopper of his earliest recordings, but he was evolving in quite a different direction. He would form a trio with two other innovators, the bassist Scott LaFaro and the drummer Paul Motian, who, along with the Ornette Coleman group of that period, would forever change the dynamics and methods of the jazz combo. No longer would a jazz group simply present a series of soloists accompanied by a rhythm section. With the innovations of these musicians, the group would improvise as an ensemble, in an attempt to both connect with the earliest jazz, in which there was constant ensemble improvisation, and advance the techniques of the jazz combo into the future. Interestingly, Miles led a group in the mid-1960s that was created around these innovations. Miles obviously continued to learn from his former sideman, and of course, Evans learned a great deal from Miles. In almost every album he recorded in the first few years after he left the sextet, Evans included a tune either written by or associated with Miles.

As a leader, Evans sometimes seemed to hide inside himself; he would sit at the piano, hunched over, his nose inches from the keyboard, almost as if he wanted to crawl inside the instrument and literally *become* the music. Some critics wondered whether Evans was really interested in communicating with his audience at that point or whether he was using the music to dig deeply into his own psyche.

Sound familiar? As different on the surface as their music seems to be, this is also the charge that was leveled at Coltrane after he became a leader. I do not think this similarity between the pianist and the saxophonist is a coincidence. Musicians influence one another in myriad ways, and the presumed differences between Evans's music and Coltrane's seem less and less real the closer you examine the work of these two geniuses. The real teacher here was Miles, who showed both Coltrane and Evans that playing jazz is based on looking deep within yourself and creating music based on what you find. There is little doubt that Evans studied Zen Buddhism for this reason: to manipulate his consciousness, to create music out of "no-mind," "the mind in contact with itself." Eventually he succeeded in overcoming the psychic barriers that faced him, and he became a genuinely great jazzman whose music came directly from his heart and soul. Indeed, some of his music is so nakedly emotional that I have found listening to it almost too wrenching. Black and white jazzmen may follow different routes, but the best of them eventually arrive at a place where they can put their lives on the line every time they play. This is certainly true of Bill Evans at his best.

Although Evans had moved on to become a leader, Miles was not finished with him. After Evans left the band, Miles briefly rehired Red Garland and then brought in Wynton Kelly, an inspired choice. But Miles conceived *Kind of Blue* with Bill Evans in mind; he wanted to use Kelly for only a single track. One reason Miles hired Evans was undoubtedly the pianist's experience playing with George Russell and his understanding of Russell's modal concept. But his reasons went even deeper.

Kind of Blue was, for Miles, an intensely personal album, one that reflects dark-hued memories and attempts to conjure spirits from his youth—one reason the album has such a ghostly ambience. Miles understood that Evans would grasp the emotional atmosphere he wanted to create. Yes, it was helpful that Evans was comfortable with modal composition and improvisation. To Miles, however, far more important than technical command was emotional empathy. It is impossible to conceive of *Kind of Blue* without Bill Evans. Thus, the black trumpetist who grew up in a black neighborhood in East St. Louis chose the white pianist from a middle-class home in Plainfield, New Jersey, to create this music that was so close to his soul. Instinctively Miles knew that Evans would be able to reach back and awaken his own apparitions, perhaps different in shape but no less haunting.

7 Cannonball's Run

We tend to look at jazz history—or any other history, for that matter—as a procession of great individuals who come along at intervals, shake the firmament, and create change. For jazz, that means we focus almost exclusively on innovators or leaders who have shaped the jazz tradition from decade to decade. Naturally we tend to give the music's greatest players virtually all the credit for the most important works of jazz. But jazz has progressed as a communal art form in which many players—some obscure, others not—have made important contributions. Great jazz albums have been made by a bassist who is able to drive the players to new heights, or have been ruined by key sidemen or the wrong drummer.

One famous example of the importance of every player in a jazz group is the "reunion" of Charlie Parker and Dizzy Gillespie that was recorded for Verve in 1950. The producer, Norman Granz, had a magnificent opportunity, and he made two good choices for the rhythm section, Thelonious Monk and Curly Russell. Monk was probably chosen at the behest of either Bird or Gillespie, since the pianist was not a Granz favorite. He probably would have preferred Oscar Peterson, who would not have adapted very well to the situation.

But then Granz made a crucial error: rather than using one of the great bop drummers of the day (for example, Max Roach or Kenny Clarke), he chose Buddy Rich for the session. Rich was a great drummer, but he simply did not fit with the other players. It should have been one of the finest moments in modern jazz history, if for no other reason than that Gillespie, Parker, and Monk—the three most important bop innovators, who at the time were at their peak—had never previously recorded together and never would again. Thus, these recordings did not achieve the level of greatness they might have if Granz had used a sympathetic drummer. (I should add, however, that the group did record a magnificent side, "Bloomdido," which includes one of my favorite Bird solos.)

Most of what has been written about *Kind of Blue* focuses on John Coltrane, Bill Evans, and of course Miles Davis himself; yet the dominance of their performances is deceptive, because any jazz album is a collaborative effort. In retrospect, I find it nearly impossible to conceive of this album without the four other musicians, and they must not be ignored.

In any case, it would certainly be difficult to ignore Cannonball Adderley, especially his presence on the bandstand. He was a huge, rotund man who, I suppose, might be called "jolly," though "ebullient" is a far better way to describe him. I once asked Miles why he used Cannonball. At the time, I believed that Adderley was not on the same level as Coltrane, Evans, and Miles, and there were many who agreed with me. Moreover, Miles had a rather childish and insensitive disdain for overweight people. He thought there was nothing wrong with saying directly to a heavy person's face, "You're too fat!" (When his former colleague Charles Mingus died, Miles said: "He was too damned fat!") When I asked him why he used Cannonball, I was surprised to see for a brief moment an undeniable sadness sweep over Miles's face. (Adderley had died relatively recently.) Miles replied, "Cannonball had a certain kind of spirit." That was all he said, but as usual with

Miles, it was enough. His statement had more than one level of meaning, though as usual, it took me a while to understand that other level.

At one time I thought that Miles's use of Adderley was the only genuine flaw in *Kind of Blue*. I no longer feel that way. Adderley certainly does bring a "certain kind of spirit" to the album, a funky joy that gives the music an added facet—and an important one. Miles, Coltrane, and Evans looked deep within themselves to create their music; Adderley buoyantly celebrated the moment. The blues were always present when Adderley played but were rarely the melancholy blues; rather, they were the music of a man who reveled in the totality of life.

Yet as I finally understood, Miles's comment about Adderley has another meaning: Miles was also referring to Adderley as a jazz populist. That is *not* the same thing as a jazz popularizer like Herbie Mann or, for that matter, Kenny G and the other players of "lite jazz" (how I hate that term). Adderley believed that jazz was still a "people's music" and strove to make it accessible, especially to black audiences—although he had many white fans as well. In fact, he often employed white players such as Joe Zawinul and Victor Feldman. If jazz had become a more elitist music since the rise of bebop, Adderley's mission seemed to be to make it once again a music for dancing and celebration.

Julian "Cannonball" Adderley was born in Tampa, Florida, in 1928, making him two years younger than Miles and Coltrane. He was given his nickname as a twist on *cannibal,* which referred to his huge appetite. His father was a musician who had played in some local bands, but he actively discouraged his son from pursuing the insecurity of jazz life. Cannonball's first instrument was the trumpet, but he soon gave it up and turned the horn over to his brother, Nat, who became a fine player in his own right (although he eventually played a cornet rather than trumpet). The two of them would later form their own band. Cannonball decided to concentrate on the alto saxophone. He led his high-school band but, after the warnings of his father, decided that it would be safer to pursue a career as a music teacher rather than as a jazz musician.

He graduated from Florida State University with a degree in music teaching. On the side, he continued to take whatever gigs he could find. Playing mainly dances, he discovered (as he would tell Nat Hentoff years later) that such gigs "made it necessary to play with drive and with a basic blues feeling to keep an audience at a dance interested." This was a lesson that would affect his playing for the rest of his career, even though as a jazzman, he was playing clubs and concerts rather than dances.

Cannonball took a job teaching at a Fort Lauderdale high school. He must have been a great teacher; for one thing, he was fluent on several instruments, including trumpet, flute, clarinet, and both the tenor and alto saxophones. In addition, he must have been entertaining to his students if his later behavior is any guide: when he was leading his own groups, Adderley enlivened his audiences with jovial mini-lectures that were both humorous and instructive, creating a warm and intimate atmosphere. At this time, jazz musicians rarely addressed the audience at all, or if they did, it was only to name the tunes and perhaps introduce the other musicians (of course, Dizzy Gillespie was one great exception). Part of this hands-off attitude toward the audience was the influence of Miles, who regarded any type of stage patter as a throwback to the minstrel era; he firmly believed that the music should speak for itself. Coltrane, after he began leading his own groups, would adopt Miles's onstage style (although *he* was not accused of being "arrogant" toward his audience). But Adderley saw nothing wrong with addressing his audience verbally; he felt that, if anything, such talk brought them closer to a kind of music—modern jazz—that many thought was over their heads.

After being inducted into the army in the early 1950s, Adderley played in several military bands. After leaving the army, he went back to teaching high school. But he was full of ambition and wanted to at least attempt being a success in the New York jazz scene. Both he and his brother, Nat, decided to venture to the big city. The story of Cannonball's "discovery" in New York is one of those jazz legends that on the surface sounds like a Hollywood fantasy. But it is the improbable truth. Soon after they arrived in New York City, Cannonball and his brother went to a now-defunct club in Greenwich Village called the Cafe Bohemia. It was at the time a favorite haunt of jazzmen; several important albums from this period were recorded live there.

The night the Adderleys went there, the bassist Oscar Pettiford was performing with his group. Pettiford was one of the great jazz bassists, a pioneer at adapting the advances of bop to the bass. He was also well known for having a peevish temper, particularly after a few drinks. On this night Pettiford's regular saxophonist, Jerome Richardson, was late because of a record date, and the bassist wanted to begin his set. He noticed that Adderley had a horn and asked the young jazzman to lend it to one of the established saxophonists who happened to be in the audience. Cannonball refused to lend his horn but said that instead *he* would like to sit in. Apparently Pettiford was offended at the brashness of this big young man but assented and let Cannonball play with the group.

Pettiford had no intention of letting Adderley off easy. Jazzmen have a long tradition of testing would-be players by choosing a tune with tricky chord changes and counting out a very fast tempo. It was a test of mettle that most burgeoning young jazzmen failed. Pettiford chose "I'll Remember April" and set off at a furious tempo. But Cannonball shocked all the musicians and "hip" elite by playing brilliantly, eating up the changes, totally unruffled by the tempo. When Jerome Richardson got to the club, he was shocked to see this unknown saxophonist on the stand. As Richardson recalls, "I came in and found this guy playing and he was blowing the walls down, and I said, 'Oh, Jesus, who the hell is this?' And I thought to myself, Well, I just lost my job."[1]

But Richardson need not have worried; not only did he continue to play with Pettiford but he also became friends with the Adderley brothers and was one of their most tireless boosters in the New York jazz scene. He was scarcely the only one; after that night at the Bohemia, the reputation of both Cannonball and Nat (who also sat in with Pettiford) spread like wildfire throughout the jazz world. The two brothers continued to play with Pettiford and soon became respected members of the jazz fraternity. Cannonball's reputation reached the stage at which he was able to become a leader in his own right, forming a group with his brother. They also received a recording contract with Savoy and began what would be a long and active recording career.

Cannonball's earliest recordings reveal that even at this point of his career, he had an unmistakably original style, although the influence of other altoists (in particular, Bird and Benny Carter) can clearly be heard. Since Charlie Parker was so important to Cannonball's development, it should come as no surprise that Nat was heavily influenced by Miles. However, like his brother, he developed his own style and became a formidable player. Incidentally, despite being so deeply influenced by Miles, Nat could not tolerate him as a human being. This antipathy can perhaps be traced to a famous incident. Miles was in a nightclub where the Adderley brothers were performing. During intermission Miles went up to Nat, took the cornet out of his hands, and acted as if he were about to hurl it to the ground, saying, "You can't play this thing, motherfucker!" Nobody ever accused Miles of being overly tactful.

Although he had a high repute among fellow musicians, Cannonball discovered what a struggle it could be to keep his own group afloat. Despite his musical prowess, dealing with all the practical and emotional difficulties of leading one's own jazz group proved to be more than he could handle at this stage of his career. After all, he had been a leader while he was living in Florida only, and he had not done particularly extensive work as a sideman in New York. He hadn't paid nearly as much "dues" as most other jazzmen on the scene. Nevertheless, he and Nat realized that seriously paying one's dues would be the only way to survive if they wanted to remain in the city.

Listening to Adderley's early albums, it becomes clear that his problems as a musician extended beyond the financial and logistical concerns of group leadership. Although no one would deny his technical facility, his style betrayed certain deficiencies. Perhaps the most outstanding problem with Adderley's playing was *taste*. It is very difficult to define taste, in particular within the context of jazz improvisation. After all, one man's tastelessness may be another man's (or woman's) ecstasy.

Is it tasteless because he plays so many notes? Well, Charlie Parker and Dizzy Gillespie played a lot of notes, yet only "moldy figs" ever called them tasteless. Certainly Coltrane played vast mountains of notes; there were those who called him tasteless, but to be succinct, they were simply wrong. Coltrane paints on a vast canvas and needs those countless notes to "get it all in." Tastelessness, at least in jazz improvisation, occurs when one plays more notes than are necessary to make a musical point. This was a large part of Adderley's problem.

Just as important, however, is his use of blues licks. As already noted, there are people who believe that all jazz expression must touch on the blues in order to be truly idiomatic; and there are many, including me, who do not agree with that position. There are certainly a number of jazzmen whose work is more blues-tinged than others—for example, Louis Armstrong or Horace Silver. But those two players, and other great jazzmen as well, are careful not to blow basic blues licks, chords, or even blue notes haphazardly, turning everything they play into funk.

Despite Cannonball's inability to keep his own group afloat, he caused a stir in the jazz scene. Although like most saxophonists of that period, he was clearly in thrall to Charlie Parker, he was just as clearly his own man. In addition to Bird, he was also influenced by such rhythm-and-blues players as Eddie "Cleanhead" Vinson (with whom he would later record) and Earl Bostic. Technically commanding, Adderley could keep pace with any of his contemporaries in jazz.

In addition, Adderley had emerged in the heart of the New York jazz scene at a very propitious time for someone with such a fervid and blues-drenched style. In 1955, the year Cannonball arrived in New York, the hard-bop movement was just beginning to dominate the East Coast jazz world. This movement was to a degree a reaction to the "cool" jazz era that was for the most part identified with West Coast (and mainly white) jazz musicians. Many jazzmen were looking back to their music's black roots, and for many of them that meant the blues.

Did jazz really develop out of the blues? The answer is yes—but only to an extent. Labeling jazz as "blues music," as one writer has done, exhibits a lack of knowledge about the true roots of jazz. Those who insist on claiming that the blues is the sole parent of jazz do so for their own narrow sociopolitical agenda. For me, one of the most inspiring aspects of the evolution of jazz is the resourcefulness and eclecticism of the musicians who have developed it. They took what they needed from a wide panoply of sources: gospel music, African rhythms, brass band music, the blues, European folk music, classical music, "Latin-tinged" music, and who knows how many other types of music. (Some have even claimed to hear in jazz Native American music and, amazingly, cantorial song.) This is what makes jazz so profoundly American—like its people, the whole of these different musical sources is greater than the rich sum of its parts.

Nevertheless, the blues have traditionally been associated with African American culture; and it certainly is true that

West Coast "cool" jazz had virtually no blues tinge at all, except when the musicians actually played blues (which was not too often). So when somebody whose playing was as steeped in blues as much as Cannonball Adderley's arrived on the East Coast, he was immediately embraced for his commitment to the black roots of jazz.

Perhaps this encouragement led Adderley to rely too heavily on blues licks. Their overuse made some musicians and critics doubt his sincerity, as they similarly doubted the sincerity of other musicians. Oscar Peterson, for example, often turned blues clichés when playing virtually any kind of tune. Miles caustically remarked that Peterson was the type of musician who had to be *taught* how to play the blues. Such clichés have often been used by jazzmen, but some musicians in the mid and late 1950s created solos with very little else except blues-oriented clichés.

Martin Williams, hailed as the dean of American jazz critics, put it this way: "I find Adderley's work unsatisfying. . . . At the end of his solos, I usually find myself asking just what he has said—in form, in melody and rhythm, and in content. . . . Adderley seems to toss off casually what he can play within the *technical* form of each piece but not within its emotional form or musical implications."[2]

In a review of a live Adderley album, Williams wrote that the tunes have "more blue notes per four-bar phrase than you might have believed possible. Indeed, the whole occasion has the air of a communal celebration in which a black middle-class determinedly seeks out its musical roots."[3]

Yet another critic of Adderley was Miles Davis. Miles had befriended Cannonball after he made his move to New York, giving him advice about using the right agent and which record companies to stay away from. He also gave him musical advice. As Cannonball later recalled it: "Miles began telling me something musically about chords, but I sort of ignored him. . . . I was a little arrogant in those days. Then about three months later I saw an interview in which Miles said I could swing, but I didn't know much about chords."[4] Make no mistake about it—Miles said these things deliberately to reach Adderley, whom he had been thinking of hiring. He undoubtedly wanted him to become more harmonically sophisticated before he would be permitted to play in Miles's group.

Despite this criticism, both Miles and Williams recognized Cannonball's great talent, and so did most of those on the scene. But the burden of leading a group made it difficult for Cannonball to focus totally on his own playing. And his group with Nat had a tough time finding enough of an audience at this early stage of their careers. Adderley was forced to accept the fact that he would not be able to keep his band together, at least not before he became a better-known name among the jazz audience.

But then Cannonball got a break, the most important of his career. Dizzy Gillespie had invited him to join his small group, and Adderley, frustrated with trying to lead his own group, decided to do it. At the time, he was playing opposite Miles at the Cafe Bohemia, the same club where he was "discovered." When he mentioned to Miles that Gillespie had asked him to join his group, the trumpeter asked Adderley why he didn't join *his* group. Cannonball replied, naturally enough, "Because you never asked me."

In October of 1957 Cannonball finally disbanded his group and accepted Miles's invitation rather than Dizzy's. He said, "Not that Dizzy is not a good teacher, but he played more commercially than Miles. Thank goodness I made the move that I did."[5]

At the time, Miles's group was a quintet—Coltrane was still with Monk. The importance of this opportunity for Adderley was more than simply Miles's penchant for "star making." For one thing, it gave the saxophonist a certain kind of legitimacy. Playing for Miles, throughout virtually the trumpeter's entire history as a leader, meant almost instant acceptance among those in the jazz scene. And since Miles toured constantly, a musician was able to garner nationwide, and even worldwide, recognition and respect.

But for Cannonball, there was an even more crucial reason that Miles was important to his career: better than just about anybody else, Miles was able to help him shape and develop his conception. As Nat Hentoff put it in an article about Cannonball, "Adderley had been mistaking speed and facility of execution for musical expression, and he learned much about editing his solos and about harmonic imagination from Davis. 'You don't have to play all those notes,' Davis would tell him."

There are many musicians (and even more jazz fans) who confuse superb technical facility with great playing. There are many jazzmen who have gained their reputations by their ability to play very fast or "all over their horn." Some musicians have regularly tried to "wow" their audiences by using circular breathing in order to hold on to a note for a lengthy period of time. Roland Kirk amazed audiences with his ability to play three wind instruments at once, and maybe blow a flute through his nose simultaneously. (It should be said, however, that he could also play brilliantly on one horn when he wanted.) But improvising beautiful and emotionally meaningful music has nothing to do with that kind of facility. After all, jazz is not a series of carnival or athletic events. It is an art form that speaks to us as deeply as any other. The best technique is that which is invisible, which does not draw the listener's attention as if the technical challenges alone constitute the essence of the music.

I have often wondered whether there is an element of racism in the way some jazzmen are admired for these purely technical qualities; such admiration is not dissimilar to the respect given, for example, Michael Jordan or Walter Payton or Mike Tyson. It is easier for some white people to admire black men and women for physical ability than for being able to create profound and intellectually stimulating artistic statements.

There have been some jazzmen who were incredibly virtuosic but also played music of great beauty and depth. Charlie Parker is one obvious example, along with fellow bopsters such as Dizzy Gillespie, Bud Powell, and Fats Navarro. To examine the flip side of the "technique" argument—this time with a very different kind of jazzman, I think it is fallacious to state that Thelonious Monk *lacked* technique. As previously noted, he developed the precise kind of technique he needed to play his own unique music. And that distinctiveness is the quality that is paramount: a jazzman's—or at least a great jazzman's—technique arises out of the specific demands of his own idiosyncratic musical conception. Ask yourself, for example, whether Clifford Brown is a "better" trumpet player than Miles Davis. From the perspective of traditional musical technique, yes. But from the more demanding jazz standard—the ability to create personal, emotionally compelling musical statements—no.

For Cannonball Adderley, then, his great technical facility perhaps stood in the way of his developing into a major jazzman. But he could not have found a better way to evolve as a musician than playing with Miles Davis. Nobody had a better understanding than Miles of how to make musical statements with an economy of notes. This is not an easy thing to learn. Many musicians have said that the important thing about improvising is knowing what *not* to play. It takes time and great patience to discover this truth. Some critics have pointed out that Miles seemed to have the ability to edit complex lines as he played, reducing them to their essentials and implying more than he actually stated.

The effect of Miles on Cannonball's development as a mature improviser is clear when one listens to the music Cannonball recorded while he was with Davis, both as part of Miles's group and as a leader in his own right. The first time Cannonball recorded while he was with Miles was on the first session for the *Milestones* album on February 4, 1958. Of course, by that time Coltrane had rejoined Miles. On the group's version of Monk's "Straight, No Chaser," Cannonball plays with a sense of purpose not heard in his earlier work. He is obviously being spurred by Coltrane to play more adventurously than he had in the past, and his harmonic language in particular is far more exploratory. From Adderley's earlier work, the contrast between him and Coltrane is not as great as one might have expected. Miles was a master at finding ways to make his musicians play over their heads. For example, often during a performance by the sextet, Miles would whisper into Coltrane's ear while Cannonball was playing, and vice versa, praising whoever was playing at the time. By doing so, he exacerbated the competitiveness between the players, which in turn caused them to take chances and not rely on clichés and trite licks.

Cannonball seems far more relaxed and assured on "Miles" ("Milestones"). In fact, his solo is one of his best on the album; his work gives credence to Miles's remark about Cannonball's "spirit"—it is genuinely joy-inducing, and the ability to elicit joy in this way should not be discounted. Cannonball may suffer from the same prejudice that makes many jazz fans downgrade Dizzy Gillespie in comparison with Charlie Parker or Miles. Darker emotions are, for some people, much deeper or more significant than the expression of joy. This view is similar to the widespread belief that a great comedy is less profound than a serious drama—but this perception is, at best, superficial.

A month after the first *Milestones* session, Cannonball recorded the only album he would do for Blue Note (that is, as a leader; he was a sideman on a date led by the trumpet player Louis Smith). The album, called *Somethin' Else,* was a true "all-star" date, and a very unusual one at that: one of the sidemen was Cannonball's boss at the time, Miles Davis. The rhythm section was suitably top-drawer: pianist Hank Jones, bassist Sam Jones (the two were not related), and the mighty Art Blakey. Although this was nominally Adderley's date, Miles clearly was the one running the show. Perhaps, then, it should not come as a surprise that this is the finest album Cannonball ever recorded as a leader. If there needs to be any further evidence of Miles's genius for giving musicians the perfect context in which to excel as improvisers, this album should provide more than necessary.

Not only is this Cannonball's best record, it also includes his finest solo—his beautifully sculpted, emotionally charged "Autumn Leaves." This solo alone proves that Adderley was capable of playing superbly when given the opportunity. Of course, Miles, in his subtle yet calculated way, strongly affected Adderley, whose playing is far more thoughtful and nuanced than most of his earlier work, and these qualities would continue to be true for years after. At the same time, Adderley retains the bluesy passion that colors most of his music. Miles also plays magnificently on the album; he was obviously at a new peak. Unfortunately, it was a peak he would never equal again, although his playing on *Kind of Blue* comes, at times, quite close. As we shall see, Adderley would also be the source of the single obvious flaw in *Kind of Blue*.

Miles's genius as a musical strategist is important in his work with Adderley—or, for that matter, with any jazzman who played in his group. Miles never jumped into anything unless he had tested the waters; he understood that his own ambitions could not be realized unless the musicians he worked with were able to follow him as he headed in new directions. I believe that this was the main reason Miles undertook the role of "sideman" to Adderley on this one date. Cannonball, as noted earlier, seems more relaxed on the first modal tune Miles recorded—"Miles" ("Milestones"). Yet Miles must have realized that the alto saxophonist was not a musician on the same exalted level as Coltrane, Bill Evans, or himself. For Adderley, Miles was in a sense both Machiavelli

and Svengali: Miles was subtly preparing for the new challenges he planned for his musicians as well as helping shape
Cannonball into a player who could prevail in the new kind of
musical freedom Miles intended to explore.

Why, then, use Adderley at all for *Kind of Blue* if Miles had
misgivings about the saxophonist? The answer takes us back
to the beginning of this chapter—Miles understood the value
of that special "spirit," that funky ebullience and joyous celebration that Cannonball brought to the music and to life
itself. Years after *Kind of Blue*, Miles would be harshly criticized by some critics—and by more than a few musicians,
too—for his explorations of jazz/rock/funk—or fusion, as this
period was labeled. He was accused of selling out, deliberately
diluting his music in order to reach a huge pop and rock audience. But the truth is, Miles was never an elitist. He always
wanted his music to reach the broadest audience possible.

Late in his own career, Cannonball himself was accused of
selling out. His answer was that if he could find a way to sell
out, he would do it in a minute. The fact that Cannonball's
blues-filled style reached those in an audience confused or put
off by Coltrane's byzantine journeys into the stratosphere or
Bill Evans's romantic introspection gave the sextet an extra
dimension. After Cannonball left the group, at the end of
1959, Miles toured with only a quintet. In his autobiography
he makes clear that without Adderley, he was not able to continue in the same direction that he had been pursuing with
the sextet. But Miles could not have gone out and simply
hired any of the alto saxophonists on the scene in order to
restore the sextet. Miles was always concerned with the primacy of sound itself, and no alto saxophonist except Adderley
could have combined with the other horns to make the glorious *sound* of the great sextet.

The recordings of the quintet that Miles used on his European tour are magnificent; Coltrane's solos, for example, virtually explode with ideas. But there is something lacking.

And Miles was right: that missing quality was a certain funky "spirit."

Rhythm sections are always vital to a great jazz album. In the case of *Kind of Blue,* the rhythm section and its sensitivity in supporting the soloists was particularly crucial. The emotional and musical ambience of *Kind of Blue* is so fragile, a responsive and inventive rhythm section is as important as brilliant soloists. Moreover, the wide disparity of styles (and especially rhythmic conceptions) in this band was so great that the rhythm section had to shift gears constantly, depending on who was soloing—not an easy thing to do. And this rhythm section was nothing short of magnificent.

The musicians in the rhythm section on *Kind of Blue* are not as famous or respected as several others from this era, including some of the jazzmen in Miles's own groups. The bassist Paul Chambers and the drummer Jimmy Cobb have never been as celebrated as, say, Chambers and Philly Joe Jones from Miles's original group, or as the Tony Williams–Ron Carter pairing in the group Miles would lead a few years later. But in many ways the Chambers-Cobb rhythm section is equal to them. It was not as innovative as, say, the Williams-Carter section, but it was the perfect rhythm section for *Kind of Blue.* No other rhythm section that I can think of could have supplied such strong but unobtrusive and sensitive support. Both Chambers and Cobb not only knew how to listen to what the soloist was doing, they were able to anticipate the flow of each solo. And with soloists like the ones on this record (and in particular, Coltrane), this was a formidable task.

It is especially astonishing to hear how mature the playing of Paul Chambers is on this record, since he was only twenty-three at the time. But Chambers was one of those remarkable prodigies that springs up in jazz from time to time. He was born in Pittsburgh in 1935 and moved to Detroit after the death of his mother. His original instrument was the tuba, but when he turned fourteen he switched to the double bass. Within a few years he was playing with some of Detroit's best jazzmen and was hired by the tenor saxophonist Paul Quinichette for a tour that wound up in New York, where Chambers finally settled. He soon became one of the most admired young bassists in jazz, playing with some of the best modernists of the time, including pianist George Wallington, trumpeter Donald Byrd, trombonists J. J. Johnson, Kai Winding, and Bennie Green. When Miles formed his first great quintet in 1955, he chose Chambers as his bassist. At the time, few bassists swung as hard as Chambers, although he was not among those who were attempting to expand the role of the instrument. That honor would go to Charles Mingus and the important bassists who somewhat later would take the bass further along an innovative path, including Scott LaFaro, Gary Peacock, and Ron Carter, the bassist who would eventually replace Chambers in the Davis quintet. For Miles, though, Chambers's ability to provide strong rhythmic impetus for a band was of paramount importance. *"Phew,"* Miles said about him, "that motherfucker can really make a band swing."

It is not surprising that Chambers became a drug addict after joining the Davis band—still nicknamed the "dope and booze" band despite the fact that Miles himself was then clean. (Still, anyone who worked in close proximity to Philly Joe Jones seemed to be drawn into heroin sooner or later.) Chambers would eventually stay with Miles until 1963, when the entire band, which by then included the tenor saxophonist Hank Mobley, broke up in a rather confused fashion. Chambers and the others in the Miles rhythm section, Wynton Kelly and Jimmy Cobb, formed a trio that was quite successful for a while; they recorded a live album with Wes Mongomery that, in my opinion, is the best album the great guitarist ever made—*Smokin' at the Half Note.*

Although Chambers was not in the vanguard of jazz bassists, his playing was tremendously influential for its drive and deep, woody sound. His good taste and penchant for playing the right notes were remarkable for someone so young. Rather than trying to overrun the soloist with his technique like many youthful hotshot bassists, his dedication was always toward being supportive of the soloist. He himself was also a superb soloist who could improvise equally well when strumming the bass or playing arco (with the bow). That may be Chambers's greatest legacy—he influenced many bassists as a soloist. And, of course, as the perfect bassist for *Kind of Blue*, he will be remembered as one of the greatest of all jazz bassists.

Jimmy Cobb never got the approbation from critics that Chambers received. I think he is one of the most underappreciated of all modern jazz drummers, and not just because he played on *Kind of Blue*. For me, at least, he is pivotal in the evolution of jazz drumming, serving as a kind of bridge between Max Roach, Roy Haynes, and Philly Joe Jones and the important drummers of the 1960s, such as Pete La Roca, Elvin Jones, and especially Tony Williams. More than any of those drummers, Cobb was, and is, a *group* drummer who understands how to pull together a band while forcefully providing perceptive support to the soloists. He never let his ego dictate his work as an accompanist; he never tried to overwhelm the soloist, nor did he take many solos himself (at least not while he was with Miles). Miles's rhythmic conception was so subtle that playing with him was a test for a drummer; the drummer could not simply bash ahead. He had to be able to listen not only to what the trumpeter was actually playing but also to its implications. As mentioned earlier, Miles became notorious for turning his back to his audience—to hear the drummer better, he said, not to shut out the audience. However the audience understood Miles's somewhat melodramatic gesture, his own comment reveals how important the drummer was; and Cobb not only played exactly what Miles needed but he did it with great drive and intelligence—a truly *musical* drummer.

Jimmy Cobb was born in Washington, D.C., in 1929. He took some lessons but was mainly self-taught. By the time he was twenty-one, he was gigging regularly, playing locally with musicians ranging from Charlie Parker and Leo Parker (they were not related) to Billie Holiday and even Pearl Bailey. He left Washington to tour with rhythm-and-blues saxophonist Earl Bostic, with whom Coltrane also played for a while. After leaving Bostic, Jimmy played with the blues singer Dinah Washington, whom he married. The relationship was volatile and eventually led to divorce. After Cobb settled in New York, he became a very busy drummer, playing with some of the top modernists, such as Stan Getz, the ubiquitous J. J. Johnson, and Cannonball Adderley, who was responsible for bringing him to Miles's attention.

Cobb joined Miles's band in 1958 amidst the chaotic sessions for the *Milestones* album. Miles was having major problems with both Red Garland and Philly Joe Jones, so Cannonball brought Cobb to the session in case Jones did not show up. Jones did eventually show up, but Red Garland, who was still supposedly the pianist in the group, did not. Miles was forced to accompany the soloists on piano and then to play without piano accompaniment when he took his own solo. At the end of the session, as Cobb remembers, "Red walked in and started to play the piano. But the shit was over! Miles was pissed, but he knew what Red and Philly Joe were about; he had been through that junkie bullshit himself. And Red and Philly Joe, in turn, felt that Miles didn't care about their problems, that he could just go home—to his great home. He didn't have to scuffle on the streets like they did." Soon after these notorious sessions, Cannonball brought Jimmy in to play a date at a club in Brooklyn, and from then on he was the sextet's drummer. (This was also the gig at which Bill Evans first played with the group.)

Playing with this sextet was both a dream come true as well as nightmare for a drummer. It was the best band in jazz, and it played *hard*, giving the drummer the opportunity to really turn loose, which is how most drummers like it. Some drummers have almost been ruined when they are forced to play mainly behind singers. Such gigs may be lucrative but are frustrating for a drummer; and, of course, Cobb knew this very well after the years of playing behind Dinah Washington. The complexity of playing behind such disparate soloists as those in Miles's band was daunting, to say the least.

Coltrane, especially, was a challenge. His intense solos became longer and longer, forcing Cobb to test his own stamina as it had never been before. One evening he was playing so hard behind a lengthy Coltrane solo that one of his sticks flew out of his hand and just missed the saxophonist's head. After the set, Coltrane chuckled and said to him, "You almost got me that time." But Cobb loved Trane's playing, as exhausting as it was just to keep pace with him.

Cobb, like the other players in the sextet, was given the freedom to develop his own style. I have often wondered whether Miles himself was actually a strong influence on Cobb because the drummer seemed at times to be paring down his style, breaking away from the complex rhythms of a drummer such as Philly Joe Jones. Cobb's work was, in fact, similar to that of Miles's best solo statements, implied rhythms rather than outright statements. Thus, Cobb streamlined jazz rhythms while still providing the strong rhythmic support that Miles demanded. Like Chambers, the drummer's ability to provide sympathetic support behind such an array of different soloists was extraordinary in itself.

Jimmy Cobb is a quiet, plainspoken, gentle, and truly sensitive man with a great sense of humor. From his demeanor one would never guess what an explosive drummer he really is. Hopefully, the high regard for *Kind of Blue* will result in reconsideration of Cobb in the pantheon of great jazz drummers.

Wynton Kelly has only a cameo role in *Kind of Blue*, but Miles's decision to use him instead of Bill Evans on one cut, the blues "Freddie Freeloader," was a stroke of genius. Kelly was a master blues player who was a *swinger* if there ever was one. Yet unlike many of his contemporaries, in addition to being funky, Kelly was also a highly lyrical player who combined his blues with a songlike character that made him unique. As Miles put it, "In Wynton Kelly we had a combination of Red Garland and Bill Evans so we could go in any direction we wanted."[6] Additionally, Kelly was one of the greatest accompanists in all of jazz. He did more than just provide support; he gave the soloist a genuine lift and was able to engage in a kind of two-way musical conversation, throwing out ideas, filling in spaces, giving drive to the entire rhythm section while never interfering with the soloist's musical direction. As Sonny Rollins pointed out, some pianists get in the way of a player's freedom or simply envelop him in chords; Kelly, on the other hand, made a soloist want to play.

Wynton Kelly was born in December 1931 in Jamaica. When he was four years old, his family moved to Brooklyn. By the time he was a teenager, he was playing in rhythm-and-blues bands, which heavily influenced his mature blues-oriented style. He went on to play with Dinah Washington (while, incidentally, Jimmy Cobb was playing drums behind the singer) and later with Eddie "Lockjaw" Davis, whose playing was like one of the "blues shouters" out of the 1940s. When Kelly was eighteen, he was hired by Dizzy Gillespie; thus, by the time he was hired by Miles Davis in 1958, he was at twenty-seven already a veteran.

Wynton Kelly is one of the greatest of all modern jazz pianists, although lately he has become almost a forgotten figure (while Bill Evans's reputation has, if anything, soared after his death—and rightly so). Kelly made dozens of albums with some of the best post-bop players, including Miles, Dizzy, Coltrane, Sonny Rollins (he was Sonny's favorite accompanist), Wayne Shorter, Hank Mobley, and dozens more. Tragically, he died at the age of thirty-nine. Among the many pianists whom he influenced were such future Miles sidemen as Victor Feldman and, especially, Herbie Hancock.

The contrast between these three jazzmen—Bill Evans, Jimmy Cobb, Paul Chambers—proves how much difference one musician can make, especially in the rhythm section, to the overall dynamics of a jazz group. With Evans, the rhythm seems slightly behind the soloist, providing a more abstract rhythmic attack. But with Kelly, the rhythm is far more aggressive, pushing the soloist forward. It is difficult *not* to swing when Kelly is in the piano chair. And the one track on *Kind of Blue* on which Kelly plays has a very different feel from the others, although in its own way it is no less compelling than the tracks on which Evans is the pianist.

Miles often pointed out that his rhythm sections *liked* playing with one another. This was certainly true for the Kelly-Cobb-Chambers team. They fit together perfectly. As pointed out, none of them were radical innovators; rather, their concern was to try to make the group swing as hard as possible and to provide strong support for the soloists. And they succeeded at it brilliantly.

These musicians—Cannonball Adderley, Paul Chambers, Jimmy Cobb, and Wynton Kelly—usually do not get much attention or credit for the success of *Kind of Blue*. But bring in, say, Philly Joe Jones instead of Jimmy Cobb, or Oscar Pettiford instead of Chambers, and the album would have been entirely different. Not necessarily worse or better, but profoundly different.

The lives and careers of all seven musicians who play on *Kind of Blue* seem almost predestined to lead each of them to the time and the place, the recording studio where this jazz masterpiece was created in March and April of 1959.

8 The Sessions

In 1999 someone had the bright idea of producing a concert in honor of the fortieth anniversary of the recording of *Kind of Blue*. The producer put together a band that included Jimmy Cobb, the only living member of the original Miles Davis sextet; the group used the same instrumentation as that of the original recording, and they played all the tunes from the album. Yet no matter how experienced those musicians were or how well they played, their performance seemed to have little relationship to *Kind of Blue*. That masterpiece was possible only with the original members of the sextet—playing together as a group—and the music could only have been created at that time, in that particular place. Anything else is a forgery. As we have seen, the roads of the great musicians who recorded *Kind of Blue* seem to have led them inescapably to a single destination: that CBS recording studio in Manhattan in 1959.

So this is our story so far: the roads traveled by seven post-bop jazzmen intersect when they join Miles Davis's sextet in 1958. At the time, Miles—who was seeking greater harmonic freedom—latches on to the theory of his old friend George Russell and begins to explore the idea of using modes, or scales, instead of chord progressions. After an initial experiment with modes for the *Milestones* album, Miles decides to do an entire album on which most of the compositions will be based on various structures founded in modes rather than in Western harmonic theory.

Which leads us to March 2, 1959. This was the first of the two dates on which *Kind of Blue* was recorded. Miles had worked on the tunes right up until the morning of the session. He had been thinking about this album for a while and had specific goals in mind. One was to steer a new course for jazz, away from Western musical theory; another goal, even more important, was to record an album on which the musicians were forced to play their solos with complete spontaneity.

In his biography of Miles, Bill Cole wrote this about the *Kind of Blue* sessions: "Much of the playing seemed too cautious due to the fact that only Miles and [Bill] Evans were familiar with the written music. . . . If the entire group could have shared in the development of these new ideas, they could have gone much further ahead."[1]

Of course, that was exactly what Miles very deliberately did not want to do. It is obvious that Cole completely misunderstood the concept behind these sessions. Miles was deliberately attempting to make his group play with a kind of spontaneity that in itself was unprecedented. Musicians have often brought new compositions to a recording studio, but the *Kind of Blue* sessions went far beyond that. Not only had all the musicians (with the exception of Evans) not seen the tunes in advance, *they had never before played music with the very structure of these tunes*. Yes, they had played the one modal tune on the *Milestones* album, but these tunes had different kinds of modal structures that were far more challenging than what they had played on "Miles."

Miles's commitment to genuine spontaneity was in itself a key innovation of *Kind of Blue*. The only session that I can think of in which this type of strategy was used was called *Crosscurrents*, led by the pianist Lennie Tristano in the late

1940s. On two tunes, he and his musicians played with absolutely no compass, no tune or chord structure, no set tempo. Although it was a fascinating experiment, it was obviously clear that Tristano's musicians, which included some great ones (the two horns on the session were Lee Konitz and Warne Marsh), were not ready for this kind of all-out freedom, although much later in their careers they eventually were able to play in a "free" context. Nobody attempted to play in a completely "free" context until the early 1960s. At that time, Ornette Coleman, using a "double quartet" (two reedmen, two trumpeters, two bassists, and two drummers) recorded *Free Jazz*, an entire album that was totally free—no set tunes or fixed tempo or chord structures. It was an audacious musical adventure. While playing with untrammeled freedom is risky, since "anything goes," the music can be simply pure cacophony. But creating a coherent musical statement in a completely "free" context is an extremely difficult challenge. In the 1960s a whole new generation of jazzmen dealt with the difficulties of truly free jazz, attempting the profound challenge of creating music as free of preset structure as possible while also offering coherence. This music is often just as difficult to listen to as it is to play. When it works, however, it is exhilarating for both musicians and listeners.

The tunes used on *Kind of Blue* were certainly not as free as that music. While giving the improviser a great deal of freedom, the tunes did have a structure that the soloists had to consider. The musicians could not, for example, play anything that happened to come into their heads. As previously noted, Miles's goal with his small groups was always to achieve freedom *with control*. This is how Miles himself put it: "If you put a musician in a place where he has to do something different from what he does all the time, then he can do that—but he's got to think differently in order to do it. He has to use his imagination, be more creative, more innovative; he's got to take more risks."[2]

This is Miles the existentialist speaking—his ultimate goal

was to make his musicians realize that they had the freedom to explore new avenues they had never before dared to enter. At the same time, Miles was able to guide their free flights in a direction that gave the album coherence and, especially, that engendered an overall mood.

In his autobiography, Miles says that his aim was not simply to achieve greater freedom but also to play music that was more "African, Eastern, less Western." Certainly this desire was as much social and political as it was musical. The times they were a-changin', especially for African Americans, and Miles was acutely aware of this.

But Miles's idea for the album went beyond the challenge of spontaneity and formal innovations. He had definite ideas about the emotional terrain he wanted to explore. For Miles, *Kind of Blue* was a memory album. In his autobiography he states that when he conceived the idea for the album, his aim was to try to re-create a memory from his boyhood. It was a memory of when he was visiting relatives in Arkansas. He remembered walking back along a country road from church at night and hearing in the distance ghostly "bad gospels" being sung in some of the black churches they walked past. It was one of those evanescent memories that we all have from childhood, more an unforgettably haunting mood than a specific memory.

In addition, Miles had seen a troupe of African dancers not long before the *Kind of Blue* sessions and was fascinated by the polyrhythms played by the drummers and the spontaneity of the dancers as they moved to those rhythms. He wanted his musicians to play music with the same graceful spontaneity. He also wanted to capture the feeling of the African music itself, its stark harmonic simplicity tied to rhythmic complexity. The sound of the African thumb piano especially moved him.

Miles, then, came into the studio on that day in March 1959 with a well-defined and exceedingly personal *sound* and mood that he wished to re-create. This was a daunting task, considering the wide latitude he insisted on giving his musicians and that they, of course, had not necessarily had the same experiences that lingered in Miles's memory. And since they performed these pieces with only minimal preparation, it was very difficult for them to be able to shape their own playing in a way that would summon up the mood and sound Miles had in mind.

It is not surprising that Miles would say years later that *Kind of Blue* was a failure. He loved the music, but it did not attain the very specific emotional ambience he was trying to evoke, nor did it really reflect the sound of the African music (especially the thumb piano) he had heard at the program of African dance.

The vagaries of jazz improvisation are too complex for anyone to be able to create such a narrow, specific sound or mood. Whatever memories the leader of a jazz group may try to evoke are greatly mitigated by the musical agenda of the musicians in his group. This was especially true of the jazzmen in the Davis sextet. The leader can try to push his musicians in a certain direction, but they can go only so far. A great leader, like Duke Ellington or Charles Mingus or Miles, chooses musicians who they believe will be to some extent sympathetic toward the leader's own ends. This is one reason that a writer has named jazz "the imperfect art." If an artist has faith in the power of spontaneity, he cannot also hope for sleekness and perfection.

Whatever happens in the studio is further complicated by the relationships among the musicians, and not just in terms of their music. Just as important are their social relationships. By the time the *Kind of Blue* sessions took place, these relationships were fairly tangled and, to an extent, tense. Undoubtedly this had a profound effect on everyone and on the music they made.

Tension, even outright anger, can either help or hinder the playing of a jazz group in the studio. The longest-lived of all jazz groups, the Modern Jazz Quartet, had a continual high degree of tension that lasted for most of the group's history. John Lewis was fascinated with the classical music tradition and often wrote pieces based on fugues or concertos, and at times played with a full orchestra. The vibist, Milt Jackson, simply loved to wail, especially on the blues. Although every member of this group was a master jazzman, I believe that this tension between Jackson and Lewis had a lot to do with their continued success. I have always thought that Jackson played his best with the MJQ, and I also think this tension accounted for his high level of performance.

Another famous example of tension in the recording studio occurred when Bill Evans made his second album—*Explorations*—with his wonderful trio. He and his bassist, Scott LaFaro, were angry at each other, supposedly because of Evans's drug addiction and the way it affected the group. Evans thought the session went badly because of the vexed feelings between the two musicians. Upon further listening, though, he was happily surprised. Knowing about this situation, one might think that the music from the session would be tense or even aggressive. Interestingly, just the opposite is true—it is some of the loveliest and most crystalline music Evans ever created.

In the case of *Kind of Blue*, there were a number of causes for tension. For one thing, at the time of the first session, the group was on the verge of disintegration. Miles was deeply troubled by the prospect of losing both Cannonball Adderley and John Coltrane. Adderley had made it clear that he wanted to try achieving success as a leader in his own right, and a few months later he did leave the band. Coltrane was also making noises about leaving the group. Miles was doing everything he could to keep Coltrane from going out on his own. He was a brilliant, almost Machiavellian manipulator, and Coltrane was becoming increasingly frustrated. As I wrote in *Ascension*, "One night in a rare fit of pique Coltrane said to saxophonist Wayne Shorter, 'You want the Miles gig? You got it. I'm finished with the Miles gig.' "[3] For the usually mild-mannered Coltrane to explode like this is ample evidence of just how much he wanted to lead his own band and of his rising irritation with Miles for making it so difficult for him to leave the sextet. He could not just walk away, because he knew, and Miles undoubtedly never let him forget, how much he had learned from the trumpeter and, of course, all the things Miles had done for him—after all, it was Miles who had made him a major jazz star. On the other hand, Coltrane's memory of the humiliation he had felt when Miles fired him in 1957 was still fresh in his mind. Yet if Miles had not done so, Coltrane probably would have died from his dual addictions. So the relationship between the two musicians at this point was uncomfortable, to say the least, and complex.

Bill Evans, of course, was officially out of the group at the time of the *Kind of Blue* sessions. But from Miles's point of view, Evans had left prematurely. He realized that with Evans the band had a special sound, one quite different from the sound of the group with Evans's predecessor, Red Garland, or the sound when Evans's successor, Wynton Kelly, became the pianist. Miles wanted to exploit that sound, and although he had done so to a degree for the "On Green Dolphin Street" session from March of the previous year, he wanted Evans to return because the sound of the group with him was the one Miles wanted to create for the album.

As for Evans himself, even briefly performing again with Miles must have been a bewildering situation. Playing with Miles had been a turning point in his life for more than one reason. It had established him as a major jazzman and gave him exposure to both the fans and the critics. But it had also been emotionally eviscerating. For one thing, he had become a drug addict; and playing with Miles had been an enervating musical challenge. Evans had never felt totally comfortable in the group. Miles's facetious racial jabs were wearying and, to an extent, were probably responsible for Evans's feeling that he had never really been "one of the guys." To make matters worse, Miles was disgusted that Evans, who was clean when he first joined the group, now had a bad drug habit. After all, that was exactly the reason he had fired Red Garland.

For Evans, the tension of the session was exacerbated by Miles's having called on his then-current pianist, Wynton Kelly, to also play on the session. Kelly was even more confused. As Jimmy Cobb remembers it: "When Wynton came to the date, he was puzzled. He said, 'I thought I was the pianist on this date.' He was wondering what Bill Evans was doing there. So I told him not to worry, that this may be different from what he was used to, but that Miles did things differently. Miles liked to fuck with musicians' heads like that, get them worried and nervous. He thought it would make them play better, and I guess he was usually right." On *Kind of Blue* Miles's strategy worked, because "Freddie Freeloader," the tune that Wynton played on, fit in perfectly with the rest of the album, as if it were all of a piece.

Of course, Miles used the same psychological strategy with the two saxophonists; he used a number of means to make them compete with each other. Probably both musicians were somewhat tired of this kind of manipulation, but for Coltrane it was especially annoying because he had worked with Miles far longer than Cannonball and undoubtedly saw through such maneuvers more than the alto saxophonist.

So the chemistry among the musicians on this particular day was volatile, to say the least. To further complicate things, the seven musicians who play on the album were not the only ones involved with this recording. There was the engineer, of course, and the A&R men, nowadays called producers.

Miles required a very special kind of person to produce his dates. Perhaps most important, he required a producer who knew what *not* to do. That is, the producer should not tell him what material to use or which musicians. Miles would ignore any such suggestions. A producer had to let Miles create his music in his own way with as little interference as possible.

The producer also had to be a musician himself, hopefully someone who was comfortable with Miles's subtle and constantly progressive musical vision. He also had to be able to have the patience to deal with Miles's mercurial personality and iron will. Most of all, he had to know *how* to listen to the music and to truly understand it because Miles had a laser-sharp bullshit detector. Fortunately, the right producer was found in time for the *Kind of Blue* sessions. His name was Teo Macero.

Teo Macero is an unpretentious, straight-talking and regular kind of guy, never self-consciously hip as one might expect for someone who throughout his life has been dealing with musicians like Miles, Mingus, and Monk. *Kind of Blue* was the first time that Macero was the producer for an entire Miles session. He was not the only producer, though; the other was Irving Townsend, who along with George Avakian (who had "discovered," or rather "rediscovered," Miles at the 1955 Newport Jazz Festival) had produced Miles's Columbia albums up to this point. The relationship between the artist Miles and the producer Teo Macero would last for more than two decades. Macero and Davis are among the most legendary pairings of artist and producer in jazz history. After *Kind of Blue* the two would go on to record a series of further jazz masterpieces, ranging from *Sketches of Spain* to *In a Silent Way* and *Bitches Brew*.

Unsurprisingly, Miles would often downgrade Macero's contribution to the success of his albums. (He said to me, "Teo just stands in the booth like a dummy, and I tell him what to do.") Those who know better understand that Miles's version is simply not so. Macero had been instrumental to both Miles and a number of other great jazzmen, including Mingus and Monk, in producing superb albums without infringing on their freedom to create and explore.

Undoubtedly Teo's empathy with these musicians arises from the fact that he himself is both a fine saxophonist and an adventurous and innovative composer. In the fifties he explored modal composition, the combination of symphony and jazz (years before the third-stream movement), atonality, and musical collage. Some of his music is quite daring and at times a bit eccentric—such as his use of two accordions in a series of pieces he recorded in the 1950s. As a saxophonist he combined a beautiful tone, not unlike that of Stan Getz, with a harmonic imagination that is surprisingly advanced. And his own road led as inevitably to *Kind of Blue* as those of the musicians themselves.

Teo Macero was a year older than Miles, having been born in 1925 in New Jersey. He became aware of music very early on because his father owned a nightclub. He first started playing saxophone in high school and often sat in with jazzmen at his father's club. Like Miles, Macero attended Juilliard, where he studied both composition and his wind instruments (including both tenor and alto saxophone, clarinet, and flute) as well as keyboards; but unlike the trumpeter, he took his courses seriously and regularly attended classes. But as with Miles, he quickly advanced to the point where he was eager to leave the school prematurely: "I was ready to get out with a bachelor's degree after two years, but they wouldn't let me go. So I kept taking courses and wound up taking master's courses and got my master's in two years and I said, 'I can't stay here for another two years.' "

Like Miles, he spent much of his time on Fifty-second Street, which was where he met one of his most important colleagues, Charles Mingus: "I used to play with his band and we would play at the [Cafe] Bohemia with other musicians, like Monk [whom he would later produce for Columbia]. It was a very nice association." Surprisingly, Macero had no problem dealing with the intermittently explosive and volatile Mingus: "We got along fine, just fine. He never gave me a problem. We did lots of shows together, lots of records, too."

The music that Macero recorded with Mingus as well as on his own is very advanced, and some of it highly experimental. Although at the time there was a bevy of musicians who were as influenced by Lester Young as Macero was, Teo's harmonic conception is far more sophisticated than their's.

In 1954 Macero got a Guggenheim grant, which helped open up new avenues for him:

> I took the money and just started giving grants all around New York, and one day one of the producers from CBS attended one of the concerts. At the end of the concert he said, "Would you like a job with Columbia?" So I asked him how much it paid. He said it was ninety bucks a week. I was only making $2,500 a year teaching blind students and mentally retarded kids. The only extra money I got was from working in the recording lab at Juilliard and the shows I did with Mingus. So I took the job.

Macero's first job at Columbia was to score some sides for Johnny Mathis. He did four sides, the composer-arranger Bob Prince did four sides, and Gil Evans did four sides—three years before recording his first monumental orchestral collaboration with Miles Davis, *Miles Ahead*.

Macero was given the opportunity to write some fairly adventurous music for Columbia, but eventually he spent most of his time producing. Although it was regular work, he found that trying to do creative and innovative projects was a continual war with the top brass:

> It was such a struggle! I mean, those guys didn't give a quarter! And I used to lick my wounds, because there were so many goddamned guys in the Columbia A&R department and they were all opinionated—they wanted this, they wanted that. So I would say, "For

chrisssakes. Just leave me alone!" I just wanted to have them leave me and the artists alone so we could make some records.

Teo first met Miles in the early fifties at Birdland. But they did not work together until a few years later:

In 1956 I did a thing with Leonard Bernstein called "This Is Jazz." And I wrote some of the examples that they used. I wrote an introduction for "Just You." Miles played the tune—it was the quintet with Coltrane and Red Garland. After that, I did some editing for the *Porgy and Bess* album. I put it all together—Gil didn't give a shit whether the splices worked or not. The tempos kept changing. I said, "Gil, listen to it. The tempos are changing." So he told me I could do whatever I wanted with the tapes.

Teo had also been involved in the first recording session of the sextet with Bill Evans, in which the group played four tunes, including "On Green Dolphin Street." But the *Kind of Blue* sessions would be the first time that he experienced the highs and lows of working with Miles. As Macero recalls:

It was a long time ago, but as I remember it, we made that record at the CBS studio on Thirtieth Street. It had to be there because that is where everything was being recorded at that time. It was just a great studio. It was a great big place, and none of the musicians had to wear earphones like today. I boxed everyone in so that there would be a physical closeness among the musicians, not like today when the musicians are spread all over the place. I used to spend most of my time outside the booth 'cause I could hear what the hell was going on. I didn't have to sit in the control booth and say, "Take one, take two." A lot of things that happened with a jazz group happened outside the control booth when the microphones were turned off. I used to stand right next to Miles with a pair of earphones on. I had to make sure that he played into the right goddamned microphone.

Even back when he first started to produce Miles, Macero had a special understanding of the trumpeter's motives for his musical direction:

I think Miles was genuinely uncomfortable with chord changes by that point, and he would cut out the changes when somebody brought him a tune. And he felt very comfortable doing that. Not that I could blame him, because it gave you a chance to expand your ideas. But I did not discuss this at any length at the sessions. Miles was not very talkative in the studio. Neither was Coltrane. We would just be there to listen, to see what was going on and put it down. Every once in a while, at the end of a take, [Miles] would motion me to come out and sit with him. And I'd go out and sit in the hall with him for ten or fifteen minutes and he would not say one word! Then he would turn to me and say, "Hey, motherfucker, you didn't like that, did you?" And I would say, "No, I didn't. It was a piece of crap." So he'd jump up and we'd do another take, and I'd go, "That's it! Good night, everybody." I did that more than once. A lot of times Miles would call me about ideas he had for an album, like those he had for *Kind of Blue*. I'd get a call from him in the middle of the night, two or three in the morning. And he would play something on trumpet or piano over the phone and then he would want a critique. So I used to lie there and listen. I helped steer him toward a lot of the musical directions that he went after.
 Recording with Miles was always easy. You might think it would be difficult, but it wasn't. I remember

with *Sketches of Spain* he didn't show up for six of the sessions because he was ill, but when he came, it was a breeze. We just went straight through it! He was always prepared. He knew what he wanted to do and how to do it. I was there just to help him in any way I could. And there was such camaraderie among the players. When Miles was there, you had to play what was right! They would play a tune for the first time, and I would say, "Let's make it!" That was my favorite expression—"Let's make it!" Of course, back then Miles's music was a little simpler than it eventually became (during his electric phase). I do remember that Gil Evans was at the *Kind of Blue* sessions. And as I recall, that introduction for "So What" was his idea—he and Miles were very tight musical partners at that time. Miles would listen to Gil. But when other musicians came to him, guys in the band, he wouldn't pay any attention to them.

Macero was usually the sole editor of Miles's albums, because the trumpeter himself had little interest in that aspect of recording:

He never came to the editing room after the recording was over. Maybe four or five times, tops, in all those years. I would just put it together and send it up to him; if he liked it, fine. If he didn't like it, I'd tell him I would do it again. But I never really did it again. Every time I sent it back to him, he would say, "Yeah, I liked it." So he was just being ornery, as usual. Miles wanted to put all kinds of shit on record. I would say to him, "Look, this has gotta go. I mean, Jesus Christ, you wanna sell Miles Davis, or you wanna sell some saxophone player or guitarist? Your first obligation is to you. You want to put in thirty choruses of the sax player—hey, be my guest! But it ain't gonna be shit. People are going to say, "Where's Miles?" He even wanted to put some curse words on a record. I told him to go to hell! I think he was just trying to be hip.

Despite all his hassles with Miles, he looks back on those riotous days with great affection:

It was fun. I'd go up to his house and we'd sit or whatever, and I used to go up there quite a bit and try to get him to do things and work on another project, and yeah, it was always fun. Miles had a mind of his own, and he didn't give a shit who we were. I once brought the head of the Columbia A&R Department. So we hung out in that little backyard of his, and finally I asked, "Where is Miles?" And I was told he had left half an hour before we had arrived. He knew I was bringing this guy up, and we had some money for him! He was doing it just to be ornery. But I would just laugh at the guy. One time he even bit my earlobe. He said, "It's such a nice white ear." He was playful. But he was very serious when it came to music.

Miles had been carefully thinking and strategizing the *Kind of Blue* sessions months before they actually took place. Bill Evans said that a couple of months before the sessions, Miles showed him some chords and asked him to try to do something with them. Evans took those chords and wrote "Blue in Green." Miles would later claim coauthorship of the tune, but Evans was always outspoken about the fact that he had been the actual composer of the lovely piece. This was an old trick of Miles's. I once asked him who wrote the tunes "Four" and "Tune Up." He replied, "Eddie Vinson." So I asked him why, then, the tunes listed Miles as sole composer. "Because I wrote them," he replied.

"But you just told me that Eddie Vinson wrote them."

"What difference does it make?" he asked with mock exasperation. I am certain that the authorship of such popular blowing vehicles meant something to Vinson.

Miles had sketched out all the other tunes for *Kind of Blue* within hours of the sessions. These were the fruits of his long months of thought about the goals he wished to achieve. All the pieces of *Kind of Blue* were finally together on Thirtieth Street in Manhattan: all seven musicians, the producer, and in his role as unofficial adviser, Gil Evans. Ever since I heard this album, I was certain that it must have been recorded late at night—how else could these musicians evoke such a mood unless the hour was late? So I was surprised, and slightly disappointed, when Jimmy Cobb told me that it had been recorded in the afternoon. On the other hand, it gave me a better appreciation of Miles's ability to create and sustain a mood.

Like many who love jazz, I have often fantasized about going back in time and being a fly on the wall during legendary recording sessions. Needless to say, the *Kind of Blue* sessions are at the top of my imaginary list—obviously pure fantasy.

Well, not altogether. We can *hear* at least the first session thanks to some audio documents that have turned up. So now we can close our eyes and dream that we are patiently waiting at the Thirtieth Street studio for the musicians to appear. Once they have arrived, all the musicians except Bill Evans gather around the piano as Miles shows them the music he has written out for the first tune, "Freddie Freeloader." This is the only tune on which Wynton Kelly is going to play, so Miles chooses to record it first so Kelly can leave after it is done. I don't think Miles did this just to be courteous to Kelly; as we have seen, Kelly was confused and more than a little upset that Evans was going to play on the rest of the album. The expedient thing to do would be to record "Freeloader" immediately so Miles would not have to deal with Kelly's consternation any further.

Most of the conversation during a Davis recording session was between the producer in the booth and Miles. In the case of *Kind of Blue* there were two producers: Teo Macero and Irving Townsend. Macero's role, however, was clearly that of an apprentice and observer. After all, working with Miles Davis required a special kind of know-how and an understanding of the man himself.

Once the musicians have worked out the general guidelines of the performance and briefly practiced playing the tunes, Miles is ready to record; then once the engineers signal their readiness, Townsend cues the band: "Take one, CO620290, no title." The "no title" designation was not unusual for Miles, who frequently did not assign titles to his tunes until they were needed for the album jacket.

A moment before the band begins to play, Miles says to Wynton Kelly, "Hey, Wyn, I want you to play after Cannon, and then we [the ensemble] come in." A short while later Miles says, "Hey, Wyn, I want you to play again after Cannon, okay?" One would have thought that it was a bit late for Miles to be giving further instructions, but this is an indication of how loose he wanted these sessions.

After the first few notes of "Freddie Freeloader," Miles signals to stop. "Too fast."

"Hey, Miles," asks Townsend, "where are you going to work? Where are you going to work?"

Miles replies, "Right here."

"Okay, but when you move back, we don't get you."

"I wasn't playing with my horn into the mike before." He changes the position of the mike so that he can play straight into it.

"We're not allowed to change the mikes around here. Against regulations," jokes Townsend.

On the second take, Miles stops again after the theme is played and tells Kelly, "You don't play no chord going into A flat."

The third attempt at "Freddie Freeloader" is a complete

take. But Miles is dissatisfied with the final improvised section in which there is a kind of duet between Kelly and Chambers. They attempt that section a few more times before Miles decides that he is dissatisfied with the ending. He listens a couple of more times and eventually concedes that the end of the complete take is best.

"Freddie Freeloader" has never received the same kind of popular and critical fascination as the other pieces on *Kind of Blue*. I imagine this may be because of the more conventional form of the tune. It is a basic twelve-bar blues, but a blues that Miles has stripped to its essence, providing as much freedom for an experienced jazzman as he does for the other pieces on the album. Most good jazzmen can play the blues virtually in their sleep (and I have witnessed jazzmen who actually did that, or at least came close to it). The challenge for great players is coming up with a fresh approach to this bedrock form. Within the hushed, ghostly atmosphere that Miles created for this session, it was as much of a challenge to the musicians as any of the other pieces; blues clichés and old funk licks were out of place, perhaps even gauche.

From the beginning of the piece, Wynton Kelly's rambunctious accompaniment creates a mood that is clearly different—at least to an extent—from the other tunes on *Kind of Blue*. He seems to prance on the keys, even as the ensemble plays the simple blues line. Miles takes the first solo, and it is a masterpiece: for me, one of the greatest blues solos in all of jazz history. It is, I believe, a solo that had been a kind of "work in progress" for a number of years. It can be traced back to such early 1950s performances as "Blue Haze" and its sequel, "Green Haze." (It is interesting to note that even back then Miles was playing with the concept of blue and blue-green, and shades of blue.) One can hear elements of this tune on Miles's solo "Bags Groove," which he recorded in 1954 with the Modern Jazz Giants, among whom were Milt Jackson and Thelonious Monk. And there were performances of similar medium-slow blues-oriented pieces that project the same mood we hear on the sound track that Miles had recorded in France for the film *Elevator to the Gallows*. There is also his solo on "Sid's Ahead" on the sextet's first album, *Milestones,* when both Philly Joe Jones and Red Garland were still in the band. In these solos, too, the music is a starkly played slow blues line in which Miles seems to be summing up everything he knows about the blues. Someone once compared Miles's sound to that of a little boy trapped in a closet, desperate to get out. We hear that deep wellspring of primal feeling in all of Miles's blues pieces, nowhere more so than in "Freddie Freeloader."

The first soloist after Miles is Coltrane, who plays with the typically fiery sense of purpose that has always characterized his blues style. His blues playing here reminds me of seeing him perform at a small out-of-the-way club like the Half Note in lower Manhattan. In late sets he would simply blow the blues for chorus after chorus, never seeming to repeat a single idea. On "Freddie Freeloader" his solo seems so over-heated with ideas that at times he cannot get them out of his horn before another comes tumultuously on its heels. It is essential Coltrane.

Cannonball follows Coltrane, and for him this kind of bluesy piece is his bread and butter. It would also seem to be a trap for Cannonball to simply throw one well-worn funky lick after another, and he does do this to a degree. But I do not know how anyone could not love this solo; it is almost as if Adderley is telling the other players to get down to the nitty-gritty. Adderley's solo is followed by a section that is fundamentally a Chambers-Kelly duet. Even at this early date, the musical empathy between the two jazzmen borders on the paranormal.

Incidentally, the tune was named for a well-known hanger-on of the jazz scene back then, not the famous Red Skelton character. Many years after the album was released, I heard an interview with the actual Freddie Freeloader. He said he appreciated Miles's using his name for the piece but told

Miles that he would have preferred it if "So What" had been named after him. Obviously, Freddie had justly earned his nickname.

With "Freddie Freeloader" now out of the way, Kelly leaves, and Bill Evans takes over the piano chair for "So What." Anyone who knew Miles was aware that this was one of his favorite expressions, a way of dismissing the grandiose, perhaps; Miles had a genius for seeing through pretension and hyperbole. The piece begins with a duet between Evans and Chambers that Gil Evans had apparently brought to the session. It is the single most difficult aspect of "So What."

After a few attempts at the opening section, Townsend complains that there is too much extraneous noise. He says, "This [section] is so quiet, and I can hear noises all the way through. I can even hear the snare drum."

Miles replies, "But that's part of it. All of that is part of it." To Miles, mistakes and even extraneous noises are part of a genuine jazz performance. Townsend concedes the point but adds that not all such noise should be allowed. After a few more attempts at the opening section, the band plays "So What" all the way through. Once again, the first complete take is the master take, without inserts.

"So What" is probably the single most famous piece on *Kind of Blue* (although in recent years "All Blues" has become almost as widely played). The composition is so simple that even a nonmusician can suss out the degree of freedom offered to the improvising jazzmen. Interestingly, the tune is constructed as an elemental call-and-response, a musical form that can be traced to early European liturgical music. And certainly call-and-response has a special place in African American music, being used for centuries in gospels and spirituals. (One wonders whether Miles was deliberately using this form to bring to life memories of the "bad gospels" he used to hear on those Arkansas roads.)

After the eerie opening passage, superbly played by Evans and Chambers, the theme comes in with Paul Chambers playing a figure that is responded to first by Bill Evans and then by the entire ensemble.

Miles takes the first solo, and it is at least as brilliantly constructed as "Freddie Freeloader." It is unlike anything else Miles had previously played. With a strict economy of notes, not one of which is superfluous, without ever resorting to double time or arpeggios, this is certainly *not* a bebop solo, nor is it reminiscent of jazz solos of a previous era. It is, in its own way, a new kind of jazz, with a lyricism that had only been hinted at by Miles and other jazzmen (most particularly Lester Young and those who were influenced by him). In it is the jazz equivalent of the impressionism of Debussy, Ravel, and Scriabin—the kind of lyrical impressionism usually associated with some European folk music. However, its emotional nuances are certainly those of Miles alone; it is not blues but a different "kind of blue," a violet perhaps. It is a kind of melancholy that does not rule out hope or transcendence.

Coltrane's solo follows Miles, and it is obvious that Trane has been picking up on the direction Miles had been taking, and is adapting it to his own style. Hearing this solo is particularly fascinating because Coltrane is, on his own stylistic terms, almost as economical as Miles. But unlike Miles, Coltrane has not yet learned how to make a totally coherent improvisation based on a modal tune. Although he is far more relaxed and less hesitant than he was on his first modal performance, "Milestones," he is still feeling his way. Of course, eventually he would become inarguably the greatest of all jazz modal improvisers.

As with "Milestones," Cannonball seems more comfortable with modes than Coltrane does. His solo is fine enough, though at times overly florid.

For Evans's solo, the piece turns again to call-and-response. The ensemble plays the two-note "So What" phrase, to which Evans responds. What is remarkable here is Evans's ability to create a solo statement despite this kind of tricky arrangement. Both Miles's simple arrangement here and Evans's improvisations are highlights of the piece, continuing the impressionistic flavor that Miles had brought to the tune.

Townsend asks, "This is just for you four guys on this next one, right?"

Miles replies, "Five. Adderley lays out on this piece."

The next piece recorded at this session is the ballad "Blue in Green." It is such a subtle, delicately constructed and lyrical piece of music that it presents its own kind of problem: the only analogous form that I can think of is a Zen koan—within the few simple lines of a koan, a Zen master can offer the transcendence of nirvana. Undoubtedly, this is why Miles said that Cannonball should lay out on "Blue in Green." Adderley's bold funk simply did not fit the mood of this piece. Although its construction is at least as simple as the other pieces on *Kind of Blue*, its melody is so fragile that the challenge of playing it can rightfully be compared to walking on eggshells.

Bill Evans—who was the true composer of the piece—plays the melody with the rich voicings that were such a key aspect of his work. On this piece alone, we have ample evidence of the truth of Miles's assertion that Evans did not simply play notes, he played a *sound*. After a few attempts, the band takes the tune all the way through Coltrane's solo. Something goes wrong, and Townsend says to the band, "That was our fault this time."

Miles disagrees. "I don't believe that." Anyone who thinks that Miles was the ultimate temperamental artist should listen to how he behaves on this session; he is patient, polite, and respectful to the producer and the engineer. Teo Macero has himself made clear that Miles was rarely difficult; one had only to understand him and to be knowledgeable about the way he worked.

On the fourth take, the jazzmen play through the complete piece, and that is the master. Evans's playing throughout the piece is simply gorgeous. Miles solos with his Harmon mute, of which he was the ultimate master. His poignant use of the mute is itself a *sound* as personal to Miles's soul as his own voice. Coltrane plays a brief solo that, once and for all, proves he did not have to lean on playing a cascade of notes. His solo is so simple, so emotionally direct and lyrically stunning that one is transfixed by its beauty. For a moment, we catch a glimpse of nirvana.

As soon as it is finished, Townsend says, "Beautiful, beautiful!" What other words could he have used? "Blue in Green" is, quite simply, beautiful.

With the three tunes in the can, the session comes to an end. A little over a month later, on April 9, the group reconvenes to complete the album's final two cuts. Miles is again in high, confident spirits; he is obviously pleased with the results of the first session. However, the two tunes planned for this session are "All Blues" and "Flamenco Sketches."

Surprisingly, Miles begins with the ballad, "Sketches." This is similar in delicacy to "Blue in Green," although it has a "Spanish tinge" (to use the phrase of Jelly Roll Morton) that makes it unique and more than a bit tricky. And in contrast to "Blue in Green," this piece does include Cannonball Adderley. I personally believe that using Cannonball on this tune was a mistake, perhaps the only truly egregious one that Miles made on the entire album.

Bill Evans opens the piece with an introduction that seems derived from some of his recent work as a leader: his version of Leonard Bernstein's "Some Other Time" and Evans's own famous "Peace Piece." Like "Blue in Green," the tempo is extremely slow; perhaps no tempo, except for the exceedingly fast, is such a challenge for an improviser to make a coherent musical statement.

After the first attempt at playing "Sketches," Miles tells Adderley that his horn squeaks. One has to wonder whether Miles is really trying to make Cannonball more conscious of what is coming out of his horn. They play several incomplete takes and one complete take, but Miles is not happy with the results. Finally, they do another complete take, and it is obviously a success. After the second complete take, Miles says to Townsend, "That was terrible, Irving."

"Don't worry about it," replies Townsend, laughing.

Perhaps the main problem with "Flamenco Sketches" is that the listener automatically compares this piece with "Blue in Green." The difference, of course, is the Spanish flavor of "Sketches." For Miles, this tune was undoubtedly a preview of his next major project, the magnificent *Sketches of Spain*. It was actually the second attempt by Miles at playing a piece influenced by flamenco. "Blues for Pablo" was part of Miles's first orchestral collaboration with Gil Evans, *Miles Ahead*. (Incidentally, two years later Coltrane would record his own modal/flamenco piece, "Ole.")

The solos by Miles, Evans, and Coltrane are all quite beautiful, if not as stunning as those on "Blue in Green." But Cannonball's brassy, rather tasteless solo almost completely dispels the darkly introspective mood so carefully built up by the other players. Nevertheless, if "Flamenco Sketches" were on any other album, it would be considered a masterpiece.

The next and final tune, "All Blues," is probably the trickiest one heard on *Kind of Blue*, which is probably why Miles chose to record it last. As it turns out, however, the band has little trouble with it, and their first attempt at playing the tune all the way through is the only take they need.

"All Blues" is an exceptionally stirring and emotionally compelling piece. It also has a special significance, since it is played in 6/8 time (although Miles originally conceived it as a straight-ahead 4/4 blues). It begins with the rhythm section setting up the mood and rhythmic direction, which gains greater focus when the two horns play an effective vamp. Miles enters with the lovely melody.

Miles is the first soloist, and he discards his mute, making a particularly dramatic entrance. Once again, he uses an economy of notes, saying exactly what he has to say without a single superfluous idea or note. This is the only piece on the album in which Cannonball Adderley is the second soloist, and he is in quite cogent form here. However, almost every other musical statement is virtually wiped out by Coltrane. His own entrance is at least as dramatic as that of Miles; Jimmy Cobb brings him in by playing a drum roll, making it clear that something momentous is about to happen, and indeed it does. Coltrane's solo here is the first time on record that the John Coltrane of the 1960s can be heard: here is the apocalyptic visionary whose scorching intensity so illuminated, and was illuminated by, the cultural climate of the sixties. (It is important to note that many of Coltrane's key performances of the 1960s were in waltz time, including his single most famous work, his raga-influenced version of "My Favorite Things.")

Bill Evans follows with a short, typically impressionistic solo, and it is probably the only way that any solo could be effective following Coltrane's.

The group ends the piece by repeating the theme heard at its beginning. When the recording is over, Miles jokes around by acting as if he were gasping for breath. But that is how Miles tended to behave when he was deeply moved. No doubt he was so proud of what the group had accomplished that joking was the only way he could respond. In two days in 1959 he and his musicians had created an indelible musical masterpiece. And I think Miles knew it.

Now the album would be readied for the public—the record jacket with its brooding photograph of Miles on the front cover, and on the back, another photo of him seated deep in thought, his trumpet held loosely between his fingers; also on the back is "Improvisation in Jazz," the famous liner notes by Bill Evans, and, of course, a listing of the personnel. *Kind of Blue* is complete. Is there anything else to say about it? Does the story of a great work of art end with its creation? What of its effect on the future, its effect not only on the art form itself but also on the careers of the artist or artists involved? In a word, what is its legacy?

9 *Blue*'s Legacy

The actual sessions during which *Kind of Blue* was recorded are certainly not the end of this story. Perhaps the most important part of the narrative is what happened after the making and release of this watershed album. As I have stated, we can almost divide the history of modern jazz into the era before *Kind of Blue* and the one after *Kind of Blue*. In a way, the album was almost a Pandora's box from which magical possibilities as well as new challenges and difficulties were loosed in the jazz world. The consequences were more than purely musical; parallel changes were taking place in American society, especially regarding the social and political realities in the lives of African Americans. Clearly, the new kinds of musical freedom that *Kind of Blue* helped launch were mirrored in like changes that went far beyond the jazz world. The careers of the musicians who had created the album would be affected by both the musical and nonmusical changes to one degree or another, in the aftermath of *Kind of Blue*. It was such a towering achievement that in a sense it overshadowed everything they accomplished from that time forward.

When *Kind of Blue* was released in 1959, it received excellent reviews (*Down Beat* gave it five stars). Although its importance to jazz history seems obvious in retrospect, at the time not everybody was pleased with the direction Miles seemed to be taking. In a *Playboy* article about the trumpeter, an unnamed drummer expressed a view that diverged from the generally favorable commentaries. He said: "A certain vitality isn't there any more. [Miles] lives a pretty lush life and his music gets kind of lush." An unnamed trombonist said that Miles had "deliberately restricted himself to a narrow range of notes and to safe ideas." And another musician told the writer, "All his talk of increasing the melodic possibilities of improvisation amounts to his reducing the number of progressions to an absolute minimum. But he doesn't fill in the chordal void with lots of melodic lines. The notes are always within the same compass, and he's not compensating for the meagerness of the progressions."[1]

This last comment is a direct criticism of *Kind of Blue* and stands as a perfect example of why musicians often make lousy critics. What he says might be technically true, but it is of interest only to fellow musicians. How can anyone listening to such beautiful music fault it for whatever he or she thinks is lacking in its *formal* conception? If ever there was a case of missing the forest for all those trees, this is it. Certainly few of the hordes of listeners who have loved *Kind of Blue* would complain that Miles should have played more notes or longer, more complex lines. Criticizing Miles for his stringent, unadorned style is like taking Hemingway to task for not writing like William Faulkner. That Miles's solos on *Kind of Blue* are so stark and spare is an essential aspect of the music's understated eloquence. For those who associated modern jazz with the complex and multinoted solos of the great beboppers, Miles's playing must have seemed like a throwback to the pre-bop era. This perspective, however, overlooks the context in which Miles's solos developed: after the torrent of notes that both Coltrane and Adderley play throughout the album, Miles's stripped-down solos create a stunning contrast.

But as someone once said, hindsight is 20/20. Nobody could have predicted the album's enormous popularity as well as the place that *Kind of Blue* would hold in jazz history. It was a pivotal event between the bop era and the key movements of the next decade or so. The album is important not because it is the first time modes were used extensively in jazz; George Russell first used modes in the late 1940s, and other musicians such as Teo Macero and Charles Mingus worked earlier with modal compositions as well.

The chief significance of *Kind of Blue*, in terms of its innovative use of modes, derives from Miles's preeminence as a leader and tastemaker. The album was viewed in the jazz scene as a kind of manifesto, and not simply a musical one. The point made earlier—that jazz movements tend to mirror changes in American society, and in particular those regarding African Americans—must be kept in the forefront of our thinking. Musicians as acutely sensitive as Miles and most other jazzmen were certainly cognizant that their search for greater freedom ran parallel to the cries of "freedom now!" that were coming from the burgeoning civil rights movement. The jazz that followed in the wake of *Kind of Blue* would, in turn, reflect the increasing militance in much of the black community and its growing focus on self-sufficiency. Many black people were wondering whether they really wanted, in James Baldwin's phrase, "to integrate into a burning house." And jazzmen, who historically have been among the great social as well as musical visionaries, were in the vanguard of these enormous upheavals.

Miles's acute sensitivity to the growing level of anger among African Americans was made crystal clear in an interview with *Playboy* in 1962 (the very first *Playboy* interview). For that interview the magazine astutely hired a black writer, Alex Haley (who would go on to write *The Autobiography of*

Malcolm X and *Roots*). Without hesitation, Miles unleashed his vitriolic feelings about the racism that existed in most of white America. While he had never been reluctant to speak his mind, the acidity of his comments shocked many readers and caused some to feel that Miles was viciously antiwhite: "When it comes to human rights, those prejudiced white people act like they own the whole damned franchise! . . . Prejudiced white people ask each other, 'Would you want your sister to marry a Negro?' It's a jive question to ask in the first place. . . . A Negro just might not want your sister."[2]

These words might not seem particularly militant to us now, but at the time, they were harsh and pointed—at least for "the man who reads *Playboy*." Of course, Miles's remarks were also right on the money.

Miles's anger about racism was greatly exacerbated by an incident in August of 1959. While playing at Birdland, he accompanied a white woman, a friend of his, to the street and flagged a cab for her. He decided to stay outside for a while and smoke a cigarette. A white cop asked him to move, despite the fact that Miles's photograph was prominent on a poster outside the club. When the cop told him a second time to move on, Miles refused (probably with an invective or two). Using his training as a prizefighter, he stepped closer to the cop in order to avoid being hit in the mouth, but (at least, according to Miles) he lost his balance.

Another cop who happened to be on the street then jumped Miles and bashed his head with a nightstick. After he was taken to the hospital, where he received several stitches for a head wound that had been gushing blood, Miles was arrested on a number of charges. They were all eventually dropped, and for a while he pursued a suit against the city. But the primary consequence of this ugly incident was to confirm to Miles that despite his wealth and celebrity, he was not immune to racist brutality.

One might have assumed that as Miles became increasingly enraged with America's racism, his music would also become more radical. But that is not what happened, at least not at first.

I have stated my belief (developed largely in retrospect) that *Kind of Blue* was the opening volley in the revolution that would dominate the jazz of the 1960s. Although not all musicians became part of the ensuing "free jazz" movement, often referred to as the "new thing" by many jazzmen, it was widely accepted as the most important movement in jazz since bop, and those in the jazz scene reacted to it one way or another. Ornette Coleman's stand at the Five Spot demonstrated, even more than *Kind of Blue*, that jazz was on the verge of enormous change, and it clearly accelerated the revolution. As with bebop, not every jazzman responded favorably to the challenge of the new music. For many, the effect of Coleman's music was startling in its audacity, and they worried that the changes would leave them behind—a fate suffered by swing Era players with the advent of the bop revolution.

One musician who had a strong negative reaction to Coleman was Cannonball Adderley. Not long after leaving the Davis sextet, Adderley wrote a piece for *Down Beat* about the evolution of his attitude toward Coleman's music, which he called a "lesson in tolerance." He describes the first time he heard Don Cherry, Ornette's trumpet-playing colleague and disciple. On that occasion Cherry was sitting in with John Coltrane: "At that time," Adderley said, "I was amazed at the gall of an apparent amateur to play with a giant in jazz, for his performance was seemingly unintelligible and insincere. I frankly felt that he was joking."[3]

But after listening closely to a couple of Coleman's early records, Adderley had a change of heart: "I have become an Ornette Coleman booster. I am sure there is a place in jazz for an innovator of this type."[4] It is very unlikely that Adderley would have been so sympathetic to Coleman's music if he himself had not been involved with Miles's modal experiments. My guess is substantiated when at the end of the piece, Cannonball concludes, "I feel that though Ornette may influence future jazz, so will George Russell's Lydian concept of tonal organization. . . . Ornette Coleman is an innovator of the first water. But he is certainly no messiah."[5]

Ornette Coleman is an extraordinary individual, a man who looks at things straight on and speaks whatever he feels to be the plain truth. Through his music he was asking a very simple question: if we jazzmen are supposed to improvise our music spontaneously, why should we be tied to some kind of harmonic structure? He told Cannonball Adderley: "Chords are just names for sounds, which really need no names at all, as names are sometimes confusing."

Further he asked, Why don't we just play our music the way we feel it rather than be a slave to harmonic progressions? What is the point of, say, using the chord progressions of "I've Got Rhythm" in order to create our own music? We are forced to go from one chord to another in a preset sequence and then at the end of a chorus go back and do the same thing all over again. Why? And why should every instrument have such a prescribed role—the horns solo, accompanied by the rhythm section. Why don't we create a musical atmosphere in which anything can happen, in which tempos can change, meters can change, soloists can play separately, play together, do whatever feels right in the moment? And why should we be anchored to the tempered scale? Why not use the kinds of nonmusical effects that have been heard in jazz since its earliest days? Screams, honks, bleats, all sounds were possible in such a liberated atmosphere.

In some ways Coleman was a true innocent whose questions about the most basic assumptions of Western music are reminiscent of the brave little boy who points out that the king is parading around naked. This same questioning of basic assumptions occurred simultaneously in the black community: Why should black people attempt to be part of a society that has treated them so inhumanely? Why try to play the game set up by those who have created deliberate barriers for

African Americans in their quest for first-class citizenship? And can one ever be truly free playing by their rules? These hard questions helped set the stage for the most turbulent decade, both musically and socially, of this past century.

For Miles Davis, these were very disturbing issues because he fully understood his own culpability in opening the Pandora's box of *Kind of Blue*. He had given Ornette's conceptions credence by putting his own imprimatur on the idea of a different kind of freedom, and he was certainly aware of the social parallels. Was he ready to turn his back completely on the Western musical tradition as well as the American society in which he had become wealthy?

Coleman represented a new kind of generation gap in jazz. As with bebop, older musicians were put off by Coleman's innovations, and most younger jazzmen were fascinated by them. For example, the great Swing Era trumpeter Roy Eldrige said, "I've listened to him all kinds of ways. I think he's jiving, baby." And Miles's former pianist Red Garland had this to say after hearing Coleman: "Nothing's happening. . . . Coleman is faking."

Yet, other jazzmen reacted quite differently. John Lewis, the leader of the Modern Jazz Quartet, went out of his way to win Coleman acceptance. And John Coltrane was particularly fascinated with Ornette's innovations.

Coleman's music is not really based on a guiding musical system, such as the modes of *Kind of Blue*, although eventually he came up with the term *harmolodics* in an attempt to classify it. But nobody, including Coleman, could really explain exactly what he meant by the term. Nor would there ever really be a logical explanation, since the idea behind Coleman's music is that the jazzman is free to play whatever he feels without being hemmed in by an established structure.

One of the first prominent musicians in the New York scene to understand Coleman's ideas was Sonny Rollins. (Sonny had actually heard and played with both Ornette and his trumpeter, Don Cherry, a few years earlier in Los Ange-

les.) In 1962 Rollins formed a band that included two musicians who had been playing regularly with Coleman: Don
Cherry and drummer Billy Higgins. Sonny had been moving
toward a freer conception before he had ever heard Coleman,
so he had a much deeper understanding of Coleman's music
than many of his contemporaries. Here is how Sonny described
the system he used at the time:

> When we were playing in the free style, or whatever you
> want to call it, we didn't play, say, a chord progression
> like C, F, G, C. What we played were phrases. But within
> those phrases there was the essence of the chord. In
> other words, every phrase that you play, within itself,
> has some kind of a logical sequence of chords. But in the
> sense that you're playing, for example, "I Got Rhythm"
> from one chord to the next chord . . . no, we didn't play
> that way. That's what Ornette and those guys were play-
> ing. So whatever phrase I would play had its own inner
> logic. It just wouldn't follow the straight C following G,
> and G following D, and D following A, or whatever it
> would be. You would play one phrase that might last for
> that duration of time, and in that phrase there would be
> a certain type of logic which would follow some kind of
> sequence. But it wouldn't be a formalized sequence. It
> wouldn't be four bars; eight bars; eight bars; sixteen
> bars, like some of the other forms that people were play-
> ing theretofore. That's how I would explain it.

This system, if it can really be called that, was very different from George Russell's Concept. Throwing off the shackles
of musical systems meant that, quite literally, anything went.
For musicians like Rollins or Coleman, two of the greatest
improvisers in the history of jazz, this new liberation meant
they were able to let their imaginations fly. But for musicians
of lesser ability, this degree of freedom resulted only in the
development of a new jazz cliché—screeches and wails of

dubious musical value. When a truly original jazzman like Albert Ayler used these kinds of sounds in a specific context, it was part of a deeply personal musical vision. But when others, in the name of "freedom," adopted the screams as a substitute for inventiveness, it was simply a way of achieving a hip cachet among a small segment of the jazz scene. Naturally it turned off many listeners.

Ironically, Miles was ambivalent about Coleman's music, despite the fact that he himself had been instrumental in the movement to liberate improvisation from harmonic complexity. At times he expressed little respect for the saxophonist and other times said things such as "I like Ornette because he doesn't play clichés." Sometimes he would say things like "Hell, just listen to the way he writes and how he plays. If you're talking psychologically, the man is all screwed-up inside."

Witnessing the excitement caused by Coleman, one might assume that Miles would have seen in it a vindication of the direction he himself had taken. Yet in the early 1960s, during the flowering of this new revolution, he took a surprising tack.

In late 1959, several months after the *Kind of Blue* sessions, Miles recorded his third large orchestral album in collaboration with Gil Evans. Miles loved the music of Spain and France, and in this album he explored what was basically Spanish "classical" and folk music. *Sketches of Spain* has been somewhat controversial; there are some who claim that it is not really jazz. Once again, Miles would reply: "So what?" *Sketches of Spain* is magnificent music, a classic as wonderful in its own way as *Kind of Blue*. It is also another experiment with streamlined harmony.

The most famous piece on the album is the first movement of *Concierto de Aranjuez*, by the Spanish composer Joaquin Rodrigos, originally composed for guitar and orchestra; Miles and Evans adapted it for the trumpet. Miles does very little improvising in this piece but still manages to create music of devastating emotional depth, and like *Kind of Blue*, it is exquisite. For Miles, this was evidence that he could interpret a piece of music as classical players do; yet he was also capable of improvising on a level that most classical players would never even attempt.

On one of the other pieces, "Saeta," a flamenco song of mourning, Miles solos on a single scale. Yet the effect is hypnotic: after a stately processional introduction, Miles, unaccompanied except for Evans's sustained, craggy chords, seems almost to literally sing through his horn, expressing the deepest levels of grief that I have never heard in any other piece of music.

But Miles outdoes even "Saeta" on the final piece of the album, "Solea." Over sizzling percussive rhythms that meld jazz with flamenco and bolero, and Evans's kaleidoscope of subtly shifting, dense tonal colors, Miles plays for more than twelve minutes—the longest solo he had ever recorded. Yet not a note is wasted; the entire performance induces in the listener a trancelike state. More than any other artist I can think of, Miles touches a part of our inner selves, perhaps hidden since childhood; the effect of his music is that primal.

It seems certain, after *Sketches of Spain* and *Kind of Blue*, that Miles was committed to the changes jazz was experiencing, partly because of his own efforts; but the only thing one can ever expect from Miles is, well, the unexpected. Miles, ever the constant existentialist, was always aware of the ramifications of his choices.

At the end of 1959 Cannonball Adderley left the group to form his own band. Coltrane remained with Miles, but he, too, was getting restless to become a leader in his own right. He had been leading his own band when Miles took time off, but he wound up going on a lengthy tour of Europe with Miles's group in 1960. It is clear from the recordings of that tour that Coltrane's time as a sideman was coming to an end. His long solos, with their onslaught of furiously played notes pouring heatedly out of his horn, now seemed out of balance with the rest of the band, far more so than his playing with the sextet or the earlier quintet. As great as the rhythm section is with Kelly, Chambers, and Cobb providing the necessary support, Coltrane often sounds like a man trying to punch his way out of a bag; he was quickly evolving out of hard bop. At times it sounds as if there are two different bands—that of Coltrane and that of Miles. The contrast between the two musicians, which had been the great strength of Miles's earlier quintet, now was totally out of whack. Instead of a sense of complementarity, their music now seemed like a seesaw with a child on one end and a three-hundred-pound man on the other. Coltrane's increasing restlessness is palpable in the music itself, and despite Miles's attempt to hold on to the saxophonist, it was clearly no longer possible.

Shortly after returning home, Coltrane did leave the band. Miles retained the superb Kelly, Chambers, and Cobb rhythm section and then tried a number of different saxophonists to fill the vacancy. On a second tour of Europe, Miles used the veteran Sonny Stitt, whom he had first met while still living in East St. Louis. Stitt was the first major acolyte of Charlie Parker (although he claimed that he had been playing in the same style before he ever heard Bird). Stitt was a surprisingly conservative choice, and in fact, Miles played mostly the more conventional numbers in his repertoire, only occasionally using modal pieces such as "So What" or "All Blues."

Stitt left the band after Miles returned home, at which time Hank Mobley was brought in to fill the saxophone chair. Mobley was a first-tier tenorman and one of the founders of the Jazz Messengers, the band that had established the hard-bop beachhead. Mobley played with what he called a "round tone," which was to a degree derived from Lester Young, but he had an aggressive rhythmic drive that set him far apart from the many saxophonists of this era who had been strongly influenced by Young. Yet compared with Coltrane or Sonny Rollins of this time (the early 1960s), Mobley was a fairly conservative player, too. For a while Miles added J. J. Johnson to the band, once again leading a sextet, and a marvelous one at that. But like Mobley, Johnson was a bopper at a time when a revolution was brewing and many musicians, including such former Miles sidemen such as Coltrane and Rollins, were pushing the envelope.

Miles's first small group album following *Kind of Blue* was a surprisingly straight-ahead affair, utilizing the quintet with Mobley. Despite the presence of Mobley, Miles had also requested that Coltrane play a kind of cameo role on the album. Miles was plainly unhappy with Mobley, and he made his feelings clear. Even when Mobley was on the bandstand playing, Miles made remarks about bringing back Coltrane or Sonny Rollins. Coltrane certainly did not want to return to Miles's group, but he still felt indebted to his former boss and agreed to play on the session.

Once again, Coltrane steals the show. One of the tunes is the Disney classic "Someday My Prince Will Come," which would eventually supply the title for the album. As Jimmy Cobb remembers it, Coltrane showed up in the studio right in the middle of the first complete take of the tune. He put together his horn while Wynton Kelly was soloing and put the horn in his mouth just in time for his own solo. That solo is nothing less than glorious. In some ways it is similar to the "sheets of sound" style he had been using a few years earlier, but the tumbling of notes is more like a geyser of pure spring water rising in the air. It is of such lyrical splendor that the first time I heard it, I actually gasped.

Coltrane also plays on the one modal piece, "Teo." But this tune is far different in mood from either the pieces on *Kind of Blue* or even "Miles," the modal tune on *Milestones*. Instead, it has a decidedly Latin flavor not unlike some of the pieces on *Sketches of Spain*. Coltrane takes an explosive solo, exhibiting the other side of the sweet lyricism heard in his solo on the album's title cut and previewing the direction his own music would take. By comparison, the rest of the album is relatively sedate—fine music, but nothing that Miles couldn't have done a few years earlier.

The following month Columbia recorded Miles in his first live performance, *Friday and Saturday Night at the Blackhawk*. The Blackhawk was a San Francisco jazz club whose intimate atmosphere was ideal for small jazz groups. With the exception of Coltrane, Miles used the same group that recorded *Someday My Prince Will Come*. Miles does play a couple of modal pieces, "So What" and "Teo," but the rest of his repertoire is much the same as he had used before *Kind of Blue*. Interestingly, the version of "So What" here is at a much faster tempo, and Miles's solo is not nearly as spare. Miles's playing and Wynton Kelly's accompaniment at times seem to become running dialogue. Their almost psychic musical relationship has been compared with that of Louis Armstrong and Earl "Fatha" Hines, especially on the classic "Weather Bird," and I think the comparison is apt. A month later the music that Miles would record at a Carnegie Hall concert with the group, as well with an orchestra led by Gil Evans, was even better. Hank Mobley's playing, especially on "So What," is some of the best of his entire career.

The music on all these albums is superb and if it had been created in, say, 1957 would be considered classic hard bop. But it is not what one would expect after the innovations of *Kind of Blue* and *Sketches of Spain*. The music seems almost perversely conservative coming from a man who was so aware of his stature as a jazz prophet. What happened?

I think the answer is simple: Miles was alarmed with the direction in which jazz was headed and decided to attempt to rein it in from its apparent headlong dash into anarchy, at least as he saw it. His goal had been to give soloists more freedom, not to lead the jazz scene into chaos. Miles was always concerned with playing music that was accessible, and he believed that if the "new thing" became the prevalent style, jazz would lose its status as "people's music." In addition,

Miles did not want to lose control of his musicians. His ability to lead a band with a coherent sense of purpose was threatened by the idea of absolute freedom. While Miles always gave his sidemen the greatest possible latitude, he still created a context that gave the music a feeling of direction. By taking a step backward, he hoped to show both the futility of free jazz and the threat that jazz might become a music for elitists, just as modern twelve-tone classical music had. Paul Bley once described the experience of seeing the Jazz Messengers play on the same bill as Ornette Coleman's group shortly after Coleman arrived in New York. The Messengers, one of the great jazz groups, nevertheless sounded hopelessly out-of-date and irrelevant compared to Coleman. Certainly Miles was aware of this. Perhaps he even felt a bit discomfited: with *Kind of Blue*, he had opened the gates of improvisational freedom; now, as so many musicians began to run through those gates toward realms of greater freedom that Miles had never imagined, he may have felt that to a degree he himself was responsible.

Eventually, though, Miles would move on. He had too deep an understanding of jazz and the necessity for innovation to try to hold back time. Miles's solution was to put together a band that would combine some aspects of the "new thing" with those aspects of the music's tradition that kept it from losing its status as "people's music." After disbanding the quintet, he put together a group that, unlike previous bands, included musicians he had never played with before. The rhythm section included the pianist Herbie Hancock, bassist Ron Carter, and the teenage drummer Tony Williams. Most of these young musicians were sympathetic to the "new thing." Carter had played and recorded extensively with Eric Dolphy and Booker Little, two of the Young Lions of the day. Williams had played with Sam Rivers, one of the most important of the "new thing" saxophonists, as well as Cecil Taylor. He had also worked with alto saxophonist Jackie McLean, himself one of the second-generation boppers who had been one of the Young Lions in the early fifties and had become fascinated with the nascent "new thing" movement, especially Ornette Coleman's innovations. Carter and Williams further expanded on the direction that rhythm sections of the late 1950s had begun to explore. Hancock was deeply influenced by Bill Evans, particularly his voicing of chords, and had also played with a number of the young radicals as well as such older ones as Sonny Rollins and Jackie McLean. The three musicians were not comfortable playing Miles's usual repertoire in a straight-ahead manner. Influenced by both the innovations of previous Davis rhythm sections (notably the one heard on *Kind of Blue*) and those of Ornette Coleman and Bill Evans's first trio, they developed a way of swinging that combined the new freedom and the hard drive of the best bop groups. Rhythm sections no longer simply wanted to give support to the soloists; they interacted with one another and the soloist, creating a sense of group improvisation that harkened back to the earliest jazz groups.

This new conception of the jazz rhythm section was directly connected to the stripped-down, or modal, nature of the music. Perhaps Miles was responding to the criticism that harmonic simplicity led to monotony and that constant group interaction might be compensation for the lack of harmonic variety. When Miles brought Wayne Shorter into the group, it became even more radical. Although Shorter was not nearly as "outside" as many of his colleagues during this era, he was nevertheless, in his own way, a true avant-gardist, which is reflected in both his playing and his composing. Many of his tunes employ unexpected harmonic twists and rhythmic intricacies that are reminiscent of Thelonious Monk's best compositions; as with Monk, Shorter's compositions are sometimes a kind of musical Möbius strip, simultaneously "inside" and "outside."

Even when this group played one of the standards that had long been in Miles's repertoire, they took the music into unexpected directions. A piece like "My Funny Valentine" could begin as a ballad, then shift to up tempo or suddenly take on Latin rhythms. Yet despite the broad freedom that the group enjoyed, it never descended into anarchy. As with *Kind of Blue*, it exhibited freedom with control. Miles never wanted to lose control as leader of the band, even though, at the same time, that control allowed the musicians creative freedom. Miles continued to play an occasional modal tune, such as "Circle," a lovely ballad on the *Miles Smiles* album. But he maintained his stance about harmony: when one of the musicians in his band submitted a tune for the group, Miles invariably simplified its harmonic structure (often claiming cowriter status as well).

It is interesting to note that during the time this group was together (both with and without Shorter), in the years 1963–68, it was not given the attention it now receives. It sounds somewhat sedate in the context of the time. In recent years, however, it has come to be regarded as a group at least equal to the Coltrane quartet, and in many ways it has proved to be even more influential. At the same time, of course, some (but certainly not all) of the most "advanced" free jazz of that time now sounds dated, purely a product of its tumultuous times.

Eventually, Miles moved into the most audacious period of his career, the jazz/rock/funk fusion of the late 1960s and early 1970s. In *Bitches Brew* and the music that followed, the harmonic freedom that he had first explored in *Kind of Blue* goes even further. Instead of modes, Miles used an ostinato bass line that serves as the harmonic center of gravity for the soloists. In many ways, Miles's fusion was an attempt to deal with the problems first confronted in *Kind of Blue*. He substituted dense electronic textures to make up for the lack of harmonic variety. So even during this period, when many critics and musicians (including some who had become famous through playing with Miles) attacked the trumpeter for "selling out," he was still trying to deal with the implications of freedom first broached on *Kind of Blue*.

The breakup of the magnificent Davis sextet that recorded *Kind of Blue* started not long after the sessions that produced the album. Of course, Bill Evans had already left the group and had been asked by Miles to return just for these sessions. But a few months after *Kind of Blue*, Cannonball left the group also, once again to try leading his own group. He had had a hard time doing this before Miles hired him, but after all, the trumpeter was a "starmaker" (to use Sonny Rollins's phrase) and Cannonball's name was far better known after touring and recording with the Davis group. Once again he used his cornetist brother, Nat, for his second horn, and he used a series of superb rhythm sections. This time he was far more successful, and he would lead a band until his premature death in 1975, a few months shy of his forty-seventh birthday.

Adderley knew how to ingratiate himself with his audience by doing something his former boss Miles had always shunned: talking freely to his listeners, discussing the music, making jokes, giving them lessons in jazz history. And it worked. For those to whom modern jazz was a mystery, Adderley's monologues went a long way toward making them comfortable with his music. Of course, he had that exuberant "spirit" that had drawn Miles to him in the first place.

Despite Adderley's success away from Miles, he became the slave to his own worst inclinations. His playing was often excessively florid and, on occasion, tasteless and trite, throwing ideas together without any regard for creating a cohesive musical statement. He often chose funk-oriented material that did not make any demands on his genuine talent. At times he seemed to turn everything he played into blues, relying on stock "funky" licks and clichés, all of which received an enthusiastic response from the less than discriminating members of his audience.

But there were times when he also played with intelligence and depth. He seemed to need to be around superior musicians in order to play up to his capacity. Two years after leaving Miles's group, Adderley recorded an album for Riverside titled *Know What I Mean?*, which made clear the impact of his having played with Miles, particularly on *Kind of Blue*. Instead of his working group, he led a quartet consisting of the Modern Jazz Quartet's rhythm section, bassist Percy Heath and drummer Connie Kay, and his colleague in the Davis sextet, Bill Evans. The title tune is a modal piece, similar in a formal sense to those on *Kind of Blue*, but with a different emotional tone, one that reflects the zestful nature of its leader. Despite its title, this piece is anything but the kind of simple funk piece that had come to dominate the Adderley repertoire. It is clear that Adderley's time in Miles's groups broadened his thinking to musical possibilities that he might otherwise have disregarded. Even later in his career, he would use occasional modal pieces, so the challenges of *Kind of Blue* never completely faded from his mind. Those challenges had opened him up to the entire concept of liberating the improviser.

Adderley would, like most of the other members of the sextet, go on to become one of the most popular jazzmen. He would be one of the first prominent musicians to use an electric piano and bass as an early synthesizer of jazz, rock, and funk. Whatever his direction, he would never totally lose his credibility with the jazz public; there is little doubt that this credibility stemmed, at least in part, from his contributions to *Kind of Blue*.

It might have seemed that George Russell would view *Kind of Blue* as vindication of the theory he had been working on since 1945. But his thoughts about the album, as well as its aftermath, were far more complicated. "I thought that *Kind of Blue* was beautiful music, of course. But I also thought that a lot of modal jazz that came out of it was a little simplistic. Too many jazzmen played simple modal tunes like "So What" and played long, long solos based on just a couple of modes. It could get very monotonous listening to that. Of course, it was different if a genius like Coltrane played that kind of piece. But very few musicians are on that level. That kind of thing was only a part of what I intended with the theory. It should have opened up all kinds of new possibilities to musicians, not produced monotony."

In fact, the release of *Kind of Blue* did not affect Russell in any direct way, except for exhibiting the potential of modes in jazz. Although he was now making a living with music, Russell continued to struggle. He had published the Concept as a book but still remained at work developing it further. One reason he needed to continue working on his theory can be traced to the music of Ornette Coleman: "When I heard Ornette, I thought, 'Whoa! How do I fit his music into my theory?' Back then I couldn't. It took a lot more work to develop the idea that I called supraverticality." With this idea, Russell was able to find a place for the performances of even the most extreme "new thing" musicians.

Not long after the *New York, New York* sessions, Russell was signed to do a series of albums for Orrin Keepnews's Riverside label. The first was titled *Ezz-thetics,* named, of course, for one of Russell's earliest compositions. Among the personnel in the band was the reedman Eric Dolphy, who would be associated with the earliest of the free-jazz musicians of the 1960s. It is a superb album not far distant in quality from *The Jazz Workshop*. Dolphy is brilliantly suited to Russell's music. He does not use typical bop licks but rather plays with a harmonic ambivalence that emphasizes the daring of Russell's writing. Finally, there were musicians, such as Dolphy and Coltrane, who understood the ramifications of Russell's theory and with it were able to build a new type of jazz.

Personally, Russell was not enamored of the more radical free-jazz players: "I thought about it. Should I go all the way to what I called the 'freedom riders'? I decided that I just could not go with them. I did not believe that music should be made with no rules at all. And I did not want to be locked into any one style. I wanted the freedom to do things in a variety of styles." Russell's attitude should not be surprising; although one of his goals was to give improvisers more freedom, the Concept was, after all, a *system* for tonal organization, not a mandate for mayhem.

Russell became increasingly uncomfortable with both the direction jazz was taking and his own struggle to gain acceptance in his home country. He was also disillusioned with American society, especially the continuing racial situation. When he received an invitation to go to Sweden to work regularly with a large band, he took it. For the next several years he lived and worked in Europe, composing and performing and, of course, continuing to develop the Concept.

While in Europe, he once again worked with young musicians who would eventually become leading figures in the European jazz scene. Two of them, saxophonist Jan Garbarek and guitarist Terje Rypdal, were among the most popular artists recording for Manfred Eicher's influential ECM label, and both musicians were deeply influenced by Russell's Concept. Garbarek, an early Coltrane acolyte, developed an idiosyncratic style, combining his native Norwegian folk music with Trane's modal improvisation, as well as elements of Arabic, Indian, and Brazilian music. The parallels between modal jazz and much of the music of the non-Western world that Coltrane had explored were taken even further by musicians such as Garbarek and Rypdal.

Russell's later music is very different from his greatest work of the 1950s and early 1960s. For one thing, he at times used electronic instruments in order to create new textures. His "vertical structure" pieces are based on the idea of the synchronicity of sound. Russell compares this effect to standing in the middle of Times Square: we hear a variety of sounds all at once and at the same time. This idea provided the basis for the direction in which he took his composing. For his compositions based on "vertical structure," Russell discovered that it was more fitting to use jazz-funk rhythm rather than just straight-ahead 4/4 swing. (Of course, he had explored different meters ever since the days of "Cubana Be, Cubana Bop.") In the early 1980s he composed a new masterpiece, "The African Game," that was based on these ideas.

Russell found a large following in Europe, where he was given the respect—and opportunities to work—that he had sought in vain in his native country. Like many expatriate jazzmen, he eventually chose to return home. When Gunther Schuller, with whom he had worked at the Brandeis concert in the 1950s, offered him a teaching position at the New England Conservatory of Music in the early 1970s, he accepted the offer.

The teaching position gave Russell an opportunity to dedicate most of his energies to writing new music and, of course, to making further developments in the Concept. He rarely saw Miles; but one night he was with a friend and decided to introduce her to the trumpeter. As Russell recalls it: "I went to Miles's famous house on West Seventy-seventh Street and was about to ring the bell when I saw a sign on the door. It read: 'Don't push this bell. If you push this bell, it's war. I feel tired in my mind, I feel tired in my body; you can call me if you have something; you can call my business manager, but don't ring the bell!' I rang the bell anyway—no reply—but I took the sign with me. I didn't like him telling people he was tired in his mind and tired in his body. We all looked to Miles as a trend, and he didn't have to let the outside world and its predators know that he was feeling weak. So I just took the sign."

Perhaps no story better conveys more pointedly the attitude of musicians toward Miles—even as accomplished a musician as Russell. Miles Davis was more than simply a great musician; he was a kind of cultural warrior, both a holy man and a cultural potentate, the kind of man who could actually save lives. (I should know—mine was one of them.)

One must wonder how Miles would have reacted to Russell's later music. Both men were on a similar track, actually,

using elements of rock and funk to give their music a freshness and social relevance that they deemed necessary for the
lifeblood of jazz. My guess is that Miles would have been fascinated by Russell's work and maybe even encouraged, once
again, to use some of Russell's new concepts to expand the
frontiers of his own music.

Russell has still not gained the renown that he is surely
due, but this does not trouble him. He knows how beautiful
and important the Concept he has devoted his life to is. As I
write, early in the year 2000, he is still—at age seventy-
seven—working on the theory, which is almost completed.
When it is finally published (it will now take up two vol-
umes), perhaps his country will finally show its appreciation
for Russell's work and his struggle to find the truth. "It is
very profound, it has a lot of different levels," says Russell
about the Concept. For him, it is more than just a theory of
music; it is, rather, a way of looking at the world from a
musical point of view, a method of discovering unity in a philosophy of sound.

The musician who was most deeply affected by both *Kind of
Blue* and Russell's theory was John Coltrane. He became the
dominant jazzman of the 1960s primarily because of his work
with modes. Through modal improvisation, Coltrane not only
blazed brave new musical paths but also was able to dig deep
within his own interior—in his pursuit of God and profound
truths about himself. Through the use of modes, Coltrane
was able to enter an expanded musical and spiritual universe.
He became a kind of shaman, a priest of the unknown, a
brave explorer of the hidden recesses of the mind and soul.

When Coltrane left Miles in 1960, it was not without reluc-
tance. After all, Miles had been more than his boss, he had
also been a mentor. But after *Kind of Blue*, Coltrane finally
knew the direction in which he wanted to take his music.
Modes gave him a chance to play both horizontally and vertically; he did not have to make a choice between mutually

exclusive categories—he could truly have his cake and eat it, too.

Leaving Miles was not easy. The trumpeter implored him to stay and was angry at him for leaving. But at this point Coltrane felt compelled to go his own way. He had been leading his own groups when Miles was not touring, and he knew that there was enough of an audience for him to be able to sustain a career as a leader. At first his group consisted of the pianist Steve Kuhn, a disciple of Bill Evans, the bassist Steve Davis, and drummer Billy Higgins, who had first gained fame playing with Ornette Coleman. But Coltrane did not feel that this group gave him the strong support he needed, particularly rhythmically. He replaced Kuhn with a young Philadelphian named McCoy Tyner. And he chose the up-and-coming drummer Elvin Jones as a replacement for Higgins. One has to wonder if Trane realized what a brilliant choice Jones was. At the time, Elvin was finally putting together all the pieces of his style. He was precisely the right drummer for the great quartet.

In his first recordings for Atlantic Records with the new group, Coltrane immediately made his direction clear. On the surface, the tune he choose as the centerpiece of his first album was surprising, to say the least: "My Favorite Things" from the Rodgers and Hammerstein musical *The Sound of Music*. It may seem strange for a man some critics had labeled, wrongly, as an "angry young tenor" to be playing such a sweet confection of a tune, but the result is closer to Indian ragas than to Broadway. Coltrane divides the piece into two scales, or modes, which he plays over a hypnotic vamp played continuously behind his soloing. Coltrane had been listening to Indian music, but the real influence was, of course, the modal music of George Russell and Miles Davis. Although the mood of Coltrane's "My Favorite Things" is quite dissimilar to that of *Kind of Blue*, it attains a swirling, watery trancelike effect. Listening to this mesmerizing tune is like staring transfixed at waves crashing on the shore on a warm summer day. It is magnificent.

"My Favorite Things" set the pattern for much of Coltrane's career, at least for the years of his first quartet (although Davis was eventually replaced by the bassist Jimmy Garrison). Since Elvin Jones had at this point fully developed his polyrhythmic conception, the density of his drumming fills in the lack of harmonic variety, giving the music abundant textural richness. Tyner developed a style that seems as obviously indebted to Coltrane as Bud Powell's style was to Charlie Parker.

Coltrane left Atlantic and signed with a new label called Impulse! owned by ABC Paramount. There he was given wide latitude to record whatever he wanted. His first project with the new company was a live recording date at the Village Vanguard. Most of the tunes are modal. One is titled "India" and was intended to be a kind of jazz raga. The longest piece, "Impressions," uses the same modal structure as "So What" but has a different melody—actually, a particularly pretty tune that Coltrane derived from Ravel. This piece and others with a similar structure alternated with the blues and became the primary basis for Coltrane's playing the incredibly long solos for which he became famous. The live Vanguard version of "Impressions" is almost fifteen minutes, a very long solo for anybody but Coltrane. He would eventually play solos on this tune and others like it for half an hour, even longer. Witnessing such performances in a club, in which Coltrane and Jones drove each other into altered states of consciousness, was an unforgettable experience; but it made one wonder whether these frenzies were not also quite self-indulgent.

Eric Dolphy, who for a short while had played in George Russell's group, was part of Coltrane's band at the time of the Vanguard date. Both Coltrane and Dolphy increasingly used the new harmonic freedom in order to bring in extramusical expressive effects. In the 1960s the use of such effects was taken to an extreme by the "new thing" musicians, who looked upon Coltrane as a spiritual godfather and mentor.

Not everyone was enthralled with Coltrane's music in this period. John Tynan characterized the playing of Coltrane and Dolphy as "anti-jazz." But throughout jazz history, critics have made such charges about the latest innovations. There was another, rather unexpected, critic of the Coltrane group—Miles Davis. Perhaps this should not be so surprising after all, since Miles almost reflexively had harsh words for the music of his sidemen after they left his band and became leaders. Miles had little regard for both Garrison and Tyner, who he insisted was heavy-handed. "The only ones who were playing with that group," he maintained years later, "were Coltrane and Elvin, who is a bad motherfucker. The others were useless. I can't stand McCoy Tyner." These complaints should be placed in context: Miles was always competitive, and in the 1960s he and his groups were clearly overshadowed by Coltrane's quartet.

Yet Miles, for the rest of his life, would remain in awe of Coltrane's playing. In my book *'Round About Midnight: A Portrait of Miles Davis*, I tell a story about a night when Miles came by my apartment for a visit. This was in the late 1970s, during the period when Miles was in "retirement" because of a series of medical problems. At this point he had not performed or even picked up the trumpet in years. I told him I had a tape that Jimmy Cobb had given me of Miles's group with Coltrane, recorded during the final tour of the Davis group before Trane left the band in 1960. Miles was reluctant to have me play it, but finally he assented. The first tune was "So What." After a typically pithy Miles solo, Coltrane played a long, deliriously powerful solo. Miles reacted visibly, shaking his head, grunting when Coltrane did something spectacular, imploring Paul Chambers to "play the right notes." But after this first tune, Miles got up to leave. He looked me in the eye, and I could see that he was full of sorrow. He said, "How could you do this to me, Eric? I thought we were friends." Naturally, I was devastated.

In 1964 Coltrane recorded his most famous work, the album-length suite *A Love Supreme*. For Coltrane, this was more than just another record; it was his spiritual testament, his gift to God. Seven years earlier he had been a junkie and an alcoholic with a career lying in ruins. Now he was the most important jazzman in the world. And he felt, rightly, he owed this new life to the spiritual awakening that had occurred during his painful withdrawal from the poisons that had crippled him. It is impossible to ignore the depth of Coltrane's spiritual devotion in *A Love Supreme*—the music seems to be almost illuminated as it fills the air. It is significant that this album, too, is rooted basically in non-Western musical traditions.

Coltrane's music would continue to evolve more and more "outside." The year after *A Love Supreme*, he recorded *Ascension*. The album consists of one piece in which several of the "new thing" jazzmen play together both as soloists and as part of a free-form ensemble creating a dense din that became famous as a way of driving out the guests at the end of a party. It is a fascinating but, I believe, ultimately unsatisfying work. However, Coltrane's audacity—challenging the audience with such difficult music, the same audience who associated him with "My Favorite Things" and his lovely *Ballads* album—was unprecedented..

By the end of 1965 Coltrane's complete allegiance to the "new thing" was clear. He had been flirting with it for years, giving moral support to many of the movement's leaders, such as Archie Shepp, Albert Ayler, and Marion Brown, all of whom were signed to Impulse! on Coltrane's urging. Shepp recorded one section of *A Love Supreme* that has never been released (it apparently has been lost, unfortunately). Neither Tyner nor Jones felt entirely comfortable with Coltrane's direction. Both were grounded in hard bop, and while remaining deeply respectful of Coltrane, they did not feel that they fit into his musical conception any longer. Coltrane's new group included his second wife, the pianist and harpist Alice McLeod Coltrane, and the "free" drummer Rashied Ali, as well as Pharaoh Sanders. Sanders was one of the fiercest of the "new thing" screamers, but he could also play with disarming lyricism when he felt like it.

For Coltrane, it must have seemed like a long journey from the "sheets of sound" and his obsession with harmony to the freedom of playing a modal tune for the first time ("Miles," on the *Milestones* album), then on to the "new thing" free jazz of the mid-1960s. If Coltrane had not discovered modes, one must wonder whether his music would have developed such spiritual and emotional depth. He often talked of "cleaning the mirror," by which he meant using improvisation to delve more intensely into his soul. Modes made it much easier to shut off his mind and simply let his intuition and spirit become the driving force in the creation of his music.

For Coltrane, his musical journey—his "quest," as I call it in my book *Ascension*—was simultaneously spiritual and musical. I do not think that he felt there was any dividing line between spiritual pursuit and the creation of music. But following the route that Coltrane traversed is more than a little disturbing. His earliest modal work, starting with his improvisations on *Kind of Blue* and continuing with his early work as a leader, has a straight melodic radiance that is basically joyous and celebratory—pieces like "My Favorite Things" and lesser-known works like "Mr. Day" or the beautiful "Equinox." *A Love Supreme* is close to these early pieces in mood, but certain sections reveal an increasingly complex spiritual vision. As Coltrane proceeded through the decade, his vision of God became darker and more mercurial. The work that followed *A Love Supreme* was another masterpiece, *Meditations*. But here the road to God is filled with pain and fierce demons; there is anguish. After facing without illusion the ultimate truth about oneself, there is the sobering knowledge that now there is no turning back.

In Coltrane's music of the last year or so of his life, freedom is total. He seems to be only beginning his exploration of the new and at times frightening landscape in which he has found himself. There are times when he sounds lost, trying to regain his bearings. The music is about shaping pure sound, not creating lyrical melodic ideas, and it is born of his steadfast gaze at the darkest aspects of his soul. Indisputably it is very difficult listening, requiring us to put aside our linear way of thinking about music. One must let the music take its course without fighting it with preconceptions. Unfortunately, in 1967 Coltrane died from cancer of the liver a few months shy of his forty-first birthday. We will never know whether he felt that he had reached the end of his quest. I doubt it. I think for Coltrane his quest was all about the inner pilgrimage, not a final destination. One thing is certain: the most intense and important years of that quest during the 1960s, and the freedom that made it possible, were set in motion by Coltrane's work on *Kind of Blue*.

Kind of Blue was almost as important to Bill Evans's career as a leader, but for a different reason. Evans had played modal music with George Russell years before making *Kind of Blue*. So the formal organization of the album was not a revelation to him. What was important was the fame that *Kind of Blue* brought him. When he joined Miles's group, he had an active career as a sideman, but for the most part, the public was hardly aware of him. Playing with Miles greatly changed that, and the popularity of *Kind of Blue* made his name as a leader.

But that is not the extent of the influence of the album on Evans's career. As we have seen, the introduction to "So What" is a duet between Evans and the band's bassist, Paul Chambers. In a way, this duet served as a model for the innovations Evans would explore with his first, and greatest, trio. Chambers, like many bassists of the period, had greatly advanced the role of bass in the jazz ensemble. It was no longer just a timekeeper for the band but instead had a melodic role, at times coming close to duetting, or even creating counterpoint, with the soloist. Oscar Pettiford and especially Charles Mingus had been active in advancing the role of the bass both melodically and rhythmically. I would not go so far as to say that the introduction to "So What" directly influenced Evans and the way he organized his first trio, but it was indicative of the changing role of the jazz rhythm section by the end of the 1950s.

But the most important way in which Evans was influenced by *Kind of Blue* is more subtle. There is no doubt that Evans became caught up in the sweeping movement toward a new kind of liberation, and he wanted his group to be, in its distinctive way, one that forged its own road toward freedom.

Evans's career had been in a state of more or less suspended animation. After returning to New York following a stay at his parents' home in Florida, he continued to work mainly as an increasingly popular sideman. He got occasional jobs working as a solo pianist but still had not established himself as a leader. However, after recording *Kind of Blue,* he decided that he had to put together his own group. He briefly led a trio that included the drummer Kenny Dennis and Jimmy Garrison, who a couple of years later became part of John Coltrane's classic quartet. But the Evans trio did not stay together. According to Peter Pettinger, the author of the Bill Evans biography *Bill Evans: How My Heart Sings*, the trio played at Basin Street East while Benny Goodman was headlining and were treated shabbily by the management. The Goodman group, on the other hand, were welcomed by management as if they were royalty. This snubbing greatly upset Dennis and Garrison, and they departed the group, leaving Evans to flounder around to find replacements. This is the kind of problem most jazzmen encounter when they try to go out as leaders without having gained sufficient fame. But Evans was determined to put together a working trio.

Early on, Evans decided that he wanted to break away from the typical piano trio. In most such groups, the piano was the dominant instrument. The bass and drums played accompaniment, and each took an occasional solo. But Evans had been involved with many of the new movements in jazz that were seeking new avenues of freedom for improvisation. Evans had a brilliant analytical mind, and he surely understood the ramifications of both the innovations of *Kind of Blue* and much of the work of George Russell, with whom he had played on some classic sides. With the beginning of a new decade, change was in the air. In his first two albums, *New Jazz Conceptions* and *Everybody Digs Bill Evans*, the pianist's group conception was based on the usual piano trio—by sheer luck. For a musician so caught up in the center of the jazz scene, he could hardly have avoided the feeling of transformation occurring around him. He wanted to create an entirely new conception for the jazz trio based on the advances jazz had been making, and in particular the advances of the most-forward-looking bassists and drummers during the latter part of the 1950s. In order to make his experiment work, he needed just the right rhythm section. By, he found it.

He had been playing fairly regular gigs with the clarinetist Tony Scott, who had been an early champion of melding jazz with what is now called world music. In October of 1959 Scott led a recording session just before leaving on a long worldwide tour. This date was a more or less straight-ahead session, if the unpredictable Scott ever did anything that could be considered "straight ahead." (Interestingly, in the 1960s he had great success with an album of duets with a Japanese koto player, titled *Music for Zen Meditation*. It would be intriguing to know what Evans thought of this album.)

At the 1959 session, Scott used Paul Motian, the drummer

who had played with Evans on his first album as a leader, and a twenty-three-year-old bassist named Scott LaFaro. Since his first albums as a leader, Evans had performed with Motian several times, including the album they recorded together, *New Jazz Conceptions*, and had been aware of the growing reputation of LaFaro. After the Tony Scott session, Evans decided that Motian and LaFaro would be ideal for the trio he wanted to form. In part, Evans's decision rested on the simple fact of the availability of the two musicians. This opportune moment, however, turned out to be a historic case of serendipity.

Evans implored his men to think of themselves as equals with the piano, not as mere accompanists. This was a giant step forward, and difficult to achieve without creating anarchy. It meant that Motian and LaFaro not only had to reinvent their roles within the trio but also had to "forget" everything they had learned about those roles. The group made a total of four albums, the final two recorded live at the Village Vanguard. These albums are a fascinating study of the development of a group. Theirs was truly revolutionary music, although its fragile lyricism makes it easy to overlook the iconoclasm of the group. Yet in its own introverted way, this trio was as radical as many of the "new thing" groups, and its innovations would be at least as enduring.

The first album, recorded by the group in December of 1959, does not sound particularly extraordinary except for LaFaro's playing, which at times was more like cello than bass; at times he seems almost to be duetting with Evans. On the next album LaFaro is bursting with energy, as if he wanted to tear apart the usual concept of a jazz bassist and create out of pure bravura a totally new direction for the bass. According to Evans, this was clear even before the advent of his first trio: "My first impression of LaFaro when we met during an audition for Chet Baker in '56 or '57 was that he was a marvelous bass player and talent, but it was bubbling out of him like a gusher. Ideas were rolling out on top of each other; he could barely handle it."

This impression of LaFaro is even stronger on the next album the group recorded, *Explorations*. LaFaro's role is now far more expanded—again, he often engages in a kind of duet with Evans—although it is still that of accompanist with occasional solos. Motian's role has grown here, too. In the final recordings of the group, *Sunday at the Village Vanguard* and *Waltz for Debby* (which was culled from the same sessions as the Sunday album), the three musicians establish true group improvisation. LaFaro now creates a secondary voice, and Motian rarely keeps strict time but instead splashes the rhythm through the ensemble. There are some who maintain that the group did not really swing—an absurd criticism. It is simply a different kind of swing. The rhythm is elastic. It breathes with the music; it is alive, not merely a metronome behind the soloist. The group demonstrated a more sophisticated and subtle swing; nevertheless, this music swings so hard that it burns. Listening to the Vanguard sessions is a somewhat unsettling experience because the ear is trained to focus on the primary lead voice, the piano. But doing so misses the entire point of the music. In many ways the trio had returned to the earliest jazz with its group improvisation. And as with *Kind of Blue*, the formal advances heard on these two albums (and to a slightly lesser extent on the two albums that preceded it) are not the only remarkable aspect of this music. Like Miles's classic album, the music is simply beautiful; it has a rarefied lyricism and intelligence that, again like *Kind of Blue*, make it endlessly engaging, no matter how many times you listen to it.

Tragically, Scott LaFaro was killed in an automobile accident ten days after the Vanguard sessions; he was twenty-five years old. But his playing with Evans has served as an inspiration for every bassist that came after him. Evans was devastated but then returned with a new trio, Chuck Israels replacing LaFaro. Following that group, Evans led a series of trios, all of them fine. His later ones were based on the same principles established by the first, but they lack the sense of discovery that made the music of the first trio so electric and unforgettable. Evans became one of the most popular of all jazzmen, both with fans and critics, but he never again played music as audaciously innovative.

He continued to make wonderful music until his death in 1980 at the age of fifty-one. Some of his music was innovative in various ways. For example, he recorded a series of albums on which he overdubbed his own playing two or three times, creating duets and trios with himself as the other players. At its best, the idea works brilliantly, although at times it is too much of a good thing. Evans, in his own way, was considered something of an avant-gardist in the 1950s and early 1960s— a consequence of his playing with George Russell, his work on *Kind of Blue*, and his first trio. By the time of his death, he had assumed the role of a musician who staked out his music for the most part in the rich, romantic lyricism that drew so many people to his playing. Not long before he died, he formed a new trio that seemed to put new life into his work, and it brought back memories, to both Evans and his followers, of that first wonderful group that was so important to the evolution of jazz.

There was one surprising (or maybe not so surprising) critic of Evans: Miles Davis. Miles once again insisted that Evans never played as well as he had with Miles's own group. And Miles took Evans to task for supposedly using only white musicians in his group. But in this Miles was dead wrong: Evans's favorite drummer was Philly Joe Jones, whom he had met, of course, when he first joined Miles's group. And Jones was not the only black musician who played with Evans. He also hired Jack DeJohnette, who became more famous when he played with . . . Miles Davis. Besides these musicians, Evans also used Freddie Hubbard, Kenny Burrell, Ron Carter, and other black jazzmen on some of his albums. So perhaps Miles was simply indulging in a little nostalgic race-baiting, just as he had done when Evans was in his group.

One more note about Bill Evans: one of the most memorable pieces on Evans's classic *Sunday at the Village Van-guard* album is titled "Jade Visions." Although it was composed by Scott LaFaro, it nevertheless brings to mind Evans's famous liner notes for *Kind of Blue*. "Jade Visions" is a lovely, fragile melody, played with a simplicity that belies its profundity. It is, in essence, a musical Zen koan—a single superfluous note, and the entire mood is destroyed. Yet Evans and his trio succeed in improvising as a group without destroying the delicacy of the piece. This is Bill Evans's triumph; he made it clear that the emotional range of jazz is infinite. There were many who thought such introverted music could not really be considered jazz. However, the emotions throughout most of *Kind of Blue* are quite similar in their delicacy to those of Evans's groups. For a musician like Bill Evans, perhaps this is one of the lasting legacies of *Kind of Blue*. The road from the earliest days of jazz, with its explosive burst of energy, to the making of *Kind of Blue* and *Sunday at the Village Vanguard* was a long one. And the cost of traveling that road was heavy indeed. Evans wound up paying for his music with his own life. A few years after kicking heroin, he became addicted to cocaine, which eventually killed him. Maybe that was the price he had to pay for putting his soul on the line every time he played.

The legacy of *Kind of Blue* goes far beyond its effect on the musicians who created it. Moreover, that legacy is complicated and, as George Russell has pointed out, not entirely positive. It became almost rote for many musicians to use a simple modal piece like "So What" for interminable and monotonous solos that succeeded in turning off much of the jazz audience.

Most of the legacy of *Kind of Blue*, however, is positive as well as extensive. There is an entire record label, ECM, which specializes in works of the same kind of introverted lyricism one hears on Miles's great album. Musicians ranging from the Norwegian saxophonist Jan Garbarek to the guitarist Bill

Frisell played music that has an indigo melodicism reminiscent of the mood of *Kind of Blue*.

More important, the album gave musicians the impetus to break away from standard Western musical procedures and discover ways of composing and improvising closer in form and spirit to that of non-Western music. The growing militancy of African Americans launched many black musicians into seeking their African roots and to renouncing the influence of the West. This need for cultural authenticity was a driving force in the 1960s, and certainly *Kind of Blue* proved that it is possible to play great, and accessible, music while using formal procedures that are very different from those of most Western music.

Perhaps the single most important legacy of *Kind of Blue* is its effect on listeners. Many fans, musicians included, have fallen in love with jazz mainly from being exposed to this beautiful album—an album that has changed lives, including my own. There are not too many works of art—any kind of art—about which such a statement can be made.

10 So What?

So then, what is it about *Kind of Blue* that gives it this singular place in jazz history? Of all the thousands of albums, of any genre, why does this one stand out? Why do new generations continue to be drawn to this music, to the extent that forty years after its initial release it remains one of the best-selling of all jazz albums? Why does it still seem so fresh and relevant to our lives? And why does it attract so many lovers? There are lovers of *Kind of Blue* all over the world. Through the "Miles List" on the World Wide Web, I regularly communicate with fans who live in an extraordinary number of different countries: Italy, France, England, Germany, Australia, Switzerland, Sweden, Japan, and others too numerous to name. And here, in the United States, there are lovers, too.

Suppose for everyone who loves *Kind of Blue* there is a different answer to the questions I have posed above? For many musicians the album has been a milestone in their lives. As the superb pianist Larry Willis put it, "It showed me not only what jazz could be but also what art is all about." This record album has changed lives, and what more can be said about any work of art? Willis is far from the only musician or music lover to feel this way.

Alice Schell, a prizewinning short-story writer who grew up in a small Pennsylvania town and now lives in Philadelphia, offered these comments:

When I was growing up in the 1940s my family did not own a large collection of records. Like most of the other African American families in town, we listened to the radio as our primary source of music; and when we did buy a record, it was sure to be a piece by one of the popular groups like the Ink Spots or the Orioles, or by vocalists like Billy Eckstine and Ella Fitzgerald. Among our favorites were several singers who gradually faded from public prominence: Nellie Lutcher, Savannah Churchill, Hadda Brooks. These were singers of popular music, and I doubt if many readers under the age of sixty ever heard of them. My family's collection included only a few records by jazz artists in addition to Eckstine and Fitzgerald. We had a few sides of Count Basie, Duke Ellington, Lionel Hampton, Illinois Jacquet.

In his CD liner notes for *Kind of Blue*, Robert Palmer describes the album as "one of those incredibly rare works equally popular among professionals and the public at large . . ." As the above paragraph suggests, I am a member of that public, a listener—not a musician or music critic. Nor am I knowledgeable enough about jazz even to call myself a true jazz fan; yet I am one of the many lovers of *Kind of Blue*, which has a special place among the albums I reach for when I want to hear music that touches me in a deep and personal way.

I was introduced to *Kind of Blue* by the author of this book over thirty years ago. When I think back to my earliest impressions, I realize that this music was not, as it has been for many others, a case of "love at first hearing." It was beautiful, of course, and I responded immediately to its quiet melancholy, but I did not listen to the record dozens of times a day or exhibit anything remotely like obsession about it. In fact, I had at least one specific dislike: hard as it is for me to believe now, I did not like Miles Davis's use of the Harmon mute. I thought the sound was thin, whiny, and self-consciously inward.

Over the years I listened to the album, sporadically at first, then more and more often. And I listened more carefully—which is to say, I began to give the music my complete attention. Something changed. Without being fully aware of what was happening, I had been quietly seduced. The third track, "Blue in Green," was largely responsible for working the spell. Even the sound of the muted trumpet began to pull me into the center of this gorgeous piece. "Blue in Green" is the shortest cut on the album, a mere five minutes and thirty-seven seconds; but like a fine lyric poem, it manages to distill tremendous feeling in that short time. And to my surprise, after many listenings, I no longer find the sound of the Harmon mute thin and whiny. As for my earlier criticism about its sense of "self-conscious inwardness," I thought to myself: did I ever really feel that way? Now the muted trumpet sounds dreamlike; it has a gossamer quality, like the edge of a memory that refuses to be fully captured. Moreover, the trumpet establishes the mood— what I call a mood of lights and shadows—and is perfectly suited to the understated effect of "Blue in Green." I love the meshed sound of the piano and bass together, and the almost piercing contrast that comes with Coltrane's eloquent solo.

I believe that artist and audience are, in a sense, collaborators. We not only receive what the artist has to give, but we also bring our own interior worlds, our feelings and memories, to the experience. For each member of the audience, then, something new is created. This artist-audience relationship accounts for the irreducible subjectivity at the core of anyone's judgments about art.

If I *were* highly knowledgeable about jazz, I would still describe Coltrane's solo on "Blue in Green" as a bitter-sweet piece of music; and there is no objective measure—only arguments (unavoidably subjective even when well buttressed by expertise)—that could make me feel other-wise. "Blue in Green" continues to be my favorite track on *Kind of Blue*, and I listen to it often enough to drive my neighbors crazy; but I have also come to love the entire album. One day several years ago I was walking in the Old City section of Philadelphia when I saw a small sign that read: "Blue in Green." I was excited by the obvious reference to *Kind of Blue*. The sign hung over the doorway of a tiny restaurant where a framed portrait of Miles Davis graced the left-hand wall inside the entrance. The sound system was not blaring Muzak. In this wonderful little eatery there was no "blaring" from the sound system at all, only the exquisite music of Miles Davis. It was not easy to hear the music above the din of conversation in the restaurant, but I recognized that Miles "sound," however faintly. (I did not know at the time that I had entered the restaurant during a minor lull, a rarity in this popular place, and the lull accounts for my being able to hear anything at all above the con-versation.) I ate a stack of delicious pancakes and walked home, where I listened once to *Kind of Blue*, the whole thing. Then I returned to the third track, as usual, and listened to "Blue in Green" again. And then another two or three or four times. Maybe five. Enough for one day.

These comments come from a lover of *Kind of Blue* who describes her opinions as "impressionistic" and confesses that she does not consider herself a knowledgeable jazz fan. There are many such "lovers" out there, for some of whom *Kind of Blue* might conceivably be the only jazz album they own. The following comments, on the other hand, come from a musician—Bill Douglass, a fine Californian bassist who has played and recorded with many jazzmen and women, including Marian McPartland and Art Lange. This is how he feels about the album:

> *Kind of Blue* has had a great influence on me, but it is only at this time in my life that I can articulate what it is. Two aspects stand out. The first is how the rhythm section approached the tunes. The material was so fresh, and the trio really found a new way to support the other soloists that was not the usual way. Certainly I was deeply influenced by that, as I am a bass player.
>
> The second aspect has to do with the overall arc of the recording, the concept that Miles had and that his fellow musicians so wonderfully put forward. Each solo is a perfect example of "telling a story" with music. Sometimes I feel that today's music lacks that depth of storytelling, the architecture of a great solo. I can return again and again to the recording and hear something new. What a marvel!

I was particularly eager to discuss *Kind of Blue* with the trumpeter-composer Dave Douglas. Now in his mid-thirties, Douglas is among the most innovative and forward-looking musicians of his generation. While comparing him with Miles Davis places an unreasonable burden around his neck, nevertheless the innovative nature of much of his music places him squarely in the same tradition. I was hoping to learn from him the importance and influence of the album on him and especially on his generation. Our conversation was extensive, and I want to record our dialogue here in order to highlight the complexity of the issues surrounding the album. His comments surprised me with their insight and sense of musical vision. I first asked him how *Kind of Blue* had affected him:

> I think it has affected all of us. In the same way that Miles used to say, "No one plays anything that isn't

influenced by Louis Armstrong." I think that for people my age, and certainly people younger, *Kind of Blue* is sort of a touchstone album, whatever we think of it. And it has certainly been listened to many hundreds of times.

Part of what is so fascinating about that record is the different improvising styles of the main soloists. There's a teacher in Boston named Charlie Banakis who gives as his first lesson to a lot of his students the task of transcribing the three horn solos from "So What." And something that's so interesting is how different each of the solos is. I think it is those differences that give a level of balance to the piece. Of course, Bill Evans also is extremely unique. But there's something there that I think is really important: that sense of balance. I think it adds depth to that particular record. In a way, that kind of depth is what you find in all of Miles's records and projects over the years, and why people keep coming back to him as one of the great musical minds of the twentieth century. He certainly found his own way to play the music, that was unique, and he wasn't afraid. In fact, he was encouraging these musical minds in his group to find their own way, which was very different from where Miles was coming from. I think you find that most noticeably in the great 1960s quintet which, in a certain sense, grew out of the *Kind of Blue* band. I think Tony Williams was very much influenced by what was going on in that earlier group—the way of accompanying and the way of breaking the time up. And that's a band that grew on the bandstand. I think that the sextet of 1957–58 also grew on the bandstand, but in a very different way.

I asked Douglas if he had a specific interest in George Russell's theory of modes.

Absolutely! I mean, I think it's a brilliant way of rein-
terpreting and studying—examining—music. I actually
studied with George Russell. I was in his class for a
semester at the New England Conservatory in, I guess,
1982—something like that. But in terms of *Kind of Blue*
and the way modes were used, I wouldn't attach too
much significance. I think one of the things about *Kind
of Blue* that's so stunning is the equal level of intellectual interest and emotional interest. In other words,
these were new ideas that were bandied about at the
time, but Miles was able to remove the ideas from intellectual concepts and turn them into something that
wasn't being thought about at all; that was very much
instinctual, intuitive, and emotional; that had its own
narrative apart from whatever the theoretical ideas were
being explored. After all, there had been many other people who previously used modes. I'm sure Gil Evans had a
lot to do with what happened in that session. [Douglas
was unaware that, according to Teo Macero, Gil Evans
was present at the *Kind of Blue* sessions.]

But it's a greatly flawed record on many levels, which
I think is very interesting. There are mistakes, and I
think it has a quality of being thrown together, which of
course is not at all the case. I think of Miles as a great
composer of groups. And his contribution was to put
together a situation that created great music. I think
that the making of *Kind of Blue* was a very haphazard,
thrown-together thing and that Miles came into the studio without a whole lot of stuff, other than the idea that
"We're gonna go in and do this with these people, and
create the music in this way." So I think you have to give
a lot of credit to that—to his mastery of "the moment,"
rather than some enormous rehearsal time and pre-
visionary work.

Perhaps that's a level where the record is a very great

influence on the music that has come after. I know that even though *Kind of Blue* has an incredibly haphazard feel, maybe that's why we want to listen to it thousands of times, over and over. To get to that depth, you hear something different each time, and you really read into each player because they're caught like deer in the headlights in that session. I know that as a producer of records myself, that has encouraged me to think about the way I lead recording dates.

While we may have brazenly come up with new compositional ideas that work, there is still the moment when it comes down to rolling the tape; there has to be that spark and flame that gets everyone up to that next level of interaction and creation. And so, almost every record I've ever made, I've done in two days. By doing it this way, I think you create that feeling and that excitement. And that comes one hundred percent from the philosophy of the way *Kind of Blue* was made. *Kind of Blue* also benefited from the photograph on the cover of the album, and the time it came out, and where everyone was in their careers—where Miles was in his career. In purely musical terms, everything was in the air at that time. There were a lot of other records that you could point to, within that same time span, that had the same musical significance and impact. However, so many different elements came together for *Kind of Blue* that it has become this iconic cultural artifact.

I asked Douglas about Miles's remark concerning a jazzman in a musical situation in which he must play above his head rather than lean on clichés and easy licks.

I think that is true, and I also think that Miles did that with himself as well—he did things that a lot of people are afraid to do. One of my favorite records is that of Art Blakey with the Jazz Messengers and Thelonius Monk.

With Bill Hartman and Johnny Griffin there is that same element, as if they had just barely got through some of those takes. Yet it's the most exciting jazz from that period, and I think it has some of the same element of mystery, which is why you can listen to it over and over again—to figure out how they did that and why. Maybe there is not even an intellectual reason why, and that is what mystery is.

I think you had to play differently in order to play with Monk. Miles really, more than a lot of people, blazed a trail for the way he wanted to play that was very specific. After a certain period you never heard him play as a sideman, or at jam sessions or anything like that. He only played in his own group. He mastered framing—at framing what he could do. I think there is a parallel in the making of *Kind of Blue* to a record like *In a Silent Way*. I get a little upset when people say that *Kind of Blue* was a fluke, that it was just a lucky coincidence. Taking records like *In a Silent Way*, I think there was very much the same process. Miles came in with a few ideas and created this whole album of music with one outlook, with one clear vision of what it was supposed to be. What he had to play on was very refined, and it forced everyone else to think that way.

I asked Douglas about the different perspectives that Miles and Coltrane had about recording. When playing live, Coltrane seemed to be committed to pure spontaneity, but while leading his own recording dates, he did just the opposite. Coltrane would do take after take, trying to attain something as close to perfection as possible. Miles, of course, tried as much as possible to make records with the same spontaneity as a live performance. Douglas replied:

I think Coltrane was a very different musician from Miles. Coltrane was obsessed with the instrumental, with the expression of what he had to say, and perhaps a lot of those takes he would throw out because they didn't sound spontaneous. Maybe he got to the technical level he wanted, but he felt as if the feeling of spontaneity was gone. He became a master of re-creating that feeling. I think that's what is interesting about all those outtakes of *Giant Steps* in the Atlantic boxed set, *The Heavyweight Champion*. On a surface level, on a peripheral level, all of those solos sound fine. But when you put them up against the one that Coltrane decided to release, they don't have that feeling that he just pulled it out of thin air. Clearly he did not, but he wanted to create that illusion.

I also think that Coltrane's interaction with composition was very different from Miles's. Maybe we are getting at something about *Kind of Blue* here. Miles was interested in achieving, especially in "All Blues," the African thumb piano feel. So his idea or vision about what the music should be interacts with Coltrane's interest in having a virtuosic solo that sounds spontaneous. And then there was Cannonball, a good-natured, brilliant kind of ebullient soloist. Those are the interactions that were going on, the vibes, the atmosphere. Coltrane was thinking more in the way that an American Indian musician would think, where the whole thing is gonna ride on elaborating on the theme in improvisation.

Now that we have all these wonderful boxed sets available, with alternate takes, you listen to Miles's quintet from the 1960s, with some of the outtakes from that, and you see that they don't achieve the atmosphere at all. There were tunes that they rehearsed that were never released because that vibe wasn't there on a piece like "I Have a Dream," the Herbie Hancock piece; there was one other outtake on there. To be able to listen to this was really a revelation. It wasn't about the idea that "Okay, we'll get some tunes that are fodder for improvising and just do our thing." The idea was more like this: "Okay, this tune isn't gonna work for us because we're not able to find our spirit with this bit of material." So maybe that applies to *Kind of Blue* in the sense that Miles happened on these ideas that, with just a very few notes, created the atmosphere that permitted everyone to do their thing.

I told Douglas about my image of this album being recorded late at night—an image that doubtless comes from the dark strain of feeling that runs throughout *Kind of Blue*. I told Douglas how surprised I was to learn from Jimmy Cobb that it was recorded in the afternoon. I just could not conceive of it—in the afternoon! Douglas responded:

> When the musicians came in, they were ready to do it. I think, as a jazz musician, that an improvising musician who is in the studio a lot . . . has seen moments when the magic just happens, and moments when the band will be knocking itself over the head trying to find the magic, and not finding it. But there is a big difference for musicians between making a record and playing live. When you record, you're creating an artifact that will live in someone's home, an object which represents the music and should not necessarily reflect a live performance. It's an object in a sleeve. I think that various musicians have a different awareness of that. I think Miles was one of the most brilliant in understanding the format of the LP, and how to make something that people could bring home and understand. . . . Other artists don't think that way.

Of course, there were those who really resisted *Kind of Blue*, including one of Miles's biographers. As we have seen, Bill Cole in his book *Miles Davis* expresses little regard for the music. He states that "although *Kind of Blue* was a commercial success and helped liberate music by less structured forms, it [nevertheless] lacked any emotional drive; [the pieces] just floated along like banners in a ticker-tape parade. Much of the playing seemed too cautious. . . . [T]he music was sluggish and low in its energy output. Here Miles was breaking out of old territory but being careful on the new ground."[1]

I have always been puzzled by Cole's remarks and would like to suggest a couple of comparisons: Is Indian music "lacking in emotional drive" because it is fundamentally meditative? Is a quiet hymn "low in energy output" because it is not foot-stomping gospel? As for Cole's comment about the music's "sluggishness," one person's "sluggish energy" is another's transcendent beauty. In his disparaging comments I suspect that Cole is referring to the fact that none of the tunes are played at a fast tempo, as if that were the only way of playing with high energy and intense emotional drive. I believe that, to an extent, this kind of thinking arises from the idea that jazz should be "masculine" in some stereotypical way—fast, rough, and bullying. Music that is sensitive and lyrical is, well . . . sort of *effeminate*. This weird kind of sexism in jazz has been prevalent for a long time. I hope we have advanced enough as a society to see now that such attitudes are not only limiting but ridiculous.

Cole also seems not to understand Miles's most important goal for the *Kind of Blue* album: to attempt to record jazz with as much spontaneity as possible. Miles once said that the day they release jazz albums with all the mistakes that are inevitable in improvisation, then they will finally produce authentic jazz records. Further, Cole makes it quite evident that, at least for him, the importance of Bill Evans on these sessions somehow made the music unauthentic, overly "European." Throughout his career Miles got whacked from both sides of racism: by those who attacked him for being antiwhite and by those who thought he hired too many white jazzmen. (Don't forget that his first band, the *Birth of the Cool* nonet, was virtually all-white and that later on during his so-called electric period he frequently used young white musicians.) Miles must have thought that these warring prejudices would, in the end, cancel each other out. Unfortunately, they never did, and he continued to be criticized from both sides.

Trying to analyze the significance of any work of art as multi-layered as *Kind of Blue* reminds me of the old fable about the four blind men and the elephant. As each of them touches a different part of the animal, they come to different conclusions about the elephant's appearance; yet all are wrong. Nonetheless, there is in us an irresistible urge to search for reasons that this album speaks to so many of us, and on such a profound level. The following summary, with several additional references, is an attempt to pull together the salient features of the album itself, i.e., the music, as well as the characteristics of the musicians and their contributions to *Kind of Blue*.

There are two primary aspects of this piece of music that have made it unique, and at first glance these two characteristics seem to have little connection to each other. The first is formal and is related to Miles Davis's use of modal structures in place of the usual harmonic progressions, and his use of this innovative context as an attempt to attain spontaneity among his musicians. We have seen how important a step this was for the evolution of jazz and in the way it reflects what was taking place in American society at the time.

One can point to a handful of records that are turning points in jazz history, and for the most part they also reflect the continuing struggle among African Americans to establish themselves as genuinely free citizens of their country. The few seminal records that come readily to mind are Louis Armstrong's first *Hot Five* recordings; the earliest sessions of Count Basie with Lester Young, Dizzy Gillespie, and Charlie Parker's earliest work such as "Shaw 'Nuff"; Miles's *Birth of the Cool* nonet sides, and Ornette Coleman's first album,

Something Else! Without question *Kind of Blue* deserves to be on this list.

It is important to remember that Miles Davis was not the first jazz musician to use modes or even to create an entire album using modes. George Russell should be given credit for having done that; he first used modes in his 1947 collaboration with Dizzy Gillespie, "Cubano Be, Cubano Bop," and then used modes in the tunes he wrote for his 1956 masterpiece, *The Jazz Workshop*. Other musicians, such as Mingus and Teo Macero, had experimented with similar forms. The difference lay in the manner in which Miles used modes. Rather than writing complex scores based on modes, as these other musicians had done, Miles put together very simple structures with the idea of giving his musicians the widest possible harmonic latitude so they could play with unhampered melodicism and at an unprecedented level of spontaneity. For Miles, modes were the door to freedom, a breaking away from the most important European element in jazz—its harmonic architecture—and a movement in the direction of African and Eastern folk music.

Another reason Miles wanted to experiment with modes was that they would offer a challenge for his musicians to create music that was really "in the moment" without leaning on the usual procedures and hackneyed phrases and licks. Miles's purpose was to make their reach exceed their grasp or, as Miles put it, to "play above what they know." Thus, as far as its formal implications are concerned, the *Kind of Blue* sessions were a kind of experiment in freedom and spontaneity that provided one of the most important opening volleys of the free-jazz revolution of the 1960s. The fact that Miles was probably the leading modern jazzman of his time gave this album a certain cachet as well as special significance; it became a manifesto about the future of jazz improvisation and composition.

So, is it simply a coincidence that an album with such historical significance in the evolution of jazz also happens to be among the most beautiful and profoundly moving pieces of music—in any genre—in this past century and probably for centuries to come; and that it has won adherents not only among musicians but also among the general public? I do not think coincidence explains these factors. I believe the album's beauty, and especially its emotional power, is related directly to its formal innovations; moreover, I think these qualities are inseparable.

There are additional formal aspects of *Kind of Blue* that make it distinctive. For one thing, it reveals and benefits from the influence of Duke Ellington, who more than any other musician except Gil Evans (with whom Miles collaborated on orchestral works as well as some of the later music of his "electric period") was central to Miles's development as a musician. Miles once said that every year musicians should get down on one knee to honor Duke Ellington. Many of the "hip" cognoscenti wondered why he was so worshipful of a musician associated with the Swing Era—a musician against whom, presumably, the modernists had rebelled. But no artist was ever more continually progressive than Duke Ellington, although he moved forward in a musical world of his own creation. The best of the boppers and post-boppers had a deep and abiding appreciation of Ellington's genius.

Miles once told me that, for him, the biggest challenge for a jazzman was establishing a *sound* that is uniquely his (or hers). "Ideas are a dime a dozen; I can just look at a picture on the wall and come up with all kinds of ideas. But finding a *sound* is hard." *Kind of Blue*, indeed, creates a sound, a very specific sound. This is why Miles was so disappointed when first Bill Evans left the band, and then Cannonball Adderley. He knew he could easily hire another pianist or alto saxophonist, but no matter how good they might be as musicians, the band could never have the same *sound*. Other eminent jazz leaders sought that same elusive quality called "sound."

By way of analogy, go back once again to Duke Ellington. No jazz musician ever had the genius for tonal coloration that characterizes Ellington's work. Duke brought musicians into his band not necessarily because they were the strongest players around, but rather for their having a tonal color that, alongside the other musicians, achieved the sound the Duke was looking for. There is a cliché about Ellington that he played his band just as a great instrumentalist plays his instrument. The cliché, in this case, is founded in truth. Ellington wrote his pieces specifically for the musicians in his band at that time. He did not write a "Concerto for Trumpet"; instead, he wrote "Concerto for Cootie," since the piece was written specifically for Cootie Williams. Another trumpetman playing the piece might play it brilliantly, but it would never be exactly what Duke had had in mind. Duke thought the same way about the ensemble—which is why he had to keep the band playing constantly, even late in his career when he probably no longer needed the money. He could not relinquish his chosen instrument, even if life was at that point nothing but an endless series of one-nighters.

This awareness of the texture of sound in his bands was part of Miles's musical world, going back even to the first group he led, the *Birth of the Cool* nonet; but in no other small group recording was Miles's awareness of tonal possibilities of the small group more obvious than on *Kind of Blue*. Replacing, say, Cannonball or Coltrane with different saxophonists would not have achieved the sound that Miles was trying to evoke, that sound of the dark, haunted roads of Arkansas with those "bad gospels" sung in the distance. It is clear that one reason he brought Wynton Kelly in for "Freddie Freeloader" is that this one tune needed a rougher and funkier texture than the others on the album, those played by Bill Evans.

In addition to wanting to blend the sounds and tonal colors of the musicians in the sextet, Miles also had a clear idea of the emotional texture he wanted his players to evoke. As different as the emotional texture is between, say, the playing of Coltrane and Evans, it took the genius of Miles Davis to perceive that in the right context they beautifully complemented each other. They created a whole truth greater than the sum of its parts, and did so with unforgettable eloquence. Even those people who question, "Where's the melody?" while listening to jazz improvisation "get" *Kind of Blue*; they "get" the *feel* of the music.

It is wondrous, at least to me, how jazzmen can dredge up not just musical inspiration but also the deepest of their emotions in such an impersonal surrounding as a recording studio. It is a process that must expose their inner selves, leaving them unusually vulnerable. Most of us do not have to face our deepest fears, desires, intense joy, or despair on a routine basis. We go through our days with a well-modulated personality that we present to the outer world; we are generally too busy to be overly introspective. In addition, looking inside oneself can also be cause for anxiety or pain, and most of us try to avoid these emotions—a case of letting sleeping dogs lie, I suppose. For the jazzman, on the other hand, his job is to create music out of the emotions he feels at the moment he is actually playing, however painful those emotions might be; there are no sleeping dogs.

Bill Evans once described what he called a "switch" that he could turn on whenever he had to sit down at the piano and improvise. As I said earlier, sometimes listening to Evans's playing (and that of most other jazzmen, for that matter), I am astounded by the naked emotion that is so clearly present in the music. Of course, every art form requires the artist to deal with the emotions engendered by his work; but in jazz the emotion is often far more raw than that of other kinds of art. Since jazz is created in the moment, there is no easy way to refine the emotion. The line between the emotion and the ensuing music is immediate and direct. In many ways this notion of creating "in the moment" is the opposite of Wordsworth's famous definition of poetry as "the spontaneous overflow of powerful feelings . . . [taking] its origin from emotion recollected in tranquillity." By virtue of his reliance on spontaneity, the improvising jazzman cannot make music by "recollecting emotion in tranquillity"; there is only the raw emotion he brings to the moment of creation.

Ultimately; turning that level of emotion off and on, using the "switch" Bill Evans described, must take its toll on the musicians. Perhaps it is not surprising, then, that jazzmen become involved with drugs or alcohol. How else does one cope with the kind of emotional roller coaster demanded by playing this music? I do not mean to provide a cop-out for the self-indulgence of some jazzmen, but I think it is clear that the creation of jazz requires a daunting ability to live a "quick change" existence.

The free-jazz movement of the 1960s was particularly notable for the rawness of the emotions it evoked, in both the musicians and the audience. At times it seemed as if it were not so much a form of music as an expression of rage or pure ecstasy. However, it would be a mistake to say that playing "free" always led in a direct line to music of greater emotional intensity. As noted, the first free-jazz recording was one led by Lennie Tristano in the late 1940s. Yet the music on that date was at least as frostily cool as the rest of Tristano's music. (I do not mean to disparage Tristano, whose music I love.)

The free-jazz movement came about at the same time as (and, in some observers' minds, because of) the explosion of the civil rights and Black Power movements and the heated emotions that it evoked among African Americans. Many black people were discovering the depth of their rage; and music—both jazz and the black popular music of the time— reflected those feelings and, in some sense, even exacerbated them, just as it had throughout African American history.

This explosive music does not mean that all jazz musicians had thoughts of injustice when they played; but it is true that there was a general feeling of *self-liberation*, a feeling of *not holding back*, a feeling that, in Jesse Jackson's famous phrase, *"I am somebody!"* The bebop revolutionaries had gone a long way in creating a wider spectrum of emotional intensity, which is not to say that the emotional tone of Louis Armstrong or Lester Young was bland. It is just that earlier musicians were more disposed to choose which emotions they wished to express. Later many musicians believed in jazz as a means of self-expression rather than as musical entertainment.

Ornette Coleman's revolutionary ideas are based on the need to connect directly with one's emotions without having to filter them through a preestablished structure. There was no intermediary. Coltrane, and those who imitated him in the 1960s, was accused of taking Coleman's raw emotionality too far. To some extent both musicians had made themselves vulnerable to the charge of being self-indulgent. But as pointed out, Coltrane's improvising was, in his own phrase, "cleaning the mirror," looking into his soul to discover ultimate truths. While recording *Kind of Blue*, he found the route that allowed him to journey even deeper inside, letting him come even closer to the final emotional and spiritual truth he sought.

It is instructive to remember Coltrane's participation in one track of George Russell's *New York, New York* album. According to Russell, after he gave the score for the tune on which Coltrane was to play, Richard Rodgers's "Manhattan," the tenorman studied it in order to work out new progressions in addition to the altered progressions that Russell had already written. Coltrane had become so committed to harmonic complexity that he could no longer simply put the tenor sax in his mouth and play. He had become harmonically ingenious and very much advanced, but this very precocity made for certain difficulties when he needed to play music directly from his heart and soul. After all, since his spiritual awakening in 1957, being able to get closer to God had become the great passion of his life. Coltrane's earlier music had always been passionate, but for *Kind of Blue* he seemed to be shedding his restraint and reaching higher than ever. His solo on "All Blues" is surely the most passionate of all his work of the 1950s, including his own *Giant Steps* album. That intensity would grow progressively stronger after he went out on his own in 1960, and as with *Kind of Blue*, most of his work during that decade would be either modal or blues.

Coltrane was not alone. I think the playing of the others for *Kind of Blue* has an emotional immediacy unheard in their previous work. In particular, the way Miles came across to the public was based very much on the persona he had deliberately chosen. Consistent with this persona, the words generally used to describe his music are *introspective, blue, stark, lonely*, even *haunted*. I think these words also describe Bill Evans and, in quite a different way, Cannonball Adderley. He comes across as the joker in the deck, without whom it would be incomplete. All of them were defined by their *Kind of Blue* personas.

When we think of the meaning of words such as *introspective, blue, stark, lonely, haunted*, we might be more surprised than ever that this album has persisted in its popularity for so long. After all, this is not happy, "good times" music, and it is not the kind of music one would expect to have much appeal beyond the core jazz audience. The fact that it is dark, brooding, dense, and introspective makes one wonder about our own lives and our society during the past century. Still, there is an edge of suppressed joy in this music that reveals the other side of the coin of despair; the music is ultimately triumphant. *Kind of Blue* embraces both sides simultaneously.

I think Miles wanted to confront his listeners with the same kind of choices he gave his musicians. He wanted us to go beyond what we knew, to expand and realize our own freedom. These goals possess a quality of enigma; therefore, the emotional currents heard on the album are mercurial. This moodshifting means, in part, that one can listen to the album over and over, yet it never loosens its grip.

We have explored the ways in which the emotional power of *Kind of Blue* accounts for its unusual popularity over time. For the musicians, however, the chief benefit derived from the use of modes, which freed the jazzmen to create melody without having to fit it into a tight harmonic architecture. It may seem obvious that music in which melody is emphasized would be immediately appealing to a wider audience, until one reflects that Ornette Coleman's music, though it was almost purely melodic, lost many jazz fans who had difficulty with his free jazz. But Ornette's music, as well as the "new thing" players who followed him, sounds atonal—whether or not it really is. But all the improvisation on *Kind of Blue* sounds *tonal* to the ear. And that, I think, has made a major difference (as well as the post-Coleman players' use of a range of extramusical effects, such as multiphonics, screams, and wails). As it had been with music of the European classical tradition, atonal music (or even polytonal music) had a difficult time finding a large audience. For some musicians, including Miles, going this route meant that jazz would lose its folk roots as "people's music" and would become music for a select minority. The "new thing" players, and those who followed them, saw the matter differently; they were unwilling to pander to the lowest common denominator for which so much of our culture seems intended. The so-called avant-garde jazz still retains that "sound of surprise," which has made so many of us love this music.

Despite all of this analysis, I find it hard to put my finger on exactly why we find *Kind of Blue* so compelling. Words are imprecise. The music is somehow ineffable; it has a quality that I can only call *spiritual*. In an article for *Theology Today,* John Michael Spencer argues that the spirituality of *Kind of Blue* is derived from both the music itself and the musical philosophy that Miles perfected for this album. Spencer tortuously attempts to find some grounds to explain the deep spirituality in this music. For example, he states that the improvisation that dominates the album "reinforced an African credo: There is no boundary between the alleged opposites of our world—the flesh versus the spirit and so forth." This may be true, but it is an idea that could apply equally to all of the best jazz. Spencer is basically correct, though, in finding an undeniable spiritual essence in this album, and thus we find yet another reason that the music seems so ageless.

It might seem difficult to label "spiritual" a record led by Miles Davis. Miles had a disdain for religion, at least on the surface. As we have previously noted, he stopped believing when he was a boy after observing that all the churches were racially segregated. He also saw organized religion as an institution focused on money and power. Miles understood spirituality to mean something very different from religion, and it is spirituality that claimed his belief. He said that he believed his deceased mother and father had come to visit him. He also said that he was visited by "all the musicians I have known who are dead, too, and part of what I am today is them. . . . Music is about the spirit and the spiritual."

That statement tells us better than any I have read why *Kind of Blue* is such profoundly spiritual music and why it is so haunting. Along with the "bad gospels" Miles heard on that Arkansas road, I believe that when he created *Kind of Blue*, he was also in touch with the specters of all the musicians who had preceded him and the players in his own group; they are the ghostly voices heard in the dark—not just Duke Ellington, Lester Young, and Charlie Parker but also Buddy Bolden blowing the first jazz trumpet in New Orleans, the ragtime pianists, the work songs, the deep "bad gospels" and the spirituals, and the drums and folk music of Africa.

The making of *Kind of Blue* had many heroes: George Russell, John Coltrane, Bill Evans, and all the rest of the brilliant musicians who were involved. Jazz is a communal art form, and any given jazz work has to be viewed from this perspective. Given the collaborative nature of jazz, it is invalid to see its history as a succession of great men. (I deliberately do not say "and women" because, in truth, they have been largely, and regrettably, ignored.) Charlie Parker did not single-handedly "invent" bebop, just as Miles never "invented" cool jazz, modal jazz, or fusion. All of the advances and greatest creations in jazz have been the accomplishments of many different musicians. This is true for the other great twentieth-century art forms, such as movies. But like film, there is a first among equals, and in film it is the director.

Kind of Blue was a triumph specifically for Miles Davis. He is the rightful auteur of the album, which is a reflection of him in so many ways: his sensibility, his musical persona, his philosophy of improvisational music. I realize that many people think of Miles as a kind of ultimate "Mr. Cool," a jaded and cynical man with little emotion invested in life. That was the (apparently convincing) front he put up in order to protect himself from those who did not understand the complex life he lived. He believed so passionately in life that he continued to put beauty into this world almost to his dying breath. He once said to me, "If you don't have anything to put into the world, you ought to get out of it."

There have been others who referred to Miles as "the Prince of Darkness." In reality, he was our angel of light. He illuminated our lives with his beautiful music in the second half of the dark and bloody twentieth century and gave many of us that rare commodity: hope.

Some years ago I was walking with Miles on the Upper West Side. Miles needed a taxi to take him to his apartment, and a taxi was a hard thing to get—especially in that area of Manhattan. Suddenly Miles turned to me and asked, "What do you want from me, Eric? What do you want me to do for you?"

I was so surprised by the question that, unfortunately, I blathered something about an old friend who wanted to interview him for the (now defunct) *SoHo News*.

"No" was Miles's quick reply.

It was one of those moments for which I wish I could enter a time machine and go back to that instant and say the thing

I felt in my heart. What I wish I had said was, "Miles, you have done more for me than virtually anybody else. And you did it long before we met. You saved my life—how much more could I ask of you?"

I think Miles would have understood.

Appendix

George Russell's long stay in the hospital during the mid-1940s turned out to be a blessing because it gave him more time, the thing he needed most, to embark on his mental journey into the heart of music.

As Russell explains it: "Miles had said he wanted to learn all the chords. So I decided to look first at the major chord and play the major scale against it. The major scale did not sound related to the major chord, in the sense that it was in unity with it. The F natural in the C-major scale was definitely the note that made the major scale sound a duality. It sounded two tetrachords: C-D-E and F, of which F was a duality. And then I started to play the Lydian scale right on the piano in St. Joseph's Hospital solarium. I would sit there playing, surrounded by fifty patients smoking cigarettes. They had TB, but they were smoking!

"It was there in the solarium that I began to play the Lydian scale. I took the second tetrachord at the G-major scale: G-A-B-C, in a C-major scale. I said to myself, 'That sounds the unity.' Then, logically, I just ran the second tetrachord at the G-major scale: D-E-F-G, and I said, 'Damn! The major scale sounds more of the unity with C than the C-major scale!' Because at least the D-E-F sharp and G resolves into a tone that's in a C-major scale, C-F-G. And the scale just absolutely sounded closer to the tonality of a C-major scale.

"Then I began looking at the modes of the G-major scale. The Ionian mode was G-A-B-C-D-E-F sharp-G. The Dorian was D-E-F-G-A-B-C sharp-G and A. The Phrygian, E-F-G-A-B-C sharp-G-A-B-C. Instead of telling musicians, 'When you see a C-major chord, play a G-major scale,' I could say, 'Play a Lydian scale.' I lifted the Lydian scale of G out of the G-major scale and put it on the tonic of C, which I called the 'C Lydian scale' forever after. It is a scale of unity with the C-major scale.

"Now that proves that a ladder of fifths is the strongest—the first interval, or the first tonically based interval to enter into the overtone series. In the overtone series, you have one C and then an octave C, which is the same note, and then a fifth of C to G. With the tonic of an interval fifth, you can go anywhere in the world and play a fifth. You can ask people to sing the note that sounds the tonical integrity of a fifth, and they are going to sing the lower tone. If you take a ladder of fifths: C-G-D-A-F sharp, the scale would be C-D-E-F natural-G-A-B. It would sound completely as if it has little to do with the unity of a C-major chord. It is not unity; it is supposed to be a duality. It is supposed to resolve to C.

"Traditional European harmony overlooked a lot. Harmony was viewed in a progressional manner, going from one chord to the five-chord and back to the one. That was considered 'harmony.' But the dictionary says that 'harmony is unity.' People completely overlooked the individual chord as a viable and individual entity that has unity and could evolve into a Lydian chromatic scale, which is all of equal temperaments.

"Stravinsky's *Rite of Spring* was recently analyzed in some bullshit way, like 'Oh, this is the first theme, and then he repeats the second in bars three and four' and so on. But what is really going on in the music? Analysis like this has no name for it.

"Ornette Coleman asked me in 1959, 'What's the tonic?' That was a hell of a question, but back then I could not answer it. Now I would say, 'It's the sun; it is the center of tonal organization in a Lydian chromatic scale. It is like gravity.'

"The Concept defined the meaning of 'horizontal' and 'vertical' playing. These terms depend on how the musician relates to the chord of the moment. The vertical player depends on the chord of the moment to access a scale that will enable him to sound the genre of the chord in an artful way. The horizontal player depends not on the chord of the moment, but rather, the chord to which chords are resolving. The non-final chords resolve to a final, and the horizontal player depends on that final, of which he picks the scale to sound over. Musicians have always chosen styles that are either vertical or horizontal. Out of a certain kind of snobbery, Coleman Hawkins, for example, liked the vertical. The vertical players had to be reasonably sophisticated musically. That went well with the bigger cities in the country—New York, Chicago, and so forth. Horizontal playing had to do with the cotton fields, and the black interpretation of English ballads. That is where the blues come from. Lester Young was the grandfather of the horizontal, and he also played vertically in a beautiful way. Bird personified the melding of horizontal and vertical.

"Western traditional music theory overlooked the vertical aspect of music, which means it left out one-third of music. The Concept is the first theory to address that missing third. No reason was ever given for why an F-major chord resolves very nicely to a C-major chord. The Concept does, because it is based on gravity. Everything I say is provable."

Notes

Chapter 1

1. John Miller Chernoff, *African Rhythm and African Sensibility* (University of Chicago Press, 1979), 36.

Chapter 2

1. *Playboy* interview with Miles Davis, March 1962.
2. Eric Nisenson, *'Round About Midnight: A Portrait of Miles Davis* (New York: Dial Press, 1983), 17.
3. Liner notes for *Birth of the Cool* (Capitol).

Chapter 3

1. Eric Nisenson, *'Round About Midnight: A Portrait of Miles Davis*, updated ed. (New York: Da Capo Press, 1996), 72.
2. Eric Nisenson, *Open Sky: Sonny Rollins's World of Improvisation* (New York: St. Martin's Press, 2000), 38.
3. Whitney Balliet, *The Sound of Surprise* (New York: E. P. Dutton & Co., 1961).
4. Joe Goldberg, *Jazz Masters of the 50s* (New York: Da Capo Press, 1965), 75.
5. Nat Hentoff, "An Afternoon with Miles Davis," *Jazz Review* (December 1958).

Chapter 4

All quotes are from my exclusive interviews with George Russell.

Chapter 5

1. John Coltrane (as told to Don DeMichael) "Coltrane on Coltrane."
    From *Down Beat: 60 Years of Jazz* (New York: Hal Leonard, 1995),
    pp. 117–18.

Chapter 6

1. Don Nelson, Bill Evans, *Down Beat: 60 Years of Jazz* (New York: Hal
    Leonard, 1965).
2. Nat Hentoff, "Introducing Bill Evans," *Jazz Review* (October 1959).
3. Ibid.
4. Ibid.
5. Hoagy Carmichael, *The Stardust Road/Sometimes I Wonder* (New
    York: Da Capo Press, 1999), 282.
6. Peter Pettinger, *How My Heart Sings* (New Haven, Ct.: Yale Univer-
    sity Press, 1998), 57.

Chapter 7

1. Nat Hentoff, "The Ascent of Cannonball," *International Musician*
    (January 1961).
2. Martin Williams, *Jazz Changes* (New York: Da Capo Press, 1970), 239.
3. Ibid.
4. Julian "Cannonball" Adderley, "Paying Dues: The Education of a
    Combo Leader," *Jazz Review* (May 1960).
5. Ibid.
6. Miles Davis (with Quincy Troupe), *Miles—The Autobiography* (New
    York: Touchstone Books, 1990), 175.

Chapter 8

1. Bill Cole, *Miles Davis* (New York: Morrow, 1974), 81.
2. Miles Davis, (with Quincy Troupe) *Miles—The Autobiography* (New
    York: Touchstone Books, 1990), 154.
3. Eric Nisenson, *Ascension—John Coltrane and His Quest* (New York:
    Da Capo Press, 1995), 79.

Chapter 9

1. Stanley Goldstein, *Playboy* (September 1961).
2. *Playboy* interview with Miles Davis, March 1962.
3. Julian "Cannonball" Adderley, "Cannonball Looks at Ornette Coleman," *Down Beat*, 1961.
4. Ibid.
5. Ibid.

Chapter 10

1. Bill Cole, *Miles Davis: A Musical Biography* (New York: William Morrow, 1974).

Index

and Miles Davis, 39, 46–47,
78–79, 102, 169–70, 184–85
drug use, 76, 78, 79–80
health, 78
musical education, 77, 94, 95
musical style, 106, 108, 158
recordings, x, 36, 41–42, 51,
84–85, 86–87, 126–27, 157,
171–72, 182–84, 185–86
recordings (*Kind of Blue*),
139–40, 152, 154, 156, 158,
161–62, 181, 183, 213–14, 216
spiritual epiphany, 75–76
Coltrane, Naima, 79–80
Columbia Records, 39, 107, 142,
143, 172
"Concerto for Billy the Kid," 99,
108
Concierto de Aranjuez (Rodrigos),
168
Cook, Willy, 56
cool-jazz (West Coast jazz
movement), 10, 12–13, 32, 33,
119, 120, 217
Corea, Chick, 92
Crawford, Jimmy, 55
Crosscurrents (album), 135–36
"Cubana Be, Cubano Bop," 62, 180,
208

Dameron, Tadd, 35
Davis, Eddie "Lockjaw," 132
Davis, Miles, 13, 63
career, 13, 23–28, 30–32, 34–35,
37, 38–49, 46, 84–85, 102,
121–22, 126, 132, 169–76
critical response to, 43, 126, 161,
162–63
drug use, 20, 27, 36–38
influence of, 16–17
and the media, 44, 45, 48, 217
"Miles List" Web site, 195
"Miles myth," 29–30
musical education and

development, 22–27, 28–29, 34,
35–36, 95, 107–8, 151–52
musicians, dealings with, 124,
148–49, 168, 171–72, 172–73,
184, 192
personality and temperament,
19–22, 27–28, 43–45, 102–3,
180–81, 214, 217–18
and racism, 162–64, 206–7
recordings, *ix*, 4, 10–11, 18–19,
25–26, 27, 33–36, 37, 38, 39–41,
42, 43, 45, 46, 47–48, 64, 70,
84–85, 106–8, 124–25, 126–27,
142, 144, 151–52, 168–69,
171–72, 175, 207
recordings (*Kind of Blue*), 134–5,
136–42, 148–58, 162, 166
and religion, 216
success of, *ix–xi*, 19, 21, 44, 45
Davis, Miles (professional
relationships)
Julian "Cannonball" Adderley,
46–47, 78–79, 113–14, 120–21,
121–22, 124–26
John Coltrane, 39, 46–47, 184–85
Bill Evans, 89, 99, 101–3, 109,
110–11, 192
Gil Evans, 28–29, 42, 43, 47–48,
63
Charlie Parker, 23, 24, 25–26, 28,
35
George Russell, 60–61, 72–73,
101, 180–81
Davis, Steve, 182, 183
Dearie, Blossom, 63
Decca, 70
DeFranco, Buddy, 98
DeJohnette, Jack, 192
Dennis, Kenny, 188
Dial label, 26, 28
"Diane," 45, 79
Dolphy, Eric, 6, 173, 178, 183–84
"Donna Lee," 28
Dorsey brothers, 7